PARENTAL
ADVISORY

PARENTAL ADVISORY

■ Music Censorship in America ■

ERIC NUZUM

Perennial

An Imprint of HarperCollins*Publishers*

HarperCollins books may be purchased for educational, business, or sales promotional use. For information please write: Special Markets Department, HarperCollins Publishers Inc., 10 East 53rd Street, New York, NY 10022.

FIRST EDITION

Designed by Jessica Shatan

Library of Congress Cataloging-in-Publication Data
Nuzum, Eric D.
    Parental advisory : music censorship in America / by Eric Nuzum.
        p.   cm.
    Includes bibliographical references and index.
    ISBN 0-688-16772-1
        1. Popular Music—Censorship—United States.   2. Music and morals.   3. Censorship—United States.   I. Title.
ML3477.N89   2001
306.4'84—dc21

01   02   03   04   05   WB/RRD   10   9

This book is dedicated to my parents,

Kenneth and Mary Lou Nuzum,

for teaching me right from wrong,

demonstrating the value of working for something you believe in,

and grimacing every time I brought home a new album.

Writing about music is like dancing about architecture. It's really a stupid thing to want to do.

—Elvis Costello

Contents

Preface

Probably the most difficult portion of this book to write is the part you are reading right now. I have struggled over many drafts of this preface. In those rejected pages, I shared information about my life, thoughts, and feelings about everything from bumper stickers to gun control to church road signs. But nothing seemed to fit. And that's why I'm sitting at my computer right now, putting the finishing touches on this book, and trying hard to prepare you to begin your process of reading it.

All I really wanted to do was share my own process of transcendence.

In the three years I spent writing and working on this book, I changed. I tested some long-held beliefs about right and wrong. Some of those tenets survived the process, others did not, and new ones were born along the way.

I hope this book has the same effect on you.

Enjoy.

Eric Nuzum
Kent, Ohio
October 2000

http://ericnuzum.com/parentaladvisory
E-mail: *letters@ericnuzum.com*

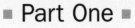

Part One

ISSUES IN

MUSIC

CENSORSHIP

"FREEDOM OF SPEECH"

An Overview of Music Censorship

Censorship is the height of vanity.
—Martha Graham

Whether or not you consider yourself a fan, it's hard to argue that the Beatles rank among the most popular and influential rock acts of all time. Although the Beatles sold millions of records, their significance cannot be measured in terms of record sales alone. They are a universal band: You'd be hard-pressed to find many members of Western civilization who haven't heard of the Beatles and their music.

When I think of the Beatles, one image always pops into my head: four mop-topped young men in suits, smiling ear to ear, and stepping off an airplane for their first visit to the United States.

What image comes to mind when you think of the Beatles?

Screaming fans? *Sgt. Pepper's Lonely Hearts Club Band*? Bed-peace?

I bet your mental picture is *not* the Fab Four dressed in white smocks, covered with raw, bloody meat, and surrounded by decapitated baby dolls. What makes me paint such a picture? That image was the original cover for the Beatles' *Yesterday and Today* album, released in June 1966.

But you'll never see that cover when you browse through the Beatles section at your local record shop. Capitol Records pulled the album cover after it had spent only a few weeks in circulation. In fact, this photo caused so much controversy that, over the band's objections, Capitol recalled every "butcher" copy of *Yesterday and Today*. They replaced it with a more benign photo of those four mop-topped young men. Incidentally, if you still own a copy of the album, look closely at the cover. To cut expenses, Capitol glued the new cover on top of many of the recalled albums, so the controversial—and highly collectible—"butcher" cover may be hiding underneath.

The problems created by the "butcher" cover pale when compared to other controversies that surrounded the Beatles that year.

Three months before releasing *Yesterday and Today*, statements made by John Lennon regarding the decrease in Christianity's popularity with teens were misreported when printed in American newspapers. His statement—"We're more popular now than Jesus"—led to numerous protests, boycotts, and public burnings of Beatles records and merchandise. There were threats of violence; the band was denounced from the pulpit and the editorial page; and parents, politicos, and school officials rallied against deteriorating moral values. Many people felt that the Beatles encouraged and personified moral decline. The Reverend Thurman H. Babbs, pastor at the New Haven Baptist Church in Cleveland, vowed to excommunicate any church member who listened to Beatles records or attended a Beatles concert. The Ku Klux Klan even nailed Beatles albums to burning crosses in South Carolina.

Lennon's comments on religion, the controversy over the "butcher" cover, and the public reaction that followed severely changed America's opinion of the Beatles. The Beatles were considered "dangerous" by the mainstream.

Was this true? Of course not. Does it matter? Again, no. Often in matters of censorship, the intended context is moot. When someone believes that music represents something entirely different perception becomes reality.

The "butcher" cover was not meant to be obscene, but rather a protest against the group's U.S. label—which they felt "butchered" their U.K. releases to make extra cash stateside. Lennon's comments were not intended to destroy Christianity, but his simply mentioning the words "Christianity" and "Beatles" in the same sentence meant that trouble was close behind.

All this begs the question: Why all the fuss over the antics of four kids playing rock music?

Throughout history many works of art and literature have been repeatedly censored. However, there seems to be an increased sensitivity when dealing with popular music. These Beatles examples illustrate one point: In matters of censorship, don't believe that content is the sole reason a work of art is censored. Actually, content makes very little difference. Censorship is less about content and much more about communication and control. This is not a new concept. As early as the third century B.C., the Chinese Ch'in dynasty recognized that one way to maintain authority and control was by prohibiting access to literature and art, even burning the imperial archives in the process.

But why the concern with pop music? Sure, music talks about sex and drugs, but so do television, movies, and the Internet. Music talks about politics and societal problems, but so do *Time* magazine and the six o'clock news. So why rock? It's simple. Few things are more anti-adult and anti-establishment then rock music.

Music, especially rock music, has always represented freedom to its fans. Freedom from authority, parents, or the boss. And ever since the start of rock music in the 1950s, there have always been those ready to campaign against it. But this is nothing new. Calls for censorship have come with the emergence of almost every new medium of communication: television, radio, the Internet, photography, telephones, and even the postal service. In fact, many other twentieth-century musical genres—like ragtime and jazz—have been met with resistance. When the saxophone was popularized in the 1920s, critics called it the "devil's flute" and thought that its low, seductive tones would cause young girls to behave immorally.[1]

Censorship has less to do with defining appropriate *expression* than it does with defining appropriate *people*. There are those in control and those who question or threaten that control. Because music offers a sense of empowerment against authority, authority feels a need to suppress and control it, lest it be their undoing. In this paradigm, censorship cooks down to its basic ingredients: racism, classism, and elitism.

Throughout the history of rock, censors haven't really cared about Chuck Berry, Ozzy Osbourne, or 2 Live Crew. What they *have* cared about is what these artists represent: change. The struggles associated with music censorship are battles between facts and opinions, between truth and assumptions. Passion overrides logic. In their ardent beliefs in concepts like patriotism, the innocence of childhood, the sanctity of church or family, people will jettison truth to satisfy their need to feel that everything will remain the same—their children will love them, their spouses will remain faithful, their retirement fund will be secure. To them, rock music threatens what they hold dearest. It expresses feelings they either don't understand or forgot about long ago; it serves as a stimulus for their children to act differently than they do; it says, "We're not gonna take it anymore," in a way that feels revolutionary.

The arguments against rock music have not changed significantly over the years, even though the issues and artists involved have. In the 1950s, adults viewed rock and roll with paranoia regarding the effects of its "tribal, jungle beats" on their children; they feared that it would cause their kids to break into fits of violence and chuck their morals out the back window of their date's Chevy. In the 1960s and 70s, the concerns were sex (again), drugs, and politics.

It's interesting that the parents of today lived through chastisement of their music, yet some choose to lobby against the music *their* children find appealing. In the 1950s, some wanted Elvis Presley run out of town, though today he is featured on a postage stamp. Did Elvis change after the 1950s? Absolutely. But given the choice, those voting on the stamp's design wanted to remember Elvis exactly the way their parents hated him. Yesterday's villain is today's hero. What once was youthful rebellion against the mainstream has become, decades later, a cultural symbol. Of course, that's now that those fifties youth *are* the mainstream. Imagine the hue and cry when Kurt Cobain or Madonna graces our postage stamps.

Laugh (or shudder) if you want, but I wouldn't bet against it.

What Is Music Censorship?

Many censors don't realize that the censorship they invoke (and, at other times, might oppose) actually compromises the ideals they work so hard to protect. Our country was founded on the principles of individual freedom and responsibility, principles embodied in the contract between the government and the governed—the Constitution of the United States. Many potential censors say that the principles of the First Amendment apply only to *government* action and therefore should not be applied to the actions of concerned citizens simply trying to establish standards of decency. While it is true that the First Amendment applies only to the *government*, should the government be the exemplar of ethics and principles in our country? Should the welfare department be the standard bearer of moral issues involving the homeless and underprivileged? Should the police department be a shining example of civility and respect of others?

When we oppose censorship—music or otherwise—we say that we, as a community, city, state, or nation, hold ourselves accountable to the same standards that our country was founded upon. Particular to music, censorship can be defined as follows:

> Music censorship is any discriminatory act that advocates or allows the suppression, control, or banning of music or music-related works against the wishes of its creator or intended audience.

Two concepts are key here (both will be explored in depth in this book): the "discriminatory" nature of censorship and its intended purpose.

Discrimination replaces logic and fact with bias. Someone who attempts to suppress content because he or she thinks it is harmful or violates community standards should be prepared to defend those claims against examination. Thousands of works of art, literature, and poetry contain references to sex, violence, and other social taboos—more references, in fact, than rock music has ever contained. If one wishes to outlaw or suppress violent or sexual content, one must be prepared to go far beyond music in order to make such suppression thorough and effective. As this book will illustrate, some have attempted this in the past; in the process, they mistakenly outlawed everything from Beethoven to the Indianapolis 500.

The second concept is understanding the intended purpose. In this country, citizens have the right to protest whatever they please. If people want to protest outside a record store to say they don't believe in the values and themes expressed by the store's merchandise, or if a community group decides to hold a rally and alternative concert to protest a local appearance by a controversial performer, then more power to them. However, the moment they switch from protesting to pressuring the store to stop carrying the merchandise in question or the concert promoter to cancel the controversial concert (thus ensuring that *no one* enjoys this music), they have crossed the line into music censorship. To carry this idea even further, music censorship is not a warning sticker; it is the fear, misinformation, lies, and intolerance that goes into creating a warning sticker in the first place, along with the intended actions that result.

Speaking of the universal parental warning sticker, what exactly does it represent? The Parents Music Resource Center (PMRC) is the organization responsible for the warning sticker emblazoned on CDs and cassettes today. The PMRC and its sticker are examples of all the layers of discrimination and futility involved in censoring music. For example, a 1994 survey of record stores in the Portland, Oregon, area found that only 8 percent of *all* CDs and cassettes on sale carry a warning sticker. However, when you examine stickering by genre, you see a slightly different story. Fifty-nine percent of rap titles carry a warning sticker, as do 13 percent of heavy metal recordings, while only 1 percent of mainstream "sugar pop" albums carry stickers.[2]

Just how effective is this tool for parents? In a 1996 survey, 37 percent of elementary school students said that their parents forbade them to buy music bearing a warning sticker; 23 percent of high-schoolers' parents forbade such purchases.[3]

Reality Break

Whatever influence rock music has on the lives of its fans pales when compared to the influence of family, church, community, peers, school, and other very tangible and real institutions in a person's life. While evidence exists that rock music has some effect on emotionally disturbed or troubled people, there is no evidence supporting the notion that rock music can make an otherwise good person go bad. Using music censorship to control problems is tantamount to, in the words of Supreme Court Justice Felix Frankfurter, burning the house to roast the pig.

But this didn't stop the censors from employing quasi-scientific surveys and bad experiments to prove their claims. Claims that fall into two categories: poor science and special-interest research.

Bad scientific method quickly becomes frightening when you realize that people actually use it as a foundation for their claims against rock music. One such project was conducted at the University of Ankara in Turkey. In 1981, researchers there determined that exposure to loud music "causes homosexuality in mice and deafness in pigs."[4] A ban on disco music was advocated as a result of their findings, under the assumption that humans would succumb to the same reactions. Needless to say, the experiment has never been repeated.

Another aspect of improper scientific method is taking research out of context. This can occur with correlation studies. It is quite popular for music censorship advocates to point to the high correlation between rap fandom and gang participation or heavy metal fandom and suicide. While it is true (and well researched) that certain genres of music attract certain types of people, it is important to remember a fundamental truth of social science: Correlation does not prove causation.

The other type of questionable research is special-interest research, or research conducted within a biased framework or hypothesis. The surest way to spot this type of research is to ask who funded it. When an organization or group commissions and funds research and is the only one to see and interpret the final analysis, it's wise to question the results. Think of the tobacco industry funding research demonstrating that there is no risk of cancer from smoking.

Most claims made against rock music result from "third-person effect": the concept that others are affected by music yet those who are making the claims are not similarly influenced. The Turkish researchers probably heard the same loud disco music their test mice heard, but they did not engage in spontaneous acts of homosexuality. Tipper Gore heard Prince's *1999*, yet, as far as we know, she didn't immediately ravish her husband, Al. Asa Carter, head of the White Citizens Council of Birmingham, listened to fifties rock ballads and didn't start dating black women. All were concerned about the actions of "more impressionable" adults and children. In their eyes, while *they* were in no danger from the evils of popular music, those in different racial, economic, or social groups were in jeopardy.

What *is* the evidence concerning how music affects the listener? Researchers Peter Christenson and Donald Roberts summarized it in one sentence: "It is not so much a case of 'you are what you hear' as 'you hear what you are.' "

In study after study, it has been demonstrated that music listeners are not attracted to or influenced by a moral or ethical message with which they do not agree; they either reject it outright or create a definition of the song's meaning that fits their belief patterns. An interesting study in this area was conducted in 1987 by social scientist Patricia Greenfield. She played Bruce Springsteen's "Born in the U.S.A." to groups of children in varying age groups and then asked them about the song and what it meant. After a group of fourth- and eighth-grade students were shown the lyric "Sent me off to a foreign land, to go kill the yellow man," they were asked who the "yellow man" was. None of the young students knew the "intended" meaning: a Vietnamese soldier. Responses included "a man who fell in yellow paint and it splashed on him" and "a man with a yellow mask."

Misinterpretations of "Born in the U.S.A." were common among college students as well, including "a yellow man is any kind of Communist." Listeners in all age brackets tended to attribute the song's theme to pride in the singer's birthplace (the U.S.A.) rather than the disillusionment the lyrics portray. They constructed a meaning for the lyrics that matched that perception.[5]

During the height of the PMRC's high jinks in 1985, probation officers in Orange County, California, asked two California State University professors to research whether or not there was any link between heavy metal music and juvenile crime. In the study, high school students were asked to identify the lyrical themes of their favorite songs. Of the 662 songs listed, only 7 percent were considered by the students to be about sex, violence, or satanism. The study participants were unable to express the themes of more than a third of their favorite songs. The professors reached the conclusion that the effect of music on the students was insignificant.

The roots of most demands to suppress music have to do with protecting children. While this is a noble cause, the facts don't support the notion that restricting music will protect anyone. Adolescence is an intense time in any person's life, full of conflict and struggle; however, it is rare that a good kid will suddenly go bad during adolescence. Studies show that most kids who commit crimes, have extreme relationship issues, or engage in sexual activity before their peers, were troubled *before* adolescence. Their issues had to do with family rather than outside influences. Most conflict in families with teenagers involves more benign issues, such as dating, leisure activities, tidiness, and punctuality.[6]

As you will see throughout this book, many other studies repeatedly back up these findings. Nonetheless, Mary Whitehouse, a speaker at the 1987 Conservative Party Conference, famously said, "You've got to get away from this silly business of having to prove things. We've got to start using our common sense and human experience. Then we might get somewhere."[7]

So if music is not a primary motivation to kill, fuck, rape, destroy, or annihilate, what is it used for? The answer is simple: as a means of communicating or socializing with others, as a diversion or escape from our troubles, as a source of information, as a way to identify ourselves as individuals, as a way to celebrate and mourn, and as a way to chronicle our experiences. However, sometimes we, as music fans, threaten the establishment in the process.

In many respects, citizens in the United States are fortunate. In 1982, Ivan Jirous, leader of the Czech band the Plastic People of the Universe, was sentenced to three and a half years in prison. His crime? Music. The court felt that his music was "creating a public nuisance." In Israel, the music of Richard Wagner is rarely performed in public because he was an anti-Semite. In Communist Russia, Dimitry Shostakovich was considered an enemy of the state for his compositions and was shunned by fellow Russians for most of his career. Zairean jazz great Franco Luambo Makiadi was jailed several times solely because he was a popular musician. Chilean folksinger Victor Jara was murdered by his own government for the political content of his songs.

Fortunately, Americans usually don't have to worry about being jailed or murdered for music—at least not yet. While these examples seem shocking, they are and were justified by an extension of the logic used to keep CDs out of a Wal-Mart store, show Elvis only from the waist up, or keep Marilyn Manson from performing in your town.

Music, like all art, mirrors the society that creates it, listens to it, and makes it a part of life. Music censorship follows that same principle. When we examine the censors, we really examine ourselves—the people who live on our block, those strangers we pass every day on our way to work, the man or woman with whom we brush shoulders on the bus. This book is about music, of course, but it is also about us—Americans. About what it means to be an American. About the actions we take when our American ideals clash with the beliefs of our fellow Americans.

Most frightening of all is how close to extremes our country has actually come—and how often.

2

"BANNED IN THE USA"

The PMRC and Music Labeling

**When politicians start talking morality,
grab your wallet and your children,
and run for your life.**
—Jon Katz

One December morning in 1984, Mary Elizabeth Gore (known as "Tipper" since she was a toddler) had just returned from a shopping trip with her eldest daughter, Karenna. Karenna had been asking to buy Prince's new hit song "Let's Go Crazy." So Tipper purchased a copy of the soundtrack to the movie *Purple Rain*. As you probably know, Tipper Gore is the wife of former Tennessee senator and vice president Al Gore. But according to Tipper, that makes no difference to the rest of the story.

When Tipper and Karenna returned to their ancestral home in Arlington, Virginia, they immediately opened the new album and put it on the family stereo. As the album played, Mrs. Gore began to notice things she didn't like. The album's fifth track, "Darling Nikki," contained some graphic descriptions of masturbation that, according to Tipper, embarrassed both her and her daughter: "I knew a girl named Nikki, guess you could say she was a sex fiend.

I met her in a hotel lobby, masturbating with a magazine." In Tipper's words, after hearing the song, "I was stunned—then I got mad."

Now let's pause and review for a moment. At the urging of her then eleven-year-old daughter, Tipper Gore had bought a copy of Prince's *Purple Rain*—the soundtrack to an R-rated movie that already had created quite a bit of controversy in the press. She'd come home and played the album in front of her four children (ages eleven, eight, six, and two) without first listening to the album to determine if the lyrics and themes were appropriate for her children. Then, when she felt embarrassed about the album's contents, she got mad.

But whom did Tipper blame for this incident? Herself? No. Her daughter? No. Tipper Gore blamed Prince. According to Gore, "Millions of Americans were buying *Purple Rain* with no idea what to expect. Thousands of parents were giving the album to their children—many even younger than my daughter."[1]

In fact, Tipper became so upset she decided to scrutinize (albeit for the first time) the popular music her children listened to and the music videos they saw on television. She sat with her children and watched Van Halen's "Hot for Teacher" video on MTV, along with Mötley Crüe's "Looks That Kill," Def Leppard's "Photograph," and the Scorpions' "Rock You Like a Hurricane." Tipper was shocked by the graphic depictions of sex and violence that she saw as commonplace in music videos and song lyrics. "The images frightened my children; they frightened me! The graphic sex and the violence were too much for us to handle."[2] She decided to do something about it.

Tipper and her friend and fellow Washington housewife Susan Baker (wife of then–Treasury Secretary James Baker) discussed the problem at length. Susan, the mother of eight children, told Tipper that several of her friends planned to start a group that would take action on the issue. She asked Tipper to lend her name to a letter that invited others to a meeting to see what they could do about excesses in rock music. The group started by Gore, Baker, and eight other wives of influential Washingtonians became known as the Parents Music Resource Center (PMRC). Within a few months, the PMRC spearheaded a public relations campaign that forever changed the way music is recorded, produced, distributed, and sold. All who came into the crosshairs of this group—and subsequent groups that were inspired by the PMRC's success—saw their lives and careers changed forever.

But events leading to the PMRC's sudden rise to prominence started several years earlier. Although the PMRC definitely was not the first organized group to lobby for censorship initiatives, society's attitudes toward music changed significantly during the 1980s—the era of the "Reagan Revolution."

The Reagan Revolution meant record national deficits, trickle-down economics, high unemployment, low wages, out-of-control defense spending, two economic recessions, and a stock market crash that rivaled Black Friday and the start of the Great Depression in 1929. Historically, we put more importance on social issues when our economy is bad and less when it is good. During the eighties, debates on issues like foreign and domestic social policy, abortion, and "family values" filled the national agenda. This also was the time when conservative Christians realized their potential power as a voting lobby, and they began to work to bring several of their social platforms to the nation's attention. One of those platforms addressed the presence of Satan in popular music.

Record burning had been a means of protest for more than twenty years, but it truly came into vogue during the late seventies and early eighties. Inspired by Dan and Steve Peters's "Why Knock Rock?" lecture series, hundreds of teens set fire to thousands of popular records that contained satanic imagery and lyrics. Record burnings were especially popular with youth groups in the Bible Belt, reaching as far as Iowa. People had been concerned with blasphemy in popular music for years (see chapter 7), but the 1980s were different. Hidden messages were "found" in rock records. These messages were commonly referred to as "backmasking."

Backmasking came to mainstream attention following a segment aired on the Praise The Lord (PTL) network on January 14, 1982. The talk show, hosted by Christina Paul Crouch, featured William H. Yarroll of the Applied Potentials Institute in Aurora, Colorado. Mr. Yarroll contended that rock musicians were members of the Church of Satan and had adopted a failed advertising gimmick known as subliminal messaging to deliver satanic messages directly into the subconscious of music listeners. According to Yarroll, most of these messages were hidden in the songs—often recorded backward and at alternate speeds. What concerned Yarroll was that these messages could be communicated directly into the listeners' minds without their own awareness.

After receiving calls and complaints from concerned constituents, California state representative, Phil Wyman, promised to look into the issue.

Wyman introduced a bill (A.B. 3741) into the California legislature as a "consumer protection statute warning of subliminal messages." He said that rock records "can manipulate our behavior without our knowledge or consent and turn us into disciples of the anti-Christ." Wyman, Yarroll, and other conservatives appeared everywhere in the popular media, defending their position and promoting the legislation. California congressman Robert Dornan introduced a similar bill into the U.S. House of Representative. Despite assurances from countless academics, psychologists, and audiologists who called the concept "silly," "without merit," and "preposterous," television, newspapers, and magazines ran hundreds of stories suggesting that the albums of artists from Led Zeppelin to the Beatles contained hidden messages that could be understood only by the "inner brain." Although conservative Christians and their concerns about satanism started the ball rolling, groups that called attention to the gratuitous sex and violence in lyrics and music videos were the ones who hit the home run.

The Reverend Donald E. Wildmon started the National Federation for Decency in 1976 to combat the sex, profanity, and violence that was seen everywhere on television. By the 1980s, Wildmon had over ten thousand contributors, and his group had spawned several other organizations focused on the moral decline depicted on television. Minister John Hurt began a movement among other Church of Christ parishes, saying, "If you ever plan to take a stand for moral decency, now is the time, while hundreds of thousands of others are moving in the same direction."[3] Hurt campaigned against the smut he found on *Saturday Night Live*, *Three's Company*, and *Charlie's Angels*, among others.

The secular and quasi-academic National Coalition on Television Violence (NCTV), founded by Illinois psychiatrist Dr. Thomas Radecki, got into the business of rating television shows for violence in August of 1980. The NCTV found programs like *Buck*

Rogers in the 25th Century and *The Dukes of Hazzard* to be prime examples of the deplorable amount of sex and violence on television. In October of 1983, once he'd gained attention for his crusade against television programming, Radecki turned his attention toward music videos. According to Radecki, "The message is that violence is normal and okay, that hostile sexual relations between men and women are common and acceptable, that heroes actively engage in torture and murder of others for fun."[4] Radecki pointed to videos such as Michael Jackson's "Thriller," Billy Idol's "Dancing with Myself," and Kansas's "Fight Fire with Fire."

While Radecki, Yarroll, and other conservatives had spent a great deal of time pointing out the evils of popular music, very little had actually been done to change it. There were record burnings, protests, and boycotts—but nothing really had much impact. And then the PTA at a small elementary school in Cincinnati, Ohio, had an idea.

Rick Allen and his family really liked the song "1999" by Prince. (Prince became the "poster boy" for music censors in the 1980s. In addition to sexually explicit lyrics that would make a sailor blush, it didn't hurt that he was black and dressed funny.) When the Allens purchased the full album and played it in the presence of their kids, they soon rushed across the living room to shut off the track "Let's Pretend We're Married." The words "Let's pretend we're married and go all night, there's nothing wrong if it feels alright" were more than they wanted their young children to know about sex. Despite Prince's reputation and the presence of printed lyrics on the album's inner sleeve, the Allens had been caught completely off guard.

Prince's *1999*, the album largely credited for starting the mid-eighties censorship movement

Rick was so upset that he decided to bring the matter to his local Parent Teacher Organization chapter at Delshire Elementary School. The Delshire PTA united with nineteen other Cincinnati

PTA chapters, vowing to take the matter of excessive debauchery in pop music all the way to the group's national convention in Las Vegas. So in June of 1984, in a city known for legalized prostitution, gambling, and eighteen-year-old strippers, the National Parent Teachers Organizations adopted a resolution urging "recording companies to put a label on record, tape, and cassette covers rating the material contained within with regard to profanity, sex, violence, or vulgarity." The only recording industry comment regarding the resolution came from a Warner Brothers Records executive who quipped, "The function of rock and roll is to annoy parents. This just proves that nothing changes."[5]

The following October, Elaine Steinkemeyer, the National PTA president, sent copies of the antirock resolution to twenty-nine major record companies. In a letter accompanying the resolution, she asked the companies to establish panels that would evaluate material similar to the ratings system used by the Motion Picture Association of America.

"A ratings system is out of the question," said a spokesperson for the Recording Industry Association of America (RIAA). "The movie industry has to deal with less than four hundred submissions a year. We have over twenty-five thousand songs. I find it a dangerous kind of precedent. It's not censorship per se, but it certainly does open a Pandora's box of unpleasant possibilities."[6] In effect, the RIAA decided to ignore the National PTA's resolution, and the matter seemed to end right there.

However, less than a year later, the recording industry found that it could not ignore the PTA and its new ally, the PMRC. This time there was much more at stake. Not freedom of expression, but lots of money. As the PMRC was being formed, Congress was considering a pet project of the RIAA: a tax on blank audiotape and home recording gear. The tax could yield hundreds of millions of dollars, and they were prepared to do just about anything to help it pass.

Cultural Fascism

Back to Tipper Gore and company. It was April of 1985 when Tipper, Susan Baker, and friends Pam Howar and Sally Nevius formed a tax-exempt nonprofit organization that was officially called the Parents Music Resource Center, or PMRC. As their first official action, they pooled about two thousand names from their respective Christmas card lists and invited friends and neighbors to a mass meeting at St. Columba's Church in Washington, D.C. The guest speaker at the meeting (which was held on May 15, 1985) was Jeff Ling, a former musician who was now the youth minister at a suburban Virginia church. Ling toured with a slide presentation that showed the horrors of rock music and its message to young people. More than 350 people attended the meeting. The only media attention devoted to the PMRC's initial public action was a brief mention in the "Style" section of the *Washington Post.*

Armed with a five-thousand-dollar start-up grant from Mike Love (of the Beach Boys) and office space donated by the Adolph Coors Foundation, the PMRC was born. Their first order of business was an official letter to the RIAA calling for the recording industry to "exercise voluntary self-restraint perhaps by developing guidelines and/or a rating system, such as that of the movie industry."

Musicians Who Made Statements Supporting the 1980s Efforts to Regulate Music

Smokey Robinson
Paul McCartney
Mike Love (Beach Boys)
Harry Connick, Jr.
Pat Boone

However, the PMRC didn't seem to want to control *all* sex and violence. A close examination of their targets shows they wanted to curb only the sex and violence that could be encountered by suburban white teenagers. Never once was a country artist, song, or video included in the PMRC's lists, nor did they feel it necessary to label opera recordings, which are notorious for their sexual and violent themes. No one in the PMRC complained about theater, paintings, or sculpture, because teenagers don't buy paintings and rarely attend the theater unaccompanied. They do buy records, and they buy millions of them.

The letter was signed by the wives of twenty influential Washington businessmen and legislators. At least four of those influential legislators sat on committees that were due to hear arguments for the Home Audio Recording Act.

The intention of the Home Audio Recording Act was to curb what the industry felt was a growing problem: home taping. The industry argued that this was a clear violation of copyright, and believed it was losing millions of dollars a year in unpurchased product. The focus of the act was to charge a special royalty tax on blank tapes and home audio equipment, such as cassette decks. The tape tax amounted to one cent per minute of tape, which had the potential of turning a $250 million annual profit. Ninety percent of this tax's proceeds would go directly to record companies and the remaining 10 percent would go to the artists. With the Home Audio Recording Act on the line, the RIAA was a lot more interested in the PMRC than in the National PTA.

In the five months following the PMRC's letter to the RIAA, more than 150 newspaper editorials were written on the PMRC's proposals. The controversy was splashed across the country's newspapers and magazines, even landing on the covers of *Newsweek* and *People*. Armed with their list of the "Filthy Fifteen," representatives from the PMRC appeared on *Donahue, Good Morning America,* NBC's *Today, The CBS Morning News, Entertainment Tonight,* and the evening news on all three major networks.

"The Filthy Fifteen"

In their first communication with the music industry, the PMRC listed fifteen artists who offended their sensibilities. Under the PMRC's original proposal, songs would be rated according to several categories: X for songs containing explicit or suggestive sexual references, D/A for the glorification of drug or alcohol abuse, V for violence, and O for references to the occult.

ARTIST	SONG	RATING
Judas Priest	"Eat Me Alive"	X
Mötley Crüe	"Bastard"	V
Prince	"Darling Nikki"	X
Sheena Easton	"Sugar Walls"	X
W.A.S.P.	"(Animal) F-U-C-K Like a Beast"	X
Mercyful Fate	"Into the Coven"	O
Vanity	"Strap on Robby Baby"	X
Def Leppard	"High 'n' Dry"	D/A
Twisted Sister	"We're Not Gonna Take It"	V
Madonna	"Dress You Up"	X
Cyndi Lauper	"She Bop"	X
AC/DC	"Let Me Put My Love into You"	X
Black Sabbath	"Trashed"	D/A
Mary Jane Girls	"My House"	X
Venom	"Possessed"	O

Twisted Sister (*left*) and Prince (*right*) were both members of the PMRC's original "Filthy Fifteen." Twisted Sister's Dee Snider was the only PMRC target to testify at the 1985 Senate hearing on record labeling. Prince became one of the focal points of the PMRC media blitz the preceding summer.

The strategy of the PMRC's media blitz was simple: get attention. And they achieved their goal by using the media to educate and inform parents "of this alarming new trend . . . towards lyrics that are sexually explicit, violent or glorify the use of drugs and alcohol." The answer, according to Susan Baker and Tipper Gore, was sixfold:

1. Print lyrics on album covers.

2. Keep explicit covers under the counter.

3. Establish a ratings system for records similar to that for films.

4. Establish a ratings system for concerts.

5. Reassess the contracts of performers who engage in violence and explicit sexual behavior onstage.

6. Establish a citizen and record-company media watch that would pressure broadcasters not to air "questionable talent."

Once they got attention, they used it to gather more. The more attention, the more pressure on the RIAA.

The PMRC repeatedly stated that their goal was not censorship but to passively assist as parents judged whether or not questionable material was appropriate for their children. Though the PMRC said they didn't think their proposals should be considered "censorship," they quickly threatened censorious action if their demands weren't met. PMRC founder Sally Nevius was quoted in *People* magazine as saying, "We want the industry to police itself. If they refuse, we're going to look into legal ways to stop what we feel is a form of contributing to the delinquency of minors."[7] Jeff Ling, by this time a paid consultant to the PMRC, commented, "Do I think [explicit music] should be out of the stores? Sure I do. And I think labelling will do that."[8]

The founders of the PMRC also talked about how they were actually rock fans. Tipper Gore often told reporters that she played drums in a high school combo and that there were many acceptable artists recording and performing music in 1985. "I have rock music in my home of my own," she told *The Christian Science Monitor,* "I am still a consumer." Susan Baker reminisced about dancing at a club called the Teenage Retreat during her high school years. "It was a neat place. They played all sorts of great rock 'n' roll—Chuck Berry, Elvis, Buddy Holly, and Fats Domino."[9] "I found my thrill on Blueberry Hill," she told a reporter, "but this stuff is different."

The PMRC didn't limit themselves to the original "Filthy Fifteen" either. As the movement escalated, so did the list of artists questioned. Heavy metal and punk seemed particularly to upset the PMRC. In one embarrassing misstep, the PMRC cited the Dead Kennedys' single "Nazi Punks Fuck Off" as a song that glorifies Nazism. A glance at the song's lyrics (or a second look at the song's title) shows otherwise.

Although Tipper and Susan were the made-for-television figureheads at the forefront of the war against rock, there were plenty of other antirock forces that were legitimate in the eyes of the media. Religious conservatives and record burners were becoming forces of change in the music industry.

Shortly after the PMRC came to the nation's attention, the Reverend Jimmy Swaggart began to pressure retailers to stop carrying rock music. As a result, Wal-Mart stores across the country started pulling all rock music magazines and controversial rock albums from their shelves. Both Sears and J. C. Penney announced that they would stop carrying records affixed with a PMRC-endorsed warning label. Some music retailers renting space in suburban malls were warned that they would be evicted if conservative protesters picketed their stores.

Inspired by the media attention devoted to the issue, Dallas radio station KAFM formed the National Music Review Council. KAFM vice president William Steding hoped to see the group spread throughout the broadcasting industry to warn consumers and broadcasters about questionable music.

Even civil rights activist and sometime presidential candidate the Reverend Jesse Jackson stated that it was time record companies accepted some responsibility for the high rate of black teenage pregnancies.

Pat Boone, vanilla pop star of the fifties, tried to bring a little peace to the battle by sharing his views on constitutional law: "Censorship should not be a bad word. No society can survive without it. I believe that the stop sign at the corner is healthy censorship. That's what the Constitution had in mind—self-imposed, majority-approved censorship."[10]

Musicians and free-speech supporters got their share of ink as well. Attorney Louis Sheinfield said, "It's scary, because the PMRC appeals to the natural fears of parents. They say rock music causes babies to have babies, teenagers to go on drugs, and teenagers to commit suicide. No one believes that these problems will go away if you suppress records. They are elevating fear over reason."[11]

Gene Simmons of KISS was quoted in *People* as saying, "Rock 'n' roll is beside the point. They're saying a small group can dictate to the masses a moral tone. Records first, then books, television, and the Bible."[12]

"I have no problem with violence when it is used for a purpose," said rock critic and anticensorship crusader Dave Marsh. "For example, in the 'Beat It' video—in which Michael Jackson unites two warring gangs through dance—the violence is used to promote racial harmony."[13]

During the national debate over the PMRC's proposals, one advocate rose above the others: lesser-known musician and composer Frank Zappa. Zappa had existed on the peripheries of popular music for twenty years. Unfortunately, before stating his opposition to the PMRC, most fans of pop music knew him only for his 1982 hit "Valley Girl," a song that spawned a national obsession with Southern California teenage girl–speak. Zappa was an underground sensation and a prolific composer and musician, having released dozens of albums. But he was also a critic of the commercial recording industry, and beginning in 1981 he released all his recordings on his own record label. When Frank Zappa learned of the proposals put forth by the PMRC, he didn't hesitate in expressing his dissatisfaction.

Zappa told the *Los Angeles Times,*

The whole thing is preposterous. It seems like the kind of campaign a bored Washington housewife would dream up when she's at a summer barbecue. The record industry is acting like a bunch of cowards. They're scared to death of the fundamentalist right and want to throw them a bone in hopes that they'll go away. But this stickering program will just start a precedent—they'll always want more.[14]

Zappa felt that the industry's interest in working with the PMRC was based on what was best for business rather than on ethical grounds:

> The RIAA has a huge financial interest in anti–home taping and piracy legislation. And guess who runs the committee that over-sees this legislation? Senator Strom Thurmond, whose wife is a member of the PMRC. I think the connection's pretty clear. The record companies are willing to chop up artists' civil rights so that they won't have to lose any potential profits from their anti–home taping and piracy campaign.[15]

Frank Zappa was right.

In a June memo, RIAA president Stanley Gortikov urged its board of directors to consider cooperating with the PMRC. In a meeting with PMRC representatives, Gortikov said he would do his best to "exercise persuasion with the record companies; in my correspondence I will start to heighten awareness."[16] On August 17, 1985, the RIAA announced that its members would work with the PMRC to develop a system of warning stickers to affix to albums whose content was questionable. But he was too late, because the issue had spun far out of the RIAA's control. The PMRC was already receiving thousands of letters and nonstop phone calls on the issue. What's more, with the slow progress of negotiations between the RIAA and the PMRC, Senator John C. Danforth of Missouri decided to step into the controversy. Several weeks later, Danforth's office announced that, in response to the issues raised by the PMRC, the Senate Committee on Commerce, Science, and Transportation would hold a record-labeling hearing on September 19, 1985.

A Government Action, or a Private Action?

According to Al and Tipper Gore, they wanted no part of congres-sional hearings and thought they were a terrible idea. However, this didn't stop Al Gore from becoming one of the most vocal and engaged senators on the committee. Further, Tipper was one of the featured witnesses who testified before her husband and sixteen other senators (four of the other senators also had wives who were deeply involved in the PMRC's activities). Yet the PMRC media machine had accelerated to such a high speed that once the hearings were announced, they quickly became the largest media event in congressional history up to that time. All the major networks, fifty press photographers, and dozens of reporters packed the ornate Senate hearing room to capacity.

The committee—called to order shortly after 9:30 A.M. on September 19—consisted of Chairman Danforth (Missouri) and Senators Packwood (Oregon), Goldwater (Arizona), Kassebaum (Kansas), Pressler (South Dakota), Gorton (Washington), Stevens (Alaska), Kasten (Wisconsin), Trible (Virginia), Hollings (South Carolina), Long (Louisiana), Inouye (Hawaii), Ford (Kentucky), Riegle (Michigan), Exon (Nebraska), Gore (Tennessee), and Rockefeller (West Virginia). After brief opening remarks and information about the day's proceedings, Chairman Danforth invited the senators to offer statements. Senator Hollings was the first speaker.

He began by proclaiming that rock music's socially redeeming value was "inaudible." Then Hollings went on to say, "I would tell you [rock] is outrageous filth, and we have got to do something about it. I would make the statement that if I could find some way constitutionally to do away with it, I would."[17]

Senator Trible followed. After misquoting Plato, Trible said that repeated exposure to the rape, incest, sexual violence, and perversion found in rock music is like "sandpaper to the soul." "It rubs raw one's sensibilities, resulting in a state of emotional numbness," said Senator Trible. "The effect on the troubled child . . . can be disastrous, pushing the child over the emotional precipice. This becomes the real social problem."[18]

Senators Gore and Hawkins also made statements, regurgitating the usual rhetoric that the PMRC's efforts were not a form of censorship but were meant only to help parents raise their children in a difficult world. They stressed that the point of the hearing should be education, not legislation.

Susan Baker and Tipper Gore

Tipper Gore (*left*) and Susan Baker (*right*) during their testimony before the Senate Committee on Commerce, Science, and Transportation

were the first to testify. Accompanying them was Jeff Ling, with his slide presentation on the evils of rock music. According to Mrs. Baker's testimony,

> The material we are concerned about cannot be compared with "Louie Louie," Cole Porter, Billie Holiday, et cetera. Cole Porter's "birds do it, bees do it," can hardly be compared with WASP's, "I f-u-c-k like a beast." There is a new element of vulgarity and violence toward women that is unprecedented.[19]

Baker's statement was interesting, particularly since all of the artists she mentioned were censored in their day (see the Chronology chapters later in this book for more information). She continued:

> Some have suggested that the records in question are only a minute element in this music. However, these records are not few, and have sold millions of copies, like Prince's "Darling Nikki," about masturbation, sold over 10 million copies. Judas Priest, the one about forced oral sex at gunpoint, has sold over 2 million copies. Quiet Riot, *Metal Health,* has songs about explicit sex, over 5 million copies. Mötley Crüe, *Shout at the Devil,* which contains violence and brutality to women, over 2 million copies.
> . . .
> There certainly are many causes for these ills in our society, but it is our contention that the pervasive messages aimed at children which promote and glorify suicide, rape, sadomasochism, and so on, have to be numbered among the contributing factors.
>   Some rock artists actually seem to encourage teen suicide. Ozzie [sic] Osbourne sings "Suicide Solution." Blue Öyster Cult sings "Don't Fear the Reaper." AC/DC sings "Shoot to Thrill." Just last week in Centerpoint, a small Texas town, a young man took his life while listening to the music of AC/DC. He was not the first.[20]

Next it was Tipper's turn.
She began by saying, "We are asking the recording industry to voluntarily assist parents who are concerned by placing a warning label on music products inappropriate for younger children due to explicit sexual or violent lyrics."

"A voluntary labeling is not censorship. Censorship implies restricting access or suppressing content. This proposal does neither. Moreover, it involves no government action,"[21] continued Mrs. Gore, wife of Senator Al Gore, while sitting in a Senate hearing room in front of seventeen of the most powerful men in the federal government.

Jeff Ling was up next. He began by showing a picture of Steve Boucher, a young man who committed suicide while listening to AC/DC's "Shoot to Thrill." Mr. Ling said that during 1985, more than six thousand young people would take their own lives, many of them encouraged by rock stars.

Ling showed slides of album covers, lyrics, and concert photos that depicted satanic imagery, violence, drug use, and explicit sex. He concluded by saying,

> How bad can it get? The list is endless. This album was released just recently by a band called the Mentors. It was released with the label Enigma Records, which also launched Mötley Crüe's career. The album includes songs like "Four-F Club: Find Her, Feel Her, Fuck Her, and Forget Her," "Free Fix for a Fuck," "Clap Queen," "My Erection Is Over," and the song "Golden Showers," which says these words, "Listen, you little slut, do as you are told, come with daddy for me to pour the gold. Golden showers. All through my excrement you shall roam. Bend up and smell my anal vapor. Your face is my toilet paper. On your face I leave a shit tower. Golden showers."[22]

While I think it is safe to say that this statement could be among the most "interesting" conclusions to any congressional testimony, it isn't accurate to use the Mentors as an example of the evils of mainstream rock and roll. The Mentors—who in addition to their unusual lyrics often performed in executioners' hoods—weren't getting rich by corrupting America's youth. The album to which Ling referred sold a total of seventy-five hundred copies—as opposed to the multimillion-selling releases bought by most teens. Most Mentors albums were sold through mail order, at concerts, or through small independent record shops. They were not found in suburban stores or on the shelves of large chain retailers.

During questioning following the testimony, several senators asked questions that were intended to clarify the PMRC's position, the group's concerns over music videos, and the role of radio broadcasters in regulating the material they air.

Then Senator Exon asked Mrs. Gore if it was correct that the PMRC was not interested in federal legislation or regulation. Mrs. Gore responded that the statement was true. Senator Exon then stated, "Well, given that and given what I think I tried to put forth as my feelings on this, Mr. Chairman, I suppose it is nice to have these hearings and discuss these things, because I think it is a concern. But I wonder, Mr. Chairman, if we are not talking about federal regulation and if we are not talking about federal legislation, what is the reason for these hearings in front of the Commerce Committee?"[23]

Following the conclusion of the question-and-answer period and testimony from other PMRC-friendly witnesses, the committee was ready to hear from the other side. Three key witnesses from the music industry testified next: Frank Zappa, John Denver, and Dee Snider of Twisted Sister. Zappa went first.

Frank Zappa testifying before the Senate hearing on record labeling

Before beginning his testimony, Zappa asked for clarification to Senator Exon's question: Was the purpose of these hearings to consider future legislation? Zappa cited Senator Hollings's opening statement as an example of an intimation made toward future legislation. Danforth informed Zappa that his role at the hearings was to testify, not to ask questions. After repeating his query, Zappa was informed that Senator Hollings had left the room, and they did not have time to second-guess the senator's earlier comments. Zappa opened by reading excerpts from his prepared statement:

> The PMRC proposal is an ill-conceived piece of nonsense which fails to deliver any real benefits to children, infringes the civil liberties of people who are not children, and promises to keep the courts busy for years dealing with the interpretational and enforcemental problems inherent in the proposal's design.

In this context, the PMRC demands are the equivalent of treating dandruff by decapitation.

The ladies' shame must be shared by the bosses at the major labels who, through the RIAA, chose to bargain away the rights of composers, performers, and retailers in order to pass H.R. 2911, The Blank Tape Tax, a private tax levied by an industry on consumers for the benefit of a select group within that industry. Is this a consumer issue? You bet it is. The major record labels need to have H.R. 2911 whiz through a few committees before anybody smells a rat. One of them is chaired by Senator Thurmond. Is it a coincidence that Mrs. Thurmond is affiliated with the PMRC?

The only way to sneak it through is to keep the public's mind on something else: Porn rock.[24]

Zappa went on to question the ethics of senators who would sit on a committee considering tax legislation that was influenced by their wives' lobbying group. He called the PMRC's proposals a terrible solution to the issue of informing parents. "Bad facts make bad law, and people who write bad laws are in my opinion more dangerous than songwriters who celebrate sexuality."[25]

Senator Gore was the first to question Zappa.

Senator Gore: I have listened to you a number of times on this issue, and I guess the statement that I want to get from you is whether or not you feel this concern is legitimate.

You feel very strongly about your position, and I understand that. You are very articulate and forceful.

But occasionally you give the impression that you think parents are just silly to be concerned at all.

Mr. Zappa: No; that is not an accurate impression.

Senator Gore: Well, please clarify it, then.

Mr. Zappa: First of all, I think it is the parents' concern; it is not the Government's concern.

Senator Gore: The PMRC agrees with you on that.

Mr. Zappa: Well, that does not come across in the way they have been speaking. The whole drift that I have gotten, based upon the media blitz that has attended the PMRC and its rise to infamy, is that they have a special plan, and it has smelled like legislation up until now.

There are too many things that look like hidden agendas involved with this. And I am a parent. I have got four children. Two of them are here. I want them to grow up in a country where they can think what they want to think, be what they want to be, and not what somebody's wife or somebody in Government makes them be.

I do not want to have that and I do not think you do either.[26]

Senator Gorton of Washington was the next to speak; however, his line of questioning was more a personal critique. He said,

I can only say that I found your statement to be boorish, incredibly and insensitively insulting to the people that were here previously; that you could manage to give the First Amendment of the Constitution of the United States a bad name, if I felt that you had the slightest understanding of it, which I do not.

You do not have the slightest understanding of the difference between Government action and private action, and you have certainly destroyed any case you might otherwise have had with this Senator.[27]

Zappa immediately queried, "Is this a private action?" Gorton would not reply, and Chairman Danforth moved on with the questioning.

Several other senators asked questions of Zappa, but most of them simply repeated points that had already been made. A few questioned Zappa about a proposal included in his testimony in which he suggested that all albums be shipped with a removable lyric sheet so parents could review the theme and lyrics before purchasing the album or allowing their children to listen.

The next witness to testify was folksinger John Denver.

Denver recalled two incidents in his career that confused people who misunderstood the meanings behind the works. His song

"Rocky Mountain High" was thought to contain drug references, and his movie *Oh, God!* was thought to be blasphemous. "Obviously, a clear case of misinterpretation," said Denver. "What assurance have I that any national panel to review my music would make any better judgment?"[28]

He continued:

Mr. Chairman, the suppression of the people of a society begins in my mind with the censorship of the written or spoken word. It was so in Nazi Germany. It is so in many places today where those in power are afraid of the consequences of an informed and educated people.

In a mature, incredibly diverse society such as ours, the access to all perspectives of an issue becomes more and more important. Those things which in our experience are undesirable generally prove to be unfurthering and sooner or later become boring. That process cannot and should not be stifled. . . .

The problem, Mr. Chairman, in my opinion, has to do with our willingness as parents to take responsibility for the upbringing of our children.

To quote a wise old man from ancient China: "If there be righteousness"—not self-righteousness; that is not part of the quote. "If there be righteousness in the heart, there will be beauty in the character. If there be beauty in the character, there will be harmony in the home. If there be harmony in the home, there will be order in the Nation. And if there be order in the Nation, there will be peace in the world."[29]

Next was the only person testifying that day whose recordings would be subject to any ratings system or warning sticker initiated by the PMRC: Dee Snider, lead singer of the heavy metal band Twisted Sister.

Snider, obviously a little overwhelmed and nervous to be speaking at the hearing, began by saying, "I am thirty years old, I am married, I have a three-year-old son. I was born and raised a Christian and I still adhere to those principles. Believe it or not, I do not smoke, I do not drink, and I do not do drugs."[30]

Snider addressed three accusations the PMRC had lodged against Twisted Sister. He began with an accusation concerning lyrics to the song "Under the Blade." The PMRC contended that the song's lyrics detailed sadomasochistic exploits. Snider told the committee that the song's theme actually described the narrator's fear of surgery and was written for the band's guitarist before he entered the hospital. According to Snider, "The only sadomasochism, bondage, and rape in this song is in the mind of Ms. Gore."

The second accusation was that the PMRC wanted Twisted Sister's biggest hit, "We're Not Gonna Take It," rated as excessively violent. Snider pointed out that the song alluded to, described, or implied absolutely no violence. Although the accompanying music video featured a child committing cartoonish violent acts in protest of his father, Snider questioned the logic of restricting any version of the *song* when the only violence was in the *video*.

The third accusation was a comment that Tipper Gore made during a television appearance regarding a Twisted Sister T-shirt that depicted a handcuffed woman. Snider resolutely denied that such a T-shirt had ever existed, and he challenged Tipper to produce it.

Snider summarized his objections to music rating and labeling by saying, "Parents can thank the PMRC for reminding them that there is no substitute for parental guidance. But that is where the PMRC's job ends."[31]

After Snider had taken questions from several senators, Al Gore asked to be acknowledged by the chair. Gore teased the nervous Snider and poked fun at his assertion that he was a Christian in the world of heavy metal. He argued with Mr. Snider about the semantics of Tipper's quoted statements. When Snider offered to present a tape recording of the statements to the committee, Gore concluded his questions.

When the hearing wrapped up at the end of that day, the issue seemed to be even more confused and diluted. Frank Zappa felt that the hearing had accomplished little. He was quoted in *Variety* as saying, "These hearings were a kangaroo court."

Wondering openly where the line was between government regulation and censorship, one industry insider asked, "Where do you stop and start? Does 'Puppy Love' mean bestiality? Does 'On the Good Ship Lollipop' mean a psychedelic trip? There's no place to stop."[32]

On November 1, 1985, after several weeks of behind-the-scenes negotiations, the RIAA and PMRC emerged to announce that they had brokered a deal that would put the issue to rest. A voluntary warning sticker, issued by the record companies, that stated "Parental Advisory—Explicit Lyrics" was introduced. This agreement came just two days after the Home Audio Recording Act received its own hearing. One of the bill's sponsors was Senator Al Gore of Tennessee.

Regulating Rock

Rather than ending the controversy surrounding music lyrics and imagery, the new labeling agreement gave potential censors something tangible with which they could work. The PMRC had generated a lot of press attention in its six short months of existence, and many politicians and activists were eager to capture some of the limelight.

Despite the fact that an agreement between the warring parties had been reached, it took nearly five years for the universal sticker to appear. Regardless, some politicians and concerned businesses used the nonexistent stickering system as a de facto obscenity standard. Almost without exception, legislation written concerning controversial lyrics in the late 1980s used the proposed sticker as a litmus test for acceptability. A problem existed because legislators didn't pay close attention to the terms of the agreement. Unlike the MPAA's system of rating movies, here there was no objective, centralized board whose job it was to evaluate lyrics. Instead, the agreement empowered each record label to oversee its own stickering policy, and that setup allowed for nonuniform, subjective criteria for stickering at each of the twenty-nine major record companies involved in the initial agreement.

Within two weeks of the labeling agreement between the PMRC and the RIAA, a flood of legislation began. On November 14, 1985, the city of San Antonio, Texas, passed a law that restricted concerts by artists whose albums carried warning stickers. Young people under the age of fourteen were banned from attending restricted concerts unless they were accompanied by a parent, and any advertisements for those concerts had to carry a warning label similar to that featured on the album. Similar legislation, passed in Jacksonville, Florida, targeted a local concert by the Beastie Boys. However, the legislation was eventually ruled unconstitutional.

By early 1986, a dozen states were considering bills that either restricted sales or banned albums that carried parental warning stickers. Among those states were Arizona, Delaware, Florida, Illinois, Iowa, Kansas, Missouri, New Mexico, Oklahoma, Pennsylvania, and Virginia. Legislation considered in Maryland received a significant amount of national exposure, and it even prompted Frank Zappa to travel to the state to testify in a hearing similar to the one held in the U.S. Senate.

The universal parental warning sticker used by all major record companies as a result of the PMRC's activities

Hoping to declare stickered records obscene and restrict their sale and display, the Maryland bill sought to amend the state's obscenity laws to include albums, tapes, and laser discs. The bill was written and introduced by delegate Judith Toth, who said she had been inspired to action by the PMRC. According to Toth's proposal, retailers would be required to place objectionable material in a separate area of their stores and seek proof of adulthood before a customer could purchase a stickered item. Toth made her intentions very clear when speaking to the press: "I say [the recording industry] is going to go broke defending themselves. Wait until we start court cases under existing laws. The purpose isn't to win; the purpose is to keep them so tied up that they don't know what hit them."[33]

During a February 1986 hearing before the Maryland State Senate Judiciary Committee on Toth's proposal, Frank Zappa again testified concerning the logic and constitutionality of labeling albums and songs. He and delegate Toth had the following exchange during his testimony:

Frank Zappa: To say that rock music is "the worst form of child abuse" and "mass child abuse" is sky-high rhetoric.

Judith Toth: We're not talking about references to sex. We're talking about references to incest. Incest. And it says, "Do it, kids! It's fine." We're talking about rape and sexual violence. . . . You've got to read this stuff to know how dirty it is.

Zappa: Did you read this? [*Laughter*] Or did you read the "synopsis"?

Toth: This is pornography.

Zappa: This is censorship. I oppose this bill for a number of reasons. First of all, there's no need for it. The idea that the lyrics to a song are going to cause "antisocial behavior" is not supported by science.

Toth: This bill is constitutional. We're talking about minors in the first place. And stop worrying about their "civil rights." Start worrying about their mental health, and about the health of our society.[34]

Eventually the bill failed, but Toth has repeatedly attempted to reintroduce it to "bring the record industry to its knees."

Frank Zappa

Most people have heard of Frank Zappa, although mostly because of his free-speech advocacy or his hit song, 1982's "Valley Girl" with daughter Moon Unit, which added words and phrases like "totally" and

"gag me with a spoon" to the American vernacular. Fewer are aware of his genius as a guitar player, composer, bandleader, satirist, and political and social commentator; still fewer realize he had more than sixty albums to his credit, many with irreverent titles such as *Thing-Fish, Lumpy Gravy, Burnt Weeny Sandwich,* and *Weasels Ripped My Flesh.*

Zappa's career in music began in the late 1960s. After a brief stint in college studying music, Zappa worked as a lounge musician in California and wrote the scores to a few B movies to finance his first studio. In 1964, Zappa joined a local band called the Soul Giants and began to introduce his own songs

Frank Zappa

through the band. Once the band was signed to MGM/Verve in 1966, the record company insisted it change its name—to become the Mothers of Invention.

It is difficult to categorize Zappa's music into understood genres. Zappa jumped into straight-ahead rock, jazz, big band, and orchestral music—sometimes mixing different genres together on the same album or even within the same composition. Throughout his career, both with the Mothers of Invention and as a solo artist, Zappa brought some of rock's most distinctive players through his bands, musicians such as Steve Vai, Adrian Belew (King Crimson), Terry Bozzio (Missing Persons), Alice Cooper, Jean-Luc Ponty, and Jack Bruce (Cream).

Zappa pioneered the concept of artist-owned and -controlled record companies, which allowed him the artistic freedom to create the music he saw fit without the pressure and misunderstandings he had endured while working with major labels early in his career. Although not a commercial "success" (on the scale of his contemporaries in music), Zappa began to receive recognition for his work late in his career. He was awarded two Grammys (in 1987 and 1993, both for instrumental albums) and was invited by Václav Havel, the president of Czechoslovakia, and life-long Zappa fan, to serve as the "Trade, Tourism, and Cultural Liaison to the West." His selfless work in the fight against music censorship in the 1980s demonstrated not only his passion for artistic freedom but his keen intellect and willingness to become a target for what he believed.

Zappa was no stranger to trouble during his career. In the early 1960s, he was arrested and charged with conspiracy to commit pornography for creating and selling fake sex tapes to an undercover police officer. Zappa used some royalty money for a minor hit he wrote for the Penguins, entitled "Memories of El Monte," to bail out his co-conspirator. Zappa also had run-ins with censors over several of his works. The song "Jewish Princess" spurred a protest filed with the FCC against Zappa by the Anti-Defamation League of the B'nai B'rith. "Let's Make the Water Turn Black" upset an executive at Verve, who thought that in the lyric "And I still remember Mama with her apron and her pad, feeding all the boys at Ed's Café," the word "pad" referred to a sanitary napkin.

After fighting prostate cancer for several years, Zappa passed away in 1993 at the age of fifty-two.

In Pennsylvania, which twenty-three years earlier considered strong antirock legislation to stop the Beatles from performing in their state, legislators introduced a bill creating Pennsylvania's own warning-label system. The bill required a fluorescent-yellow warning label on any album containing lyrics that "explicitly describe, advocate, or encourage suicide, incest, bestiality, sado-masochism, rape, or involuntary deviate sexual intercourse. [Or] advocate or encourage murder, ethnic intimidation, the use of illegal drugs, or the excessive or illegal use of alcohol."[35] The Pennsylvania legislation placed the burden of enforcement on the retailer. As the national debate on labeling continued, retailers saw the storm coming and began to make policy decisions based on the nonexistent stickering system.

In California, the Dead Kennedys' Jello Biafra was prosecuted under the California state penal code for "Distribution of Harmful Material to Minors," the first case of a musician's being prosecuted for the contents of his or her record album. The band's album *Frankenchrist* contained a poster that included a painting by Swiss artist H. R. Giger (entitled *Landscape #20, Where Are We Coming From?*). Tipper Gore took credit for Biafra's prosecution in several press interviews. The PMRC issued a statement on the trial:

> The PMRC feels that the poster and the Dead Kennedys album *Frankenchrist* is a blatant example of pornography and failure to provide truth in packaging. The warning sticker which was placed on the shrink-wrap, not on the album itself, claims that the poster is a work of art some may find repulsive and offensive. This does not relay the explicit nature of the poster and does not adequately warn parents to the contents of the album. The right to consumer information prior to purchasing a product is a time-honored principle in this country. This is clearly a violation of that principle.[36]

The case was eventually thrown out of court, and the judge forbade the prosecution to file new charges.

Concerned about losing their leases because of local obscenity laws or protests, many mall retailers voluntarily added their own warning stickers or restricted the viewing and sale of contentious titles. Others attempted to appease concerned consumers by announcing that they would not sell any labeled music in their stores. According to a music buyer for Wal-Mart, "Our customers told us loud and clear, they want to let their children shop in our music departments without having to worry about them purchasing stickered product."

In one incident, Meyer Music in the Pacific Northwest created its own stickering program to warn parents about potentially objectionable albums. Frank Zappa's high profile as an anticensorship advocate led the retailer's labeling committee to assume that his music must be controversial. After affixing a label warning of "explicit lyrics" to Zappa's *Jazz from Hell* album and placing the stickered album in their stores, it was brought to their attention that the album was entirely instrumental.

There was new action afoot on the national level as well. Several congressional representatives, frustrated by the lack of implementation of the PMRC/RIAA agreement, began to grumble about federal regulations of objectionable lyrics. An anonymous congressperson commissioned a secret congressional research study into the constitutionality of federal legislation to enforce the stickering system. Supporters of the Child Protection and Obscenity Enforcement Act hoped that the legislation could be used to prosecute retailers who carried albums considered obscene under local statutes.

By 1989, the recording industry felt the pinch from both legislators and retailers. Compounding this squeeze was the growing popularity of rap music, which was inciting its own share of controversy. The National Association of Record Manufacturers (NARM) started to pressure the RIAA to seriously review the long-dormant agreement with the PMRC and issue a universal warning sticker. Several labels considered adopting their own labeling standards, and there was talk about expanding perimeters beyond explicit lyrics. Several labels were considering internal proposals to sticker albums that contained lyrics derogatory to women, homosexuals, and ethnic minorities.

In late 1989, the PMRC once again cranked up its media machine to try to force the RIAA to follow through on its promise of a universal warning sticker. In a commentary published in *Billboard* in February of 1989, Tipper Gore and Susan Baker wrote that RIAA member labels had repeatedly violated the spirit of the agreement by releasing albums from artists such as the Beastie

Boys, Metallica, and Mötley Crüe without attempting to warn consumers about the content.

In a rare editorial stance against the PMRC, *Billboard* highlighted one of the flawed principles in the RIAA/PMRC agreement: "Even in cases where the meaning is ambiguous, defending our children from bad thoughts can easily become a smokescreen for weeding out socially or politically oriented lyrics that are perceived to threaten the established order."[37]

It became obvious to the RIAA that there was no easy way out of the controversy, and the path of least resistance was to honor its five-year-old pact with the PMRC. In March of 1990, the RIAA debuted its universal warning sticker. In addition to providing uniform artwork, the RIAA issued a statement that served as the only policy guideline to member record companies:

> To facilitate the exercise of parental discretion on behalf of younger children, participating RIAA member recording companies will identify future releases of their recordings with lyric content relating to explicit sex, explicit violence, or explicit substance abuse. Such recordings, where contractually permissible, either will be identified with a packaging inscription that will state: *"Explicit Lyrics—Parental Advisory"* . . . or such recordings will display printed lyrics.[38]

Reaction was swift. Hundreds of titles began to bear the simple black-and-white, postage-stamp-size sticker, while many music retailers used its adaptation to further restrict sales and create merchandising standards for stickered product. In a fairly common policy statement, one large chain retailer, Super Club Music Corp., instructed employees to restrict sales on all stickered products and to remove any merchandise that spawned local controversy.

Alternative Stickers

Several artists created their own stickers for their releases. Following are a few examples:

Ice-T (from *Freedom of Speech*):

ICE-T; X-Rated; Parents Strongly Cautioned; Some material may be X-tra hype and inappropriate for squares and suckers.

Dead Kennedys (from *Frankenchrist*):

Warning: The inside fold-out to this record cover is a work of art by H. R. Giger that some people may find shocking, repulsive, and offensive. Life can be that way sometimes.

The Cure (from *Standing on a Beach*):

The song "Killing an Arab" has absolutely no racist overtones whatsoever. It is a song that decries the existence of all prejudice and consequent violence. The Cure condemns its use in furthering anti-Arab feeling.

Frank Zappa (from *Frank Zappa Meets The Mothers of Prevention* and *Thing-Fish*):

This album contains material which a truly free society would neither fear nor suppress.

In some socially retarded areas, religious fanatics and ultra-conservative political organizations violate your First Amendment rights by attempting to censor rock & roll albums. We feel that this is un-Constitutional and un-American.

As an alternative to their government-supported programs (designed to keep you docile and ignorant), Barking Pumpkin is pleased to provide stimulating digital audio entertainment for those of you who have outgrown the ordinary.

The language and concepts contained herein are guaranteed not to cause eternal torment in the place where the guy with the horns and the pointed stick conducts his business.

This guarantee is as real as the threats of the video fundamentalists who use attacks on rock music in their attempt to transform America into a nation of check-mailing nincompoops (in the name of Jesus Christ).

If there is a hell, its fires wait for them, not us.

Wal-Mart immediately announced a policy that its stores would no longer carry music products that bore the universal sticker. Record companies anxious to maintain access to Wal-Mart's impressive customer base persuaded some "stickered" artists to release a "clean" version of their albums to sell at large retailers like Wal-Mart, Kmart, and Target. Bestselling artists such as Beck, White Zombie, Nirvana, Ice-T, and hundreds of others began to edit their music or cover artwork to facilitate sales at larger retailers. Many other retailers deliberately (or in some cases accidentally) followed the discount stores' lead and began to stock the sanitized version rather than the release in its intended form.

With the exception of laws in Delaware, Missouri, Florida, and Pennsylvania, all legislation dealing with controversial music was dropped following the sticker standard. That respite lasted less than a year. By late 1990, the controversy surrounding 2 Live Crew's *As Nasty as They Wanna Be* had legislators in six states declaring the album legally obscene and introducing proposals to restrict sale of 2 Live Crew albums and other stickered products. By the end of 1991, more than a dozen new controversial music legislative proposals were introduced around the country.

PMRC Postmortem

Though the PMRC still exists, its influence and public visibility are considerably diminished. Even today, the PMRC calls for further refinements to stickering standards, but the record industry has reverted to its mute state. During its history, the PMRC had more of an impact than most people in the music industry would like to admit. At the beginning of the controversy in 1985, despite Tipper Gore's insistence to the contrary, only 22 percent of adults felt it was desirable or necessary for records to be rated. By 1991, that number had risen to as high as 53 percent.

Interest in Tipper Gore's PMRC activities resurfaced when her husband was nominated for vice president in 1992. News of her reemergence on the political scene prompted James Hetfield, the lead singer of Metallica, to say that "it makes me want to clean my guns."[39]

In 1993, Tipper quietly resigned from the PMRC, saying through a spokesperson that "the PMRC accomplished what it set out to do." But has it? The only people who should be happy with the stickering system are the retailers who feel that it helps them demonstrate accountability to concerned consumers and the record companies who use it as a promotional vehicle for controversial rap and alternative artists such as Snoop Dogg, Eminem, and Marilyn Manson. As soon as protestors lobby against an artist, record-label faxes start churning out press releases attempting to turn the controversy into press exposure—and thus, album sales. Most telling of all, none of the PMRC's original "Filthy Fifteen" carry the parental warning sticker Tipper and Susan Baker insisted that they needed.

Since her retirement from the PMRC, Tipper has turned her attention to the plight of the homeless and mentally ill.

Songs That Mention Tipper Gore

Todd Rundgren	"Jesse"
Warrant	"Ode to Tipper Gore"
Ice-T	"Freedom of Speech" and "KKK Bitch"
Frank Zappa	"Porn Wars"
Ramones	"Censorshit"
Megadeath	"Hook in Mouth"
Alice Donut	"Tipper Gore"

3

"HAPPINESS IS A WARM GUN"

Violence

■

**Times have not become more violent.
They have just become more televised.**
—Marilyn Manson

On April 20, 1999, at about 11:30 A.M., two young men—eighteen-year-old Eric Harris and seventeen-year-old Dylan Klebold—walked into Columbine High School in Littleton, Colorado, carrying a duffel bag and wearing long black trench coats. Inside the duffel bag were a TEC DC-9 semiautomatic pistol, two sawed-off shotguns, a nine-millimeter automatic rifle, and nearly thirty homemade pipe bombs and grenades. When the boys entered the cafeteria, which was filled with about nine hundred students, they threw a grenade into the air and began shooting. One of the boys was heard exclaiming, "It's a good day to die." After a shooting rampage that lasted the better part of two hours, Eric and Dylan had killed a teacher and twelve fellow Columbine students, and they had injured more than twenty others. The boys then shot themselves in the mouth. Though it was reported that the boys had targeted jocks, blacks, and Christians, many of the dead had been shot indiscriminately; one boy still held a pencil in one hand when police retrieved his body.

Before the bodies were cold, most major news organizations in the country were running continuous coverage of the event. And for weeks after that, the story was featured by every newspaper, magazine, television channel, and on-line service. In just the fourth month of 1999, Columbine already had won the distinction of being the "tragedy of the year."

The focus of the story quickly changed from gory details about the events to a witch-hunt in which the goal was to look for someone or something to blame. As details of the unhappy and unfortunate lives of these two young killers began to emerge, one culprit was on the tip of everyone's tongue: the media.

Harris and Klebold had been fans of "Goth" culture, violent video games and movies, and the Internet. In the weeks that followed the shootings, a seemingly never-ending parade of activists, politicians, parents, and special-interest groups called for the censorship of the music, movies, Web sites, and games that some felt were the training grounds that turned two boys into ruthless killers. Industrial rock band KMFDM received heightened attention because the lyrics to its song "Son of a Gun" appeared on Eric Harris's Web site. In its entire career, it was the most attention KMFDM had ever had. After it was rumored that Harris and Klebold were fans of Marilyn Manson's music, newspapers printed photos of him.

Many felt that children were not safe at school, at home in front of the television set, on-line, or in even the most "family-friendly" music store. In a Gallup poll released in the weeks following the Columbine shootings, 80 percent of American adults were said to feel that the Internet bore some blame for the tragedy, and about 46 percent placed responsibility on music. The entertainment industry became Public Enemy Number One.

One piece of information did not get much exposure during this time: a study released by the FBI concerning crime rates in the United States. The report stated that in 1998, violent crime had declined 7 percent, bringing it to its lowest levels since World War II. In addition, this was the fifth consecutive yearly decline in both violent and property crimes. The last time violent crime was at such a low ebb in this country there was no Internet, no television, no video games. The popularity of these media, especially the Internet, has exploded in recent years, but the rate of crime, even among teenagers, had decreased. If there were a connection, you'd expect the opposite.

But this information didn't seem to dissuade anyone; in fact, calls for the necessity of censorship grew more strident.

Shock Waves

Within hours of the Columbine tragedy, many people realized that expressing some level of insight into the situation was a way to score easy coverage. It seemed that every member of Congress held a press conference that evening, and every day for weeks following, promising action to ensure that the rest of America's youth would be safe at school.

Within weeks several congressional efforts were under way to address violent media. Representative Henry Hyde (best known as the lead prosecutor during the Senate's impeachment trial of President Clinton) proposed an amendment to a juvenile crime bill that required music retailers to furnish lyric sheets "on demand" to parents or concerned community members. Two days later, Hyde announced he would instead ask for a "sense of Congress resolution" (a nonbinding request) that the lyrics be made available. He promised to introduce new legislation banning the sale to minors of movies, video games, and music that contained graphic sex or violence.

Senator Orrin Hatch felt that the Columbine tragedy was the result of too much violence in the media and not enough prayer in schools. Said Hatch, "It seems the only time we tolerate prayer in school these days is when people come to on-school memorials in the wake of tragedies."[1] Two of his fellow senators, Joseph Lieberman of Connecticut and John McCain of Arizona, introduced the 21st Century Media Responsibility Act. They proposed amending the Cigarette Labeling and Advertising Act—the law that keeps a tight grip on cigarette packaging and advertising practices—to include entertainment, thus requiring warning stickers to appear on all entertainment products. Their proposal also called for the strict regulation of advertising for entertainment. Senator Lieberman was quoted as saying the measure "won't single-handedly stop media standards from falling, or substitute for industry self-restraint. But it will help make ratings a more useful tool for parents who want to shield their kids from potentially harmful entertainment products."[2] Lieberman further hinted that the act, if passed, could result in criminal prosecutions of entertainment executives.

When asked about the media's role in the shootings, President Clinton warned that the music industry should "consider the consequences" of producing violent music. Clinton later called for a Federal Trade Commission inquiry into the marketing practices of the entertainment industry, an inquiry that would be similar to a probe of the tobacco industry's marketing two years earlier.

Stating that "over the past several years, our society seems to have become increasingly flooded with music with lyrics that glorify suicide, torture and murder," Senator Sam Brownback of Kansas called for Senate hearings into the role violent media played in the Columbine shootings. In the three years preceding the shootings, Brownback had held two separate hearings before the Senate Commerce Committee regarding the suggested influence of rock and rap lyrics on youth and the ineffectiveness of the PMRC/RIAA sticker. One hearing featured ten witnesses, including several other senators, conservative commentator William Bennett, and representatives of several industry and advocacy groups. Brownback did not invite any witnesses to represent the music and entertainment industries.

Reactions from concerned church and community groups were as equally quick and unrelenting as those of the legislators. A group calling themselves "Be Level-Headed," led by youth pastor Tim Bach, lobbied for the cancellation of the Hard Rock Rockfest outside of Atlanta, Georgia. The group's name was a take off on "Beheaded," a song by one of the concert's performers, the Offspring. The group thought that particular song was excessively violent and inappropriate in the wake of the Littleton tragedy. The advocacy group also took issue with another Rockfest act, Silverchair, for its song "Suicidal Dream." The concert was held as planned, with a hundred protesters outside and 127,000 attendees. Although both Offspring and Silverchair performed at the festival, neither included the songs highlighted by the protest group.

The group Focus on the Family issued many statements on the

tragedy, including allegations from Bob Waliszewski, manager of the group's Youth Culture Department. He said that Marilyn Manson and gangsta rap could be linked to Columbine and other incidents of school violence. Waliszewski quotes Debby Pelley, a teacher at Westside Middle School in Jonesboro, Arkansas, where a similar shooting had occurred a year earlier. Pelley spoke of the perpetrator's interest in rap music: "He brought it to school with him and listened to it on the bus, tried listening to it in the classes. Even played a song about coming to school and killing all the kids."[3] Waliszewski also cited a connection between Marilyn Manson and a youth murder in Mississippi, saying, "Are there young people getting the message that 'killing everyone' is glamorous and acceptable? For me, these recent shootings leave little doubt."[4]

The efforts of these interest groups seemed to pay off. A CNN/*USA Today* poll conducted ten days after the tragedy stated that 65 percent of the American public felt that the federal government should do more to regulate violence on the Internet, 58 percent wanted more video games regulation, and 48 percent wanted to see more government regulation of popular music. The poll found that at that time, only 17 percent felt that the government should exercise less regulation, and 31 percent felt that the current level of federal control over music was appropriate.

Schools across the country banned anything relating to Goth culture, including black clothing, piercings, selected rock T-shirts, trench coats, even Walkmans (fearing that kids could be secretly listening to violent music). One overly cautious high school in Salt Lake City expelled a student for wearing a shirt emblazoned with the word "Vegan." Officials feared that veganism was linked to the "Straight Edge" movement (groups of young people who are militant in their refusal to drink alcohol or take drugs) and therefore could be gang-related, much like the "Trench Coat Mafia" at Columbine High School.

The media focused heavy attention on Harris's and Klebold's interests. The National School Safety Center issued a widely publicized checklist of danger signs in children, including mood swings, a fondness for violent TV or video games, cursing, depression, and antisocial behavior and attitudes.[5] The *New York Post* featured an article headed, "Telltale signs your kids might be ready to explode." Accompanying the article were pictures of Marilyn

Manson, Hitler, three children in Goth makeup and clothing, and a young person with multiple facial piercings.

Manson became the poster child of the post-Columbine anti-media advocates. Early in the event's coverage, rumors circulated that Harris and Klebold were both big fans of Marilyn Manson. Manson quickly canceled an upcoming appearance in the Denver area, later canceling the final five dates on his 1999 tour because of negative media. ABC's *20/20* ran a segment on Manson and Goth culture; the *New York Daily News* ran a Columbine-related story mentioning the band. A school superintendent in Portsmouth, New Hampshire, forbade students to wear Manson T-shirts at school, saying that "parents are welcome to challenge me in court."[6] Dale Shugars, a state legislator from Michigan, attended a Manson concert and afterward called for an investigation into the band's role in the Columbine killings. When speaking of a suggested rise in drug use and violence among teens, Shugars said, "I think he [Manson] promotes it and can be part of the blame."[7]

Senator Brownback, along with eight other senators, sent a letter to Seagram's, the parent company of Manson's record label, calling for the company "to cease and desist profiteering from peddling violence to young people"; they further suggested that the company drop Marilyn Manson. The letter went on to say, "Out of respect for the 13 innocent victims in Colorado, sympathy for their grieving families, and concern for young people everywhere, we ask you to strongly reconsider which lyrics the Seagrams corporation chooses to legitimize and popularize."[8]

Within a month of the Columbine killings, a Manson-authored rebuttal appeared in *Rolling Stone* magazine. "It is sad to think that the first few people on Earth needed no books, movies, games, or music to inspire cold-blooded murder," said Manson, referring to the biblical story of Cain and Abel. Manson said he felt that American society is no more violent now than it ever has been:

We applaud the creation of a bomb whose sole purpose is to destroy all of mankind, and we grow up watching our President's brains splattered all over Texas. Times have not become more violent. They have just become more televised. It's no wonder that kids are growing up more cynical; they have a lot of information in front of them. They can see that they are living in a world that's made of bullshit.

Manson believed that examining Harris's and Klebold's interests for signs of culpability made no sense. "Did we look for James Huberty's inspiration when he gunned down people at McDonald's? What did Timothy McVeigh like to watch? What about David Koresh, Jim Jones? When it comes down to who's to blame . . . throw a rock and you'll hit someone who's guilty."[9]

After all this Marilyn Manson bashing, it was revealed several weeks later that, in fact, Harris and Klebold didn't even like Marilyn Manson. While they were fans of other industrial and Goth bands, such as KMFDM and Rammstein, they didn't care for Manson at all and owned none of his CDs. They reportedly thought Manson was lame.

What other perspectives have we gained now that the dust has settled on this tragedy? The first obvious lesson is that whatever level of influence music had on Harris and Klebold, it pales when compared with other factors in their lives.

Like most instigators of school violence, Harris and Klebold had a brief history of getting into trouble, they were white, they came from middle-class families, and they lived in a suburban area. Despite their minor troubles with the law, the year they spent building bombs in the family garage, and the arsenal of weapons stashed in their rooms, the boys were generally considered to be well parented. Additionally, despite the negative-toned rhetoric that marked Harris's Web site and diaries; some occasional mild threats; their love for "first-person shooter" video games, hard music, and violent movies, the two were not considered to be unusually aggressive or violent toward others. So what went wrong? These boys were not "programmed" for violence by entertainment media, they were hardwired for it—both suffering from emotional disturbances that festered relatively unnoticed.

So who or what is responsible for the Littleton tragedy? Nothing and no one. Events like the Littleton shooting are so complex and statistically infrequent and random that there is no way to find that magic bullet of blame. It isn't the music, movies, video games, not the parents, classmates, friends, or community. Incidents like the Columbine shootings are freak accidents.

Every day in the United States, three children are murdered or die as the result of abuse from a household member. That is a little more than a thousand murders committed annually by someone living under the same roof. The average number of children who die in school violence is two to five a year. That means that a child is approximately 547 times more likely to be killed by someone they live with than to die in a school massacre. In a "banner" year like 1999 (thanks to the Columbine shootings), the chances drop to 84 times more likely to be murdered by a relative. A child is more likely to be maimed by a shark, struck by lightning twice, or killed by debris falling from a plane than to be killed in a school massacre. Yet do politicians call for shark netting around beaches? No. Does Focus on the Family call for lightning rods around playgrounds? No. Children are safer at school than almost anywhere else. Murder is the second leading cause of death among children (second only to car crashes), yet only 1 percent of those murders occur in a school.

Are children more at risk of being harmed by an emotionally disturbed youth? Again, there is no reason to believe so. The rate of emotional disturbance among young children is actually lower than among adults, and the rate of teen emotional disturbance is exactly the same as that for adults.

When community leaders or politicians struggle to make sense of tragedy or try to be "the person with an answer" to a stupefying situation like the Columbine tragedy, they simply can't state the obvious: that there always will be risk in the world; abnormal things happen. As statistically small as these events are, there is no way to quantify or qualify them accurately enough to stop them. Instead, society's leaders look to something they don't understand—such as music—and start pointing fingers. Complicating these situations is a news industry that is more concerned with "scooping" the competition and filling airtime than with telling the whole story.

Not to minimize the Littleton incident or make it anything less than the heart-wrenching tragedy it was, but dramatics and sound bites aside, are times really dramatically different from when rock and roll first surfaced in the 1950s? History demonstrates not. In fact, the presence of violent lyrics and themes in music is not new.

History Repeats and Repeats and Repeats

Juvenile delinquency was a major issue on the national agenda in the 1950s. There *was* an increase in the number of youth crimes; however, that was because there were *more* juveniles. Regardless, delinquency was the big family issue of the era, and it was on the agenda of every preacher, politician, and community leader. The coincidental evolution of rock during the same era led many to ask how the new popular music genre related to the surge in teen violence. Adults attending record hops and rock and roll shows were appalled at the new dances associated with rock music. They saw the wild jumping, thrashing, and screaming as violent behavior. In several instances, concerned adults interpreted the dancing as fighting and rioting, causing the birth of two rumors: first, that rock hops and concerts were nothing more than riots and rumbles set to music; second, that the steady beats of rock music were a catalyst for violence.

In 1955 and again in 1958, Congress held hearings into the suggested link between rock music and juvenile delinquency. During the later hearing, Frank Sinatra was invited to speak. He called rock music "the most brutal, ugly, desperate, vicious form of expression it has been my misfortune to hear."

The media had a field day quoting any social scientist willing to bash pop music. A. D. Buchmueller, executive director of the Child Study Association, speculated that rock music could be the cause for youth violence and aggression. Psychiatrist Dr. Francis Braceland called rock music "cannibalistic and tribalistic," blaming its heavy beats and loud presentation for spontaneous outbreaks of lawlessness and chaos. *Time* magazine, in its first reports on rock and roll, referred to it as "jungle" and "juvenile delinquency" music; the magazine likened concerts and hops to "Hitler mass meetings." In 1956, *Variety* claimed that rock music was responsible for "a staggering wave of juvenile violence and mayhem" and quoted the head of the Pennsylvania Chiefs of Police Association, who had described rock as "an incentive for teenage arrest."[10] The *Encyclopaedia Britannica* coined the term "insistent savagery" to describe rock music and its effects on young people.

The spread of these concerns resulted in widespread cancellations of rock concerts in Cleveland; in New Haven and Bridgeport, Connecticut; in Boston; in Atlanta; in Jersey City and Asbury Park,

New Jersey; in Burbank, California; and in Portsmouth, New Hampshire—all in 1955 alone.

Concerns over teen violence caused radio stations to cease playing Link Wray's hit single "Rumble," even though it had no lyrics. The instrumental classic was thought to be dangerous simply because of its title. When Wray and his band appeared on Dick Clark's *American Bandstand* in 1959, Clark introduced the band but would not say the song's title.

In 1960, Ray Peterson's "Tell Laura I Love Her" was branded as "tasteless and vulgar" because it told the story of a dying stock car driver. Several radio stations refused to play the song, calling it the "Death Disk."

In 1962, the Radio Trade Practices Committee recommended the screening of all lyrics for references to violence. The committee recommended that the National Association of Broadcasters (NAB) empower its Code Committee to establish a screening system to use on rock records before they received airplay at any NAB station. The committee felt that the review was necessary "due to the proliferation of songs dealing with raw sex and violence beaming directly and singularly at children and teenagers."[11]

In an effort to curb violence that songs could inspire, several jukebox vendors and providers removed records and/or entire machines. In San Antonio, Texas, during the summer of 1956, the parks department removed jukeboxes from every city swimming pool, fearing that the "jumpy, hot" music would spur fights among teens. They felt that the music also attracted an undesirable element—teens who "loitered around the pools with no intention of going in swimming."[12] In 1967, Los Angeles jukebox distributor David Solish feared that rock and R&B music were responsible for violence and rioting in Watts. Anticipating that the music would only entice the "ethnics" to riot, loot, and burn to an even greater degree, Solish removed all "inflammatory" titles from his jukeboxes.

A year later, officials in Chicago asked radio stations to stop playing the new Rolling Stones hit "Street Fightin' Man" because they worried that the song would aggravate the tension and violence surrounding the Democratic National Convention.

Although violence continued to appear in rock themes and lyrics throughout the 1970s and early 1980s, censorship was rarely invoked. Music video's evolution added a new twist.

With video, creative directors were able to add a new sensory experience to music—a visual element.

Dr. Thomas Radecki, founder of the National Coalition on Television Violence (NCTV), summarized the opinion of the nonacademic social conservatives when he said, "The intensive sadistic and sexual violence of a large number of rock music videos is overwhelming. It's shocking to see this subculture of hate and violence becoming a fast-growing element of rock music entertainment for the young."[13] The NCTV, a watchdog group that monitors television violence, conducted a study in 1983. They determined that MTV broadcasts eighteen acts of violence every hour, and that 22 percent of all videos contained violence between men and women. Furthermore, Radecki's group claimed that 13 percent of all videos contained "sadistic violence where the attacker actually took pleasure out of committing the violence."[14]

One 1980s academic study into the presence of violence in music videos reported that 56.5 percent of all concept videos showed violent acts—a determination that initially appeared to complement the NCTV study. However, the study also showed that music videos were significantly less violent than prime-time network television programs (of which 75 percent contained violence).

Through the mid-eighties, several communities lobbied for the removal of MTV from their local cable systems, in large part because of the violent themes contained in many of the channel's featured videos. To fight the controversy, MTV eventually added a screening system that often rejected videos for their content (see chapter 5).

Things really got ugly when the PMRC was formed in 1985. Although only two of the PMRC's original "Filthy Fifteen" were added to the list because of violence, claims that rock songs advocated violence, suicide, and rape were always chief among the group's complaints.

During the 1985 Senate hearings into rock lyrics, artwork, and record labeling, the senators were anxious for the witnesses to begin to cite examples of violence in music. Florida senator Paula Hawkins's opening statements included album covers from Def Leppard (showing a burning building), Wendy O. Williams (in which she is standing among flames), and W.A.S.P. (in which a man has a table-saw blade protruding from his crotch).

During his testimony, Jeff Ling told senators and audience members that the slide show he would present demonstrated the level of violence and sex in contemporary rock music. Ling began his presentation by showing photos and telling the stories of several young rock fans who had taken their lives as a result of exposure to rock music. He highlighted the video for Twisted Sister's "We're Not Gonna Take It," noting that while the song did not *seem* to condone violence, the accompanying concept video featured a young man deliberately causing injury to his father.

Ling quoted lyrics from Judas Priest, AC/DC, Great White—even the Jacksons—demonstrating an "unacceptable" level of violence in each. He showed KISS, W.A.S.P., and Mötley Crüe album covers that featured violent and murderous acts. According to Ling, "today the element of brutal, violent erotica has exploded in rock music in an unprecedented way. Many albums today include songs that encourage suicide, violent revenge, sexual violence, and violence just for the sake of violence."[15]

The PMRC's argument was effective. When the RIAA, PMRC, and the National PTA agreed to a universal parental warning sticker on November 1, 1985, the agreement included an provision about affixing the label on any album that featured violence. However, the agreement contained no operating definitions or guidelines to clarify what could be considered "violence." During the next several years, widespread changes in retail policy forced any content deemed excessively violent to be regulated and restricted. By the mid-nineties, more than thirty pieces of local and state legislation were introduced that included restrictions on the sale of "violent music." Beyond rape, murder, and physical harm, rarely did the legislation define "violent content."

In one instance of oversensitivity to violence in music, the Cure rereleased an early single, "Killing an Arab," on its greatest-hits collection, and complaints soon followed that the group was advocating violence against Middle Easterners. The band's leader, Robert Smith, wrote to radio stations and asked them not to play the song.

Radio station WSOU of Seton Hall University in Newark, New Jersey, pulled all its heavy metal records in 1988, fearing that the music could cause young people to kill themselves. A local sixteen-year-old boy had committed suicide with an Ozzy Osbourne tape in his pocket. The station's faculty adviser, Michael Collazo, felt that it was "only a matter of time before another teen commits suicide and investigators blame the music the child heard on WSOU."[16] Following protests against the station, Collazo eventually allowed deejays to add a small number of metal acts to the playlists.

In 1997, two alternative albums faced problems over their content. The Crucifucks featured a photo of a dead policeman on the cover of their album *Our Will Be Done*, which spawned a lawsuit that was meant to punish the band for what some felt amounted to advocation of violence against law enforcement officers. According to Fraternal Order of Police spokesman Richard Costello, "I'm hoping for every last dime these people have, up to the penny in their loafers, if we can get it." Also that year, the English band Prodigy saw its album *The Fat of the Land* yanked from retail stores because of the single "Smack My Bitch Up." The song's lyrics contained only two phrases, "Change my pitch up. Smack my bitch up," repeated throughout the song. The band's lead singer, Liam Howlett, contends that the phrase refers to doing anything with intensity and has nothing to do with violence toward women.

Another source of controversy over violent content in popular music is gangsta rap, which repeatedly comes under heavy fire from critics who believe that the music adds to the cycle of violence surrounding its young fans. While many of rap's messages involve topics like sex, politics, economic conditions, and racism, many of these issues are addressed through the trappings of violence: as a form of conflict resolution, to establish power, or as a means to demonstrate or prove loyalty to a group or cause. In gangsta culture, allegiances are measured by an individual's willingness to kill or die. As with many elements of rap culture, mainstream society tries to shoehorn rap into its own model of understanding. It results in a perception of rap as misogynistic, violent, and chaotic. Critics of rap seem unable to differentiate between singing or rapping *about* something and condoning that something.

Suicide Solution

Suicide is nothing new; however, since heavy metal developed its own identity and a certain type of listener became associated with it, critics, parents, and community and religious leaders have claimed that heavy metal is a central cause in self-inflicted youth violence. This is not true, but it is very difficult to shrug off completely any influence that rock themes and lyrics may have on an already disturbed child. While it may be possible to prove a correlation between teens who commit suicide and an interest in heavy metal music, it is not so easy to demonstrate—or disprove—any cause-and-effect relationship.

During the Senate hearings into record labeling in the fall of 1985, Jeff Ling claimed that of the six thousand adolescents who took their lives in 1984, "many of these young people find encouragement from some rock stars who present death as a positive, almost attractive alternative."[17] The most famous incidents that alleged rock music's influence on teen suicide came to the public's attention as a result of lawsuits.

In 1985, singer Ozzy Osbourne was a defendant in the first of two suits blaming his song "Suicide Solution" for encouraging the suicides of several young fans. A California couple blamed Osbourne and his record company, CBS Records, for the death of their nineteen-year-old son, John McCollum (*McCollum v. CBS*). They claimed that the lyrics— "Where to hide, suicide is the only way out. Don't you know what it's really about?"—convinced their child that the proper solution to his troubles was suicide. The young man had shot himself in the temple with a .22-caliber handgun while listening to the song on headphones. The parents acknowledged that the boy had had emotional problems, but they felt he was "particularly susceptible to the suggestions of the lyrics found on record albums." The family's lawyer suggested that Osbourne should face criminal charges, because it was a felony in California to encourage a young person to commit suicide. The courts ruled in Osbourne's favor, saying the parents had not proven a connection between the song and the boy's suicide.

John McCollum, Sr., posing with the Ozzy Osbourne album *Speak of the Devil*. McCollum was one of several parents who sued Osbourne, claiming that his music was the catalyst to their children's suicides.

In 1991, Osbourne and his record label were again sued—this time by the parents of a Georgia boy in *Waller* v. *Osbourne*. Following the suicide death of their son, the parents of Michael Waller sued for $9 million. Like the plaintiffs in the earlier Osbourne suit, they claimed that the child repeatedly listened to "Suicide Solution." The court found no "culpable incitement" and did not agree with the parents' claim. An appeals court agreed with the decision, and in 1992, the U.S. Supreme Court let the ruling stand without comment.

Speaking of the controversy, Osbourne said that the theme behind "Suicide Solution" was the drinking death of his friend, former AC/DC frontman Bon Scott. He felt that the song was a warning against the slow suicide of alcoholism. "Do you honestly think that, as a married man with six kids, I want to see anyone injured?" he asked. According to Osbourne's attorney, Howard Weitzmann, "Romeo and Juliet cannot be blamed for the many lovers' suicides that have happened over the years. Movies that were seen by millions of people do not result in chain saw massacres."[18]

In 1986, the families of two young men from Reno, Nevada, sued the British heavy metal band Judas Priest for $6.2 million, claiming

Singer Ozzy Osbourne

the band's album *Stained Class* aided in the young men's deaths. The victims, eighteen-year-old Ray Belknap and twenty-year-old Jay Vance, agreed to a suicide pact. Before carrying out the pact, the boys went on a two-day spree of drinking, drugs, and petty crime. They eventually took turns placing a shotgun in their mouths and pulling the trigger. Belknap was killed instantly; Vance survived—literally blowing off his face with the shotgun, however. Vance underwent extensive, painful facial reconstructive surgery for three years before dying from an overdose of prescription drugs.

Both Belnap and Vance had been in and out of trouble for years. Vance had run away from home thirteen times, and both his parents admitted to beating the boy regularly and severely. A school psychiatrist had expressed concerns over his violent behavior as early as the second grade. He attacked his mother with a hammer while he was still in grade school and was institutionalized for attempting suicide at age eleven. Ray Belknap also grew up in a violent household; both he and his mother were beaten and abused by his stepfather.

During the trial, the families' attorney contended that many people grow up in violent households, yet they don't commit suicide. Their basic argument was that *Stained Class* contained hidden messages that encouraged youth to kill themselves; they ignored the fact that millions of other kids had listened to *Stained Class* without attempting suicide.

The prosecution played tape of several songs on the album, alleging that the album contained the phrase "do it," audible only through the subconscious. They wanted to demonstrate that if several of the songs were played backward, phrases such as "try suicide," "suicide is in," and "sing my evil spirit" could be heard. An important prosecution witness was Wilson Bryan Key, a proponent of the theory that evil subliminal messages have an impact on people. He had previously found disturbing subliminal messages hidden in Ritz crackers, five-dollar bills, and Howard Johnson restaurant place mats.

The band's attorneys focused their case on the lack of evidence that the messages actually (and deliberately) existed, let alone that they caused listeners to alter their "normal" behavior. In his testimony, Judas Priest singer Rob Halford had the courtroom in stitches when he presented a tape of other "subliminal messages" he found in *Stained Class*. Reversing the phrase "They won't take our love away," the court hears "Hey, look, Ma, my chair's broken." In reversing the phrase "strategic force, they will not," heard instead is "It's so fishy, personally I owe it." And finally, "Stand by for exciter, salvation is his task" reverses to "I asked her for a peppermint, I asked for her to get one."[19]

Suicidal tunes

There are many individuals and groups who claim a link between rock music and suicide. Following is a list of artists and songs most often associated with inspiring young people to kill themselves:

Pink Floyd   "Comfortably Numb"
                    "Goodbye Cruel World"

John Lennon	"Cold Turkey"
AC/DC	"Highway to Hell"
	"Shoot to Thrill"
	"Hell's Bells"
Ozzy Osbourne	"Suicide Solution"
Blue Öyster Cult	"Don't Fear the Reaper"
Black Sabbath	"Killing Yourself to Live"
	"After Forever"
Metallica	"Fade to Black"

The judge quickly ruled in the band's favor, although in his decision he admitted to a belief in the existence and influence of subliminal messages. He stated that the families had not done a convincing job of establishing their presence in the Judas Priest album, however.

One case not involving litigation but frequently mentioned by antimetal advocates (including Jeff Ling in his testimony during the 1985 Senate hearings) is the suicide of fourteen-year-old Steve Boucher in 1981. Like many young men his age, Steve developed an interest in KISS when he entered his teen years. As time went on, Steve became more and more obsessed with heavy metal music and less involved with his school and peers. He plastered the walls of his room with heavy metal posters, and covered his school notebooks with the logos of his favorite bands, like AC/DC. His parents' lack of respect for his musical tastes formed a wall between Steve and his family, who were completely unaware of the themes and lyrics of the songs in which he centered his life. According to his father, George Boucher, "I didn't like the music, and I couldn't care less about what the words were." His mother noted that Steve attempted on many occasions to share his music with her: "He would say, 'Listen to this—even you would like this.' But I would just say, 'Steve, I don't like this. Go to your room and listen to it— I don't like it.' "[20] Steve withdrew into his music more and more, eventually using it to avoid contact with almost everyone.

Fights over Steve's interest in music occurred often in the Boucher house. When the family moved to a different home, Steve wanted to redecorate his room with posters and memorabilia of his favorite bands, but at first his mother refused to allow it. Later, they agreed that an AC/DC calendar could hang on the inside of the door to his room. As Steve grew increasingly distant from his family and the world around him, he began to use drugs. He also began to exhibit signs of someone contemplating suicide: withdrawing more and more, telling his sister of his intentions, and asking his father about the family's insurance policies. Steve eventually took a shotgun given to him by his grandfather, put the barrel to his head, and pulled the trigger. His body, discovered by his sister, was lying directly under the AC/DC calendar he had argued about with his mother.

After Steve's death, the Bouchers were understandably devastated, and they wanted answers. According to George Boucher, "The music gives suicide credibility—it promotes it, encourages it, and advertises it. This is anti-church . . . it's a kind of a cult. It's advertising hell—trying to sell hell." Added Steve's mother, Sandee, "I read some of the lyrics to several people and they said that it amounts to murder."[21]

Fourteen-year-old Steve Boucher committed suicide by shooting himself through the forehead. His parents attributed his problems to an obsession with heavy metal music.

In their examination of the link between rock music and teen suicide, ministers Dan and Steve Peters have concluded, "If a teenager has listened to his favorite rock star sing to him six hours a day or more, telling him the solution is suicide, how can any parent, who averages approximately two minutes of conversation with his child each day, convince him life is worth living?"[22] However, looking to anything, especially music, as the sole culprit in examining teen suicide is overly simplistic.

Several studies have shown that children with poor academic skills, poor social standing in school, experience with drug use, bad family relationships, and a history of juvenile delinquency are all more likely to be fans of heavy metal music than are their peers.[23] Attempts at self-inflicted violence are also more prevalent among heavy metal fans than among fans of other musical genres. Twenty percent of male heavy metal fans and 60 percent of females reported that they had attempted to hurt or kill themselves in the six months preceding their interviews, compared to 8 percent of other males and 14 percent of other females.[24] It should be noted that there is no scientifically valid proof that heavy metal music or fandom is the cause of suicidal feelings or tendencies. The evidence simply demonstrates that troubled youth are more likely to be attracted to harder music. Choice of music is another symptom of a problem rather than the problem itself.

An exception occurs when a disenfranchised youth begins to use rock music containing Gothic, mystical, or fantastic imagery as a substitute for reality and relationships with others. Music can be a very personal and real experience, but it certainly is not a proper substitute for human interaction and relationships. When an obsessed young person realizes that music provides only tempo-rary solace, such a revelation may aggravate and accentuate feel-ings of loneliness and despair. In those instances, a troubled fan's interactions can exacerbate despondent feelings. In other words, by the time music plays a role in these children's lives, things have already progressed to a desperate point. It is worth noting that such obsessive cases comprise a very small percentage of teens in trouble. Since they are shocking and rare, they make it into the evening newscasts. There is an old axiom in television news, "If it bleeds, it leads."

Blinding Me with Science

The suggestion of a connection between suicide and heavy rock music begs a further question: Can rock music encourage, suggest, or spur violence among teens?

Most of what we know about links between violence and the media results from studies of the effects of television. There have been many studies into the probability that viewing violence on television encourages the viewer to be more violent or aggressive in real life (though the results of many of these studies have been questioned upon further examination).

Despite the fact that the average U.S. family watches television six hours a day, there is a misconception that children spend more time watching television than listening to music. This isn't true. Most young music fans spend considerably more time being exposed to music than to television. The confusion comes in an important distinction between the two media. Watching television is an "active" medium, while listening to music is more often a "passive" medium. For the most part, television viewing requires your relatively undivided attention. Music, on the other hand—be it listening to a cassette, a CD, or the radio—is a companion medium: something you have on while doing something else. While there are times when everyone sits back and listens to music, the majority of interactions with music, regardless of one's age, tend to take place while other things are being done.

Most studies agree that there is some probable link between watching violence on television or in the movies and heightened levels of aggression. That said, despite hundreds of studies into the subject, researchers on both sides of the issue have had a hard time determining the precise cause-and-effect relationship between visual media and aggression and violence. The degree of the influence is also unknown.

Looking at the influence of music on aggression and violence, there is very little to support the belief that the small amount of evidence presented in studies concerning television can be transferred to music. Despite assertions by music's critics, all media are not created equal, and our reactions to each are not the same.

Critics and censors of rock music also manipulate studies to make them apply to music. Often, they take crime statistics, suicide rates, or individual incidents of violence and explain them to their audience in graphic detail. Then they claim that anyone who used common sense could see that there *must* be a causal relationship.

For example, in his book *Painted Black,* Carl Raschke attempts to link violence and sex to music by saying, "And if no one can blame rock music directly for the 300 percent rise in adolescent suicides or the 7 percent increase in teenage pregnancies, it *may surely* be more than a negligible factor."[25] By following his statistical quote with the phrase "it *may surely* be more than a negligible factor," Raschke used the emphasized phrase to attempt to draw a "commonsense" connection between this statistic and his opinion. And he avoided allowing himself to be painted into a corner for lack of evidence.[26]

To understand the possible relationship between popular music and violence, it is important to follow several steps. First, gauge the level of violence in popular music. While some genres of music (such as gangsta rap and heavy metal) have more violence than others, the fairest way to approach an analysis of music is by look-

ing at the music that touches the most people. In other words, ana-
lyze the most popular music selections. The PMRC claimed that
60 percent of popular songs in the Top 40 charts contained violence, murder, or rape in their lyrics or core themes. However, the
truth is significantly different. In a study of all songs that entered
the Top 40 charts between 1980 and 1990, researchers found that
only 8 percent contained references to violence, and only 1 percent
had murder or violence as their core theme.[27] Even by the most
conservative threshold of violence, 92 percent of popular tunes
have stepped out of consideration.

Of those remaining songs, ask if the listener can understand
the "correct" theme of the song. Some of the earliest research
into lyric comprehension was conducted by Serge Denisoff and
Mark Levine in 1965. They asked college students in the San
Francisco area about the popular and controversial Barry
McGuire protest song "Eve of Destruction." Some people feared
that its lyrics about war and nuclear destruction would depress
children and young listeners, giving them nihilistic attitudes.
Although the song's lyrics were fairly straightforward ("Eastern
world it is explodin', violence flarin' and bullets loadin'. You're
old enough to kill, but not for votin' "), the researchers won-
dered if students got the message. From the study results, it was
quite obvious they did not: Four hundred students were sur-
veyed; 14 percent "correctly" interpreted the song, 45 percent
showed partial understanding of the lyrical concepts, and the
remaining 41 percent did not understand or were unable to suggest a potential meaning.

Several similar studies into perception of violent or antisocial
song lyrics have yielded comparable results. In 1972, a group of
Michigan high school students from a variety of racial, social, and
economic backgrounds were asked to identify the meanings of several current hit songs that dealt with violence, drugs, hypocrisy,
and indifference. Of the 430 students polled, just 10 to 30 percent
could give "correct" interpretations of the songs, another 20 to 60
percent gave incorrect or vague responses, and the remainder
refused to answer.

The PMRC has alleged that music is more dangerous than
movies or television because children listen to songs again and
again, compared to one or two viewings of a movie or television

show. A mid-eighties study of teenagers in
suggests that they are unacquainted with the
of songs to which they listen repeatedly. More t
participated in the study were asked to identify
songs; they then were asked to identify the core
these three songs. More than one-third of the re   ....ould
not identify *any* theme in their favorite songs. T... reasons they
gave for not understanding the songs' meanings? They didn't care.
Quotes from the study participants back this up: "I don't listen to
the words, only how the song sounds. I don't give a damn what
they say"; "[It's] a punk song—it's not supposed to mean anything"; and "I have no idea. Do you listen to the words of songs
when you're dancing?"[28] Other studies reveal that even if young
people understand the lyrics, their interpretations of themes and
application of those themes to their lives can be wildly diverse and
different (see chapter 9).

So if a song does indeed contain violent references, and a young
person actually understands and comprehends the lyrics and
themes as the artist intended—is there any potential for influence
and damage? The answer is no. Repeated studies demonstrate that
children are uncomfortable with, or even reject outright, songs
that contain moral or ethical themes that conflict with their own
beliefs. Children are firm believers that music can influence other
children, but if they encounter songs that conflict with belief patterns—even by their favorite performers—they either construct a
"new" song theme that fits with their beliefs, or they tune out the
song.

The difficulty in examining violence is understanding what it is
and isn't. A lack of clarity regarding what should be considered
violence can dramatically affect the results of any survey. The basic
problem is that one person's interpretation of violence may not be
shared by a second observer. Most people would agree that punch-
ing someone square in the face is an act of violence, but is it an act
of violence when an impassioned singer throws a microphone
stand to the floor? Should a drive-by shooting be placed in the
same category as the antics of the Three Stooges or Wile E. Coy-
ote's attempts to capture the Road Runner? Some believe that all
acts of heterosexual intercourse are acts of violence against
women—do you believe that? Using any subjective constant in a

study brings up validity issues, because the concept of
"...ce" is subject to a wide degree of interpretation.

Furthermore, accurate statistical analysis depends upon random
sampling conducted on a large enough scale that it statistically
represents the topic or group being studied. In the NCTV studies
into the presence of violence in music videos mentioned earlier, five
paid observers with no stated credentials were asked to watch
MTV and catalog instances of "violence." No further instructions
or definitions were given. When a group such as the NCTV
attempts to create statistical realities out of subjective judgments,
the edges begin to blur. Unfortunately, when researchers capture
media headlines by reporting that the amount of violence in music
or videos is excessive, few reporters question the methodology
used.

4

"COVER ME"

Album Cover Art

■

There should be warning labels for politicians.
—Derek Smalls, bassist for Spinal Tap

When one looks at the big picture of censorship in America, one quickly notes how relatively small and oblique music censorship is compared to other forms of expression, such as books, movies, and visual art. In fact, controversy surrounding visual art mediums, particularly film, have created a foundation for much of what we know about the constitutional rights of artists and art fans.

After the development of film, the movie industry quickly grew into its position as the first mass medium involving visual images. Soon after that, critics began to highlight what is the primary dilemma in any mass medium: Not everyone is interested in the same type of entertainment. Some people will appreciate certain offerings; others will find their content to be boring, uninteresting, inaccurate, or even offensive, blasphemous, and degenerate. Before 1951, film was not recognized as constitutionally protected free speech. Thus many government agencies, state film boards, and licensing committees regularly censored films, sometimes simply to avoid controversy.

Censorship in other visual arts—such as painting, sculpture, photography, and performance art—is usually centered on the way these arts are funded in this country, such as the battles against federal funding for the National Endowment for the Arts and the 1990 obscenity trial in Cincinnati involving a museum director's choice to show a Robert Mapplethorpe exhibit (Mapplethorpe's supposedly "obscene" photography triggered protests and controversies that had a chilling effect on the fine arts community that still lasts today). Since many artists and arts organizations rely on government funding, grant agencies, and/or private foundations, some critics feel that it is their right to lament the fact that tax and community dollars are funding filth, pornography, and art that is unfit to be seen by children and other concerned citizens.

Obviously, censorship in the visual arts is a much larger subject than can be covered in this book. However, these incidents illustrate the controversy surrounding artistic forms of expression outside of the music industry. It is no surprise that music controversy and resulting censorship have been significant. Yet some of the controversies have little or nothing to do with the music itself. Rather, such musical controversies target the visual art that identifies, packages, and promotes music.

When record covers were first created, they were intended to be just that: covers, or protectors, of the records themselves. Most recording companies used the same cover style and design for all the artists' singles on their roster. Usually they featured a company logo and a punch hole in the center so the record's label information could be seen. During the swing era, the concept of record "albums," or collections of recordings, began to develop. Record companies quickly realized that a visual element would add to the desirability of the product, and they began to create unique designs for each album (a similar concept was used to sell sheet music during its heyday decades earlier). By the time rock and roll evolved in the 1950s, companies still produced album covers containing a simple photo or rendering of the artist and basic information about the product (song order, copyright info, etc.). However, companies soon realized that an attractive, sexy, or provocative picture would help sell albums—so they started to produce more album covers that excited the senses. It was the birth of album art-work as a promotional and sales tool. Artists and their record companies understood that an album's artwork and packaging could powerfully establish an artist's visual identity to the audience. Of course, this was long before MTV.

Album covers caused controversy from the beginnings of rock. In the 1950s, photos of dancing teens or musicians were thought to promote hedonism, promiscuity, lewdness, and disdain for authority. For many years, racial prejudice kept record companies from showing interracial dancing on album covers.

In the 1960s, album covers began to be appreciated as art, and with that newfound appreciation came the baggage associated with public art. During the psychedelic period of the late 1960s, elaborate, colorful artwork adorned many album covers. These kaleidoscopic covers were thought by conservatives to be glorified drug advertisements. As heavy metal developed in the late sixties and early seventies, much of the religious and Gothic imagery associated with this genre caused considerable consternation from rock's critics. Albums by Black Sabbath, Meat Loaf, Uriah Heep, Iron Maiden, and Ozzy Osbourne regularly contained artwork that featured horrific demons and monsters. Some thought this imagery supported demonic worship and satanism.

Album artwork for the British group Led Zeppelin caused a great deal of controversy. Although none of the artwork was particularly offensive, critics felt that the mysterious album art themes *had* to contain some kind of subversive message. The inner sleeve of the group's 1976 album, *Presence,* featured several benign-looking photographs, each showing a bizarre black rectangular object as its

The original cover of *Blind Faith*

centerpiece. Some were convinced that this black object had occult significance.

And don't forget sex and violence. Sex has been regularly used on album covers to sell music—be it a handsome picture of New

Kids on the Block, a scantily clad Madonna, or a nude Anabella Lwin of Bow Wow Wow. Violence has been another cause of controversy, from Judas Priest's *British Steel* (featuring fingers sinking into the edges of a razor blade), to AC/DC's *Powerage* (showing the band's guitarist reeling from electricity moving through his body).

Hundreds of record covers have caused controversy; however, the number of actual censorship incidents resulting from an album's artwork is comparatively small. Small, but significant.

The Enemy Within

Most examples of album artwork censorship is the result of an artist's record company giving in to internal or external pressures. On several occasions, record companies have released albums in the United States with different artwork from that issued in Europe, a practice followed partly out of fear that more conservative American audiences would not understand certain imagery. In 1971, executives at David Bowie's record label were uncomfortable with the cover photograph for his album *The Man Who Sold the World,* which featured Bowie dressed in drag. The American edition featured a cartoon drawing of a cowboy. In 1968, concerns over the original cover photograph for the American release of Jimi Hendrix's *Electric Ladyland* caused his record company to

The original cover of Jimi Hendrix's *Electric Ladyland*, which has never been released in the United States

issue the album in the United States with an alternative photograph. The original, released on the British pressing of the album, featured more than a dozen young, naked women in a photograph that spans the front and back album covers. Subsequent reissues of the album also have not included the original photograph. That same year, London Records refused to release the original artwork for the Rolling Stones' album *Beggars Banquet,* which featured a graffiti-covered bathroom wall. Instead, the company released the album with a cover that showed a formal banquet invitation (the original artwork was restored for the CD reissue). In 1969, Atco Records released the self-titled album from Blind Faith with two different album covers. The original featured a topless eleven-year-old girl holding a phallic-looking model airplane and pointing it toward her lower abdomen. The second, more benign, album cover (featuring a simple photo of the band) was eventually dropped by the label because it did not sell as well as the original.

Record companies also have censored artists who sneaked objectionable content onto record albums without a company's knowledge or consent. In 1967, the group Moby Grape released its self-titled album with a photo of the band members on the cover. But drummer Skip Spence had "flipped off" the camera, placing his middle finger against the washboard he was holding. Once the label discovered this, they hired an airbrush artist to

The original band photo that appeared on Moby Grape's self-titled debut (*left*) and the airbrushed version (*right*). The airbrushed version was created to remove the middle finger extended over the washboard.

"amputate" the offending appendage from additional pressings of the album.

The group Mom's Apple Pie also pulled a joke on its label, Capitol Records. The photo on their self-titled debut featured an innocent-looking farm wife holding an apple pie with a single slice removed. A keen eye could spot that a photograph of a vagina had been inserted in place of the missing pie wedge. The company immediately recalled and reissued the album, although the album was a dismal failure and few copies of the original still exist.

Capitol Records was also involved in one of the best-known incidents of a record label's censoring an album's artwork. In 1966, Capitol recalled *Yesterday and Today* by the Beatles. During the height of the Beatles' popularity in the 1960s, Capitol commonly "shaved" a song or two from each British Beatles album. The label held these cut songs, allowing the company to create an "extra" Beatles album every couple of years. The Beatles didn't like the practice, but were contractually unable to stop it. As a form of protest, they had a photographer take their picture wearing butcher's smocks and covered with decapitated baby dolls and bloody meat. The idea was to show the band as "butchers"—hinting at how their American record company had butchered their British albums to make records like *Yesterday*

The Beatles' original "butcher" cover for *Yesterday and Today* (*left*), and the version released after the album's recall (*right*). Note that on the alternative cover the band is wearing mismatched and ill-fitting clothes in protest of having to produce another photograph for the album.

and Today. Shortly after the album's release, complete with the butcher cover, retailers began to receive complaints about the graphic image on the cover. Though the cover was tame by today's standards, record merchants still returned the album to Capitol because of customer protests. Capitol quickly recalled the record from retailers and ordered the band to take a photo to replace the butcher cover on future releases. But Capitol had a problem. They had recalled thousands of butcher cover albums that they could not use. Simply tossing them into the garbage would be very costly. Capitol decided to paste the new cover photograph on top of the old one, allowing the recalled albums to be shipped back to retailers for sale and minimizing the financial impact of the recall. As a result, the butcher cover became one of the most collectible and valuable album covers in rock history. Many magazines and Web sites provide instructions on how to examine vintage copies of *Yesterday and Today* to see if the butcher cover lies underneath. Many also provide instructions on how to remove the pasted-on photo to reveal an undamaged original.

Record companies have not always been the ones censoring album artwork. In January of 1969, John Lennon and Yoko Ono raised quite a stir with the cover of their album *Two Virgins* because it contained a full frontal nude photo of the couple on the cover (and a nude photo from the back view on the verso). New York City police seized 30,000 copies of the record while the U.S. Customs service sued to prevent copies of the album from being

The front and back covers of Lennon and Ono's *Two Virgins*

How the album *Two Virgins* was widely distributed, in a brown paper wrapper

imported. FBI director J. Edgar Hoover considered the cover morally reprehensible and vowed to keep it out of the country. In Chicago, a record store was closed by the vice squad for selling *Two Virgins*. Because of the controversial photographs, Capitol Records (which distributed all the Beatles records in the United States) passed the rights to the *Two Virgins* album to Tetragrammaton Records. Eventually Tetragrammaton distributed the album in a brown paper wrapper.

Although album covers continued to evolve and attract controversy through the 1970s and 1980s, it wasn't until the PMRC gave potential censors a renewed feeling of empowerment (or fear) that album cover artwork once again became a cause for censorship.

Following the PMRC's rise to fame in 1985, many artists fell victim to pressure against their record companies over artwork. In 1989, some retailers refused to carry Prince's album *Lovesexy* because the cover featured a naked photograph of Prince, though his genitalia were not visible. That same

The original cover of Guns N' Roses *Appetite for Destruction*

year, complaints from retailers over Guns N' Roses' debut album *Appetite for Destruction* prompted the band's label, Geffen Records, to change the cover art before the album became a hit. The original cover sported a painting by Robert Williams (also titled *Appetite for Destruction*) that the band had originally seen on a postcard in a Chicago art museum. The graphic painting is a cartoon rendition of a beaten and bloody woman whose underwear is pulled down around her ankles. After the album became a huge hit (with the alternative cover), protests began. Protesters paraded outside Cymbaline Records in Santa Cruz, California, with signs reading CYMBALINE SUPPORTS RAPE and CYMBALINE SUPPORTS CHILD MOLESTATION. Yet the only copies of the album that Cymbaline had in stock featured the replacement cover, not the Williams painting. Protesters admitted that they had waited until the group had achieved more notoriety, feeling that the Guns N' Roses' popularity would help attract more attention to their cause of "healthy images of women and children in the media."

Both studio releases from the group Jane's Addiction received a significant amount of protest from retailers over sculptures (created by the band's singer Perry Farrell) that were featured on the album covers. Despite threats to drop the record, the band's label, Warner Brothers, stuck behind their desire not to change the cover of their debut, *Nothing's Shocking,* which featured a sculpture of two naked women attached at the hip like conjoined twins, their heads afire. However, the record label pressured the band to rethink the cover of their follow-up album, *Ritual de lo Habitual.* This sculpture featured two naked women cuddling with a naked man who resembled Perry Farrell. Though the bodies were partially covered by a satin cloth, the genitalia of one of the women and the man are exposed. Farrell was perplexed by the controversy, saying, "Every time we were at a meeting, they'd bring up

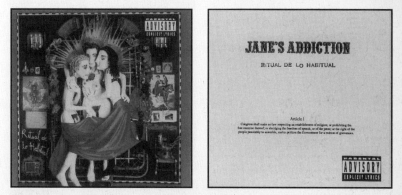

Under pressure from their record company over the original cover of *Ritual de lo Habitual,* Jane's Addiction created a second cover with virtually no artwork (*right*). It did, however, include the text of the First Amendment.

the fact that they find the penis objectionable. Like the cock's too much."[1] Under growing pressure, the band agreed to release an alternative cover for the album, which was entirely white and featured only the band's name, the album title, and the text of the First Amendment to the Constitution. Once both album covers were put out for sale, Warner executives admitted that the original was significantly outselling the alternative and that the original cover had met with very little resistance.

Controversial rapper Ice-T also found himself locking horns with Warner Brothers over the cover of his album *Home Invasion*. Fresh from the controversy that surrounded his song "Cop Killer," Warner refused to release the album because of its lyrical themes and cover artwork. The album's cover featured a painting of a young white male listening to rap music on his headphones and surrounded by images of murder, violence against women, and African history and culture. Ice-T opted to be released from his Warner contract rather than change the album, and eventually he released *Home Invasion* on a small, independent label.

The most notorious case of record artwork censorship involved the Dead Kennedys' album *Frankenchrist*. While the album's cover features a rather humorous photo of Shriners riding minicars in a parade, the source of controversy was actually a poster included

Following the controversy surrounding the Dead Kennedys' *Frankenchrist,* many supporters were surprised to see the album's cover (*left*)—mistakenly believing that the cover art was the issue at stake. The source of the album's controversy was a poster that featured a painting by artist H. R. Giger (*right*) that was folded inside the album cover.

inside the jacket. The poster featured a painting by Swiss surrealist H. R. Giger (best known for his Academy Award–winning art design work for the 1980 film *Alien*). The painting, entitled, *Landscape #20, Where Are We Coming From?*, depicts about a dozen sets of penises and vaginas. Before the painting appeared on the *Frankenchrist* poster, it had toured extensively (including exhibits at several museums in the United States) and was featured in the book *Twentieth Century Masters of Erotic Art*. The genital images are interlocking, so it seems that each "person" is both penetrating and being penetrated. According to lead singer Jello Biafra,

> It's the greatest metaphor I've ever seen for consumer culture on parade. The painting portrayed a vortex of exploitation, that vicious circle of greed where one of us will exploit another for gain and wind up looking over our shoulder lest someone do the same to us in return. . . . I felt that we should include this piece of artwork as a kind of crowning statement of what the record was trying to say musically, lyrically, and visually.[2]

However, assistant Los Angeles city attorney Michael Guarino did not agree. He claimed that the painting was obscene, pornographic, and unfit for children. Guarino charged Biafra and several business associates with violating Section 313.1 of the California state penal code, or "Distribution of Harmful Matter to Minors." Guarino said the poster depicted "dead body parts." The PMRC's Susan Baker described Giger's painting as depicting "numerous sets of diseased genitalia engaged in anal intercourse." Though charges were eventually dropped against Biafra (see chapter 17 for details on the trial), afterward the poster was no longer included in the album, though purchasers could return a coupon—which included an affidavit stating that one was at least eighteen years of age—in order to receive a copy of the *Frankenchrist* poster for a nominal fee.

Retail Hell
Another aftermath of the PMRC's blitz against music in the mid-eighties was a new policy at mass merchandisers such as Wal-Mart and Kmart, plus several large chain retailers, stating they would

not carry any albums bearing a universal parental warning sticker. Several retailers (including both Wal-Mart and Kmart) also expanded that list to include any album featuring objectionable artwork on the cover (no guidelines or definitions of what constituted "objectionable" were offered). Since Wal-Mart alone sells about one out of every ten albums sold in the United States, record companies were eager to please the retail giants and began to alter their products to fit the merchandisers' criteria. In addition to song title and lyric alterations to relieve an album of its warning sticker, the labels began to offer different artwork on the album covers. Where at one time record companies would simply add a sticker that conveniently covered up the controversial part of the album cover or offer the album in some type of wrapper (as with the *Two Virgins* album discussed earlier or the Rolling Stones' *Dirty Work,* which was wrapped in red paper to cover certain words), now record companies routinely issue two versions of the album—the original and a "clean" or "edited" version.

One of the first victims of the influence of discount retailers was the Scorpions' *Love at First Bite.* The original cover featured a partially nude couple locking limbs while the man tattooed a scorpion on the woman's thigh. The record company had showed the original cover to retailers without much ado. However, once the record was offered for sale, Wal-Mart complained, and PolyGram quickly rereleased the album with a different cover.

The cover of John Mellencamp's album *Mr. Happy Go Lucky* features Mellencamp with two children and a dog. In the background are portraits of Jesus and a devil. In the "clean" version for sale at large retailers like Wal-Mart or Blockbuster, the Jesus and devil have been airbrushed out. Albums by the group White Zombie (and a solo album by group leader Rob Zombie) have been altered to remove potentially offensive material and gain access to the discounters' shelves (see "Zombies for Sale," p. 80–82).

Nirvana's second studio album *In Utero,* released after the multiplatinum success of their debut album *Nevermind,* was originally turned down by the large retailers because of the cover and the dreaded warning sticker. Once the album reached the number-one spot on the pop charts (and still was not for sale at discount retailers), Wal-Mart and Geffen Records struck a deal. On the "clean" version of the album, the band would change one song's title from

The original version of the back cover of Nirvana's *In Utero* (*left*), along with the "clean" version (*right*) for sale at large retailers

"Rape Me" to "Waif Me" (though even in the "clean" version's interior booklet pages, the song title and song lyrics still contain the original title and the phrase "rape me"), and the back cover would be altered to remove the images of several fetuses. The "clean" version was then offered for sale at the retailers without a warning sticker, though the actual musical content of the album had not changed at all.

Under such policies, album artwork and content from other artists such as 311, Type O Negative, Primitive Radio Gods, Beck, Jackyl, plus a large number of rap artists such as Ice Cube, Snoop Doggy Dogg, and Outkast have been "sanitized" for the buyer's "protection." Despite decisions by other retailers, including Wal-Mart, to carry Ministry's *Dark Side of the Spoon*, Kmart decided not to sell the album because it objected to the cover artwork, which featured a naked overweight woman dressed in a dunce cap, repeatedly writing "I will be God" on a chalkboard.

These policies have backfired on several occasions, causing unwanted publicity for the retailers' policies. One such example was Wal-Mart's public announcement that it would stop carrying the breakthrough album by the Goo Goo Dolls, *A Boy Named Goo,* because they felt the cover art depicted a child-abuse victim. The press had a field day with the announcement, demonstrating that the cover photo was not of an abused child but of a toddler covered in "goo." This was reminiscent of a similar controversy

Officials at Wal-Mart banned this Goo Goo Dolls album because they mistakenly thought the cover depicted child abuse.

Critics called for boycotts of Bruce Springsteen's *Born in the U.S.A.* because they thought Bruce was urinating on the American flag.

almost a decade earlier, when critics had called for boycotts of Bruce Springsteen's album *Born in the U.S.A.* because they mistakenly thought the cover showed Bruce urinating on an American flag.

Album artwork in today's mainstream music industry differs from that of the era that spawned a sense of artistic creativity in the medium. Album artwork with true artistic significance is a rarity in today's music business. Now it's simply a matter of "packaging": a promotional item used to sell the record, usually with little or no input from the artists themselves. Album artwork also has lost its power to define an artist's image, losing ground to MTV and Internet Web sites. Grand vision or promotional tool, advertising or art, the images that cover and protect the music we purchase reflect the values of the industry that creates them: money first—integrity, morals, and ethics bringing up the rear.

Zombies for Sale: Clean, Edited, and Sanitized for Your Protection

It is important to note that retailers (such as Wal-Mart) are not the ones who decide what to add or remove from album artwork. They simply decide whether or not to purchase the album; changes are left entirely to the label. Who knows what it is about White Zombie that makes them offensive, but their label, Geffen Records, has tried to appease large retailers by taking some rather drastic measures to "sanitize" the album covers of several releases.

For a collection of White Zombie remixes, *Supersexy Swingin' Sounds*, retailers declined to stock the album because it featured nude women throughout the CD and cassette booklets. To make peace, Geffen had a

The "original" (*left*) and "clean" (*right*) cover art for a collection of White Zombie remixes

Interior of booklet accompanying White Zombie's *Supersexy Swingin' Sounds*. The "clean" version (*bottom*) featured computer-generated swimsuits to cover the models.

"clean" version of the artwork created by digitally adding swimwear to all the models. After viewing the now bikini-clad babes, the retailers agreed to stock the album.

When group leader Rob Zombie released his solo album, *Hellbilly Deluxe,* he couldn't shed his stigma with retailers—who rejected the CD because of lyrics and artwork. Geffen altered some songs,

The "original" (*left*) and "clean" (*right*) versions of Rob Zombie's solo album, *Hellbilly Deluxe*

changed a song title to remove a reference to a "whore," removed the lyrics from the booklet, and substantially altered the artwork featured on the front and back covers and the interior booklet. On the front cover alone, four changes were made: An X scratched into Zombie's forehead, a pentagram, and a series of skulls and crossbones were removed from the artwork, plus the phrase "SATAN-A-PHONIC" was deleted. Rob Zombie has been quoted as saying the alterations to his work are "lame," but he's never made an attempt to stop them.

5

"I WANT MY MTV"

MTV and Music Videos

◼

**The introduction of novel fashion in music
is a thing to beware of as endangering
the whole fabric of society.**
—Plato

After the birth of rock and roll, the evolution of music video is among the most significant events in the history of music. However, when MTV was launched in August of 1981, staffers had to travel to Fort Lee, New Jersey, to view the channel's debut (featuring the infamous first video shown that evening, "Video Killed the Radio Star"), because cable operators in their home base of Manhattan didn't think the channel would amount to much of anything. At the time, the creation of MTV was such a nonevent that it was largely ignored by the press, and it received no headline exposure during its first three months on-air.

MTV was born before cable television blossomed. Cable in the 1970s did not feature specialty channels like CNN, the Golf Channel, or Nickelodeon; instead, it featured retransmission of broadcast signals to areas where normal signals were weak. With the advent of movie channels and a few other original programming channels for cable, the big operators (such as MTV's parent,

Warner) started to conduct research into programming ideas that might prove to be effective.

Warner executives developed a channel that was targeted toward fifteen- to thirty-five-year-old fans of an emerging marketing tool created by record companies to promote artists: music videos.

Until then, music and television were a strange marriage. Both the music and television industries sensed that ratings and promotional potential existed if popular rock acts could be brought onto television variety shows. When Ed Sullivan, not considered a big fan of rock music and its performers, began to schedule hot rock and roll acts regularly on his television show, he was rewarded with an incredible boost in ratings, all because America's youth flocked to the television to catch a glimpse of their idols performing live. Since the evolution of rock as a popular medium, television had tried to create specialty programs that could exploit rock's popularity by adding that enticing visual component. In the coming years, that visual component would be refined even as it defined society and culture.

In the 1950s, Lucky Strike's *Your Hit Parade* featured a group of actors pantomiming story lines to the accompaniment of the week's seven most popular rock songs (selected, of course, by Lucky Strike's advertising agency). Several years later, Dick Clark's *American Bandstand* featured teen dancers shakin' their groove things to the current hits.

By the 1960s, television producers were attempting to capitalize on rock's popularity by creating new television variety shows like *Shindig* and *Hullabaloo*. Those shows featured "safer" popular music (such as the Righteous Brothers) and were hosted by popular movie or television stars (like Jerry Lewis or Zsa Zsa Gabor). However, the combination led to low ratings. *American Bandstand* was the only show with staying power. Also during the 1960s, television produced its first creation aimed at rock audiences: Don Kirshner's prefab group and show *The Monkees*. Television networks also began a trend of offering rather benign musicians opportunities to stage their own variety shows (such as *Sonny and Cher* and *Donny and Marie*).

By the late 1970s, American television's attempts to latch on to mainstream rock coattails consisted of two basic formulas: the dance show (e.g., *American Bandstand*) and the featured musical performance (live or lip-synched). Popular music-themed shows in the 1970s were, again, *American Bandstand* plus *Soul Train; In Concert; Midnight Special;* and, to some extent, *Saturday Night Live.*

It was during the 1970s that record companies began to reexamine television as a serious alternative to the high costs of concert tour support and promotion. Companies began to produce ready-made performance and conceptual videos that were distributed to various television programs. While the music video concept did not really take off in the United States, the idea blossomed in England, where television shows like *Top of the Pops* and *Ready! Steady! Go!* ate up these promotional clips. It's worth noting that the popularity of music videos in Europe is cited as the reason that many of MTV's early success stories were British: There simply were more videos available from English artists.

But television was unpopular with many musicians. In addition to poor sound quality of television broadcasts, artists were regularly asked to edit song lyrics to conform to the rules of network Standards and Practices departments. Producers of *The Ed Sullivan Show* asked the Doors and the Rolling Stones to change song lyrics, even suggesting the replacement words. The Doors' Jim Morrison agreed to a lyric change backstage, but then sang the original lyrics on television. Mick Jagger, lead singer of the Rolling Stones, insisted that he didn't alter his lyrics during their appearance but he actually mumbled the lyric, making it unintelligible. During a taping of *American Bandstand*, Curtis Mayfield was surprised to learn that producers had edited certain phrases from his song "Pusherman." This lack of enthusiasm on the part of the musicians, plus the large costs involved in producing videos, left the pool of available clips relatively small.

During these early years, video availability was a big problem. The average Top 40 radio station in the United States has a playlist that features about 300 songs each week. MTV's initial rotation was about 125 videos. Thus, MTV featured many unknown bands—not from any altruistic desire to break new music but because American record companies' hesitation to produce and provide video clips forced the channel to play nearly everything available. Adding to the frustration was cable's lack of popularity in major metropolitan areas. That fact made MTV a hard sell to advertisers, who were slow to buy time on an unknown network—especially a network they could not even view themselves. MTV was a huge gamble. But the channel's originators felt they had a concept that could not fail.

The concept of MTV was anything but what it appeared to be on the surface. MTV was meant to be cool. It was designed to look spontaneous—like something that had just popped up from a cool nightclub, college fraternity house, or the basement of someone you'd want to have as your best friend. The veejays (mostly former FM radio disc jockeys or bit actors) rehearsed their patter about the videos with the goal of making it seem off-the-cuff and *un*rehearsed. They were encouraged to ride out mistakes to add to the DIY feel. Sets were meticulously constructed to have a thrift-store look. Graphics used in MTV positioning promos and imaging were cutting edge, flashy, and meant to overload the senses with a feeling of hip euphoria. To appeal to viewer desires for social change and the need to buck the establishment, MTV devoted airtime to trendy causes like USA for Africa and Rock the Vote. MTV knew what its target demographic thought was cool, and that's what MTV delivered.

But under the young, hip exterior was a corporate machine that would have shocked many early fans and viewers. MTV's commitment was to itself and to its own brand preservation. In the words of television critic Tom Shales:

> Political and social content is almost entirely missing from MTV because it is built on the illusion that rock music is a political and social system in itself; that the world is divided into pro-rock and anti-rock forces, that to be a fan of the music or of particular groups is somehow to stand for something.[1]

MTV wasn't trying to buck the establishment—MTV was the establishment. According to one record-label executive, "The purpose of MTV is not to bring culture to the great unwashed. The purpose of MTV is to make money for MTV."[2]

Today, MTV and its various owners have turned it into a veritable cash machine—turning yearly profits upward of $100 million. These profits are generated from advertising revenues and successful branding efforts: MTV caps and jackets, *Beavis and Butthead* merchandise, *The Real World* books, MTV-themed compilation CDs, and so on. What has gone into creating that brand is no happy accident.

Former MTV researcher Marshall Cohen once said, "We believe [MTV] was the most researched channel in history."[3] While the service was still in its conceptual stage, MTV polled hundreds of teenagers and twenty-somethings to see if the idea would fly. Each week, fifteen hundred to three thousand phone surveys were conducted by the network to identify the video clips favored by target listeners, which videos they wanted to view more (or less) often, and what their opinions were concerning MTV and its programming.

MTV's attention to detail paid off. A poll of high school students several years after the channel's debut found that 85 percent of those with cable regularly watched MTV; 80 percent of a separate survey group reported viewing MTV more than two hours each day.[4] Once record labels noticed that MTV sold records, they began to pour millions into video production. MTV became a phenomenon; however, MTV's strong image also was a burden, because its importance in the music business eventually placed it squarely in the censors' view. While MTV did not produce the videos, as the messenger it was considered guilty by association.

The Case Against MTV and Music Videos

Almost since its inception, MTV has been lambasted for the imagery it airs. During the 1980s, a rash of academic studies concerning music videos appeared. When it came to race, gender roles, and violence, the results were none too flattering. One study found that men in music videos were usually portrayed in stereotypical male working roles: firefighters, mechanics, and doctors. Men on MTV comprised 94 percent of the police officers and 90 percent of the business executives. Women were portrayed in stereotypical roles as well: cheerleaders, secretaries, and librarians. Ninety-five percent of all characters of color were portrayed as athletes, entertainers, or other non-white-collar roles.[5]

According to the National Coalition on Television Violence, a majority of music videos contained excessive violence. Videos that the NCTV found particularly disturbing included Pat Benatar's "Anxiety," "You Might Think" by the Cars, "Come Dancing" by the Kinks, T-Bone Burnett's "Murder Weapon," "Fight Fire with Fire" by Kansas, Lionel Richie's "Penny Lover," and "Eat It" by Weird Al Yankovic. To emphasize what he considered to be positive images on MTV, NCTV head Thomas Radecki identified several artists he thought should be applauded for the "prosocial" values in their videos. Among that group were the Romantics, Donna Summer, U2, and Missing Persons (whose lead singer paraded through the video wearing a revealing bikini made of clear plastic tubing and discarded scraps of vinyl). In viewing these videos, it is apparent that interpretations of what constitutes violence and "prosocial" values are highly subjective.

One group suspiciously absent from much of the debate concerning music videos is the Parents Music Resource Center. While the PMRC initially lobbied heavily for warning labels displayed on a screen whenever video clips containing violent or sexually explicit lyrics or imagery were shown, the group backed down when it realized it was fairly powerless to control MTV. Federal Communications Commission guidelines for cable channels are far more lenient than for traditional TV broadcasters, and any action by MTV had to be voluntary. In an attempt to defuse the "Washington Wives" interest in MTV, the network invited PMRC representatives to visit their offices to discuss the standards and practices employed in video selection. Eventually, the attention given to music videos by the NCTV and PMRC had a chilling effect on MTV, which began to reject or request edits for a significantly higher percentage of submitted videos. When this action began, MTV was in a heated battle of its own, trying to save itself from the wrath of censors.

Censoring MTV

"You have to understand the pressure MTV is under," stated one former MTV exec. "If cable operators are pressured by the townships they're in, they'll put the pressure on MTV. If they really get in a battle, they'll consider jerking the channel."[6] While MTV was a runaway hit and a powerful force in the music industry, it had an Achilles' heel: carriage. Since first coming to the air in 1981, MTV found carriage by cable subscribers to be an uphill battle. Many cable providers resisted adding the network, because extra channels required extra cable capacity and distribution equipment. The cable companies were understandably hesitant to sink their profits into those kinds of investments. MTV first caught on in the suburbs and rural areas where cable was most popular, but it had a tougher time gaining carriage in major markets. While MTV did well in Wichita, Indianapolis, and Spokane, the large advertising agencies were located in major cities like Los Angeles and New York—areas slow to begin airing the network.

As MTV grew and carriage became less of a pressing concern, the issues quickly switched to maintaining distribution points during the explosion of the cable industry and weathering the controversy kicked up by the NCTV and other groups. A single decision to remove MTV from a cable system could translate into permanently lost access to hundreds of thousands of homes, easily eliminating entire markets. In the view of its detractors, MTV "the messenger" was just as flawed as the videos it presented. MTV's first sign of trouble came in the little town of Emporia, Virginia.

Shortly after Pembroke Cablevision added MTV in the summer of 1983, Roger Wilcher, the supervisor of youth activities at a local Baptist church in Emporia, felt that something should be done about it. Wilcher found the network "vulgar and distasteful" and thought that adults had an obligation to provide some "moral guidelines."[7] He began to lobby the city council to remove MTV from the cable system. In turn, the city council passed a resolution requiring Pembroke to remove the network from its standard cable offerings, but it allowed the cable operator to offer MTV as a premium service for an extra ten dollars a month. Few were happy with the council's decision—Wilcher and his friends wanted MTV completely removed from the cable system; network viewers were now required to pay an additional fee for a service they didn't object to; and MTV had lost access to more than 1,500 homes. A survey later determined that of the 1,659 Pembroke subscribers, only 28 percent wanted the service restricted.

The following year, 1984, saw several other attacks against MTV. Mormon bishop and landlord Leo Weidner banned MTV from the cable system in his Provo, Utah, apartment complex. He believed that MTV was a bad influence on his tenants, who were mostly students from nearby Brigham Young University. Weidner thought that music videos were "pornographic," even though he admitted he had never seen one. In May of that year, Surgeon General C. Everett Koop threw his opinion into the ring during a speech at a Southern medical college. He claimed that video fans had become "saturated with what I think is going to make them have trouble having satisfying relationships with the opposite sex . . . when you're raised with rock music that uses both pornography and violence."[8] Koop's statements were widely quoted, though he had no scientific evidence to support his claims.

On the East Coast that July, two born-again Christian women circulated a petition demanding the removal of the "decadent, morally degrading, and evil" video music network from their local cable system in Weymouth, Massachusetts. Local officials tried to offer a compromise: a channel-blocker that could be installed in any home to prevent MTV's signal from entering the television set. This solution did not satisfy the crusaders, and MTV was eventually removed from the cable system.

The channel-blocker compromise was a little more successful in Texarkana, Texas, after the city's board of directors objected to the sight of Cher's leather-thong-covered, tattooed buttocks flashing on their televisions in her clip for "If I Could Turn Back Time." Dimension Cable System offered the single channel "traps" to its 22,000 subscribers, which seemed to please the opposition. In the ensuing years, there have been only forty requests for the blocking device from Dimension subscribers (that's less than two-hundredths of one percent).

A major battle ensued when Tele-Community Antenna (TCA)— serving 420,000 subscribers in Texas, Mississippi, and Arkansas— decided to drop the music network in the summer of 1991. TCA labeled the channel as "borderline pornographic" and claimed to have received complaints from parents, teachers, and local government agencies. Following the ban, several local groups began actively campaigning to have the network restored to their cable systems. An Amarillo, Texas, radio station produced a pro-MTV rap song, and several petition drives were conducted to get back their MTV. Because almost half a million homes were at stake, MTV heavily invested in advertising to support the protesters who were trying to get the channel restored. TCA quickly caved under the pressure, and MTV was back on the system two weeks later.

A similar situation occurred in November of that year when Sammons Communications tried to replace MTV with the less provocative Video Jukebox Network on its fifty-five cable systems in nineteen states. Sammons initially wanted to switch MTV to a pay service, emulating the situation in Virginia eight years earlier. MTV refused, fearing the loss of advertising revenue. Soon after Sammons dropped MTV, several groups circulated petitions and organized protests against the cable giant. MTV again stepped in, running local television ads featuring Paula Abdul and Phil Collins, asking listeners to demand the return of the service to their cable system. Four months later, Sammons restored MTV.

MTV as Censor

There is a duality to MTV. Although it has taken some serious knocks from censors over the years, MTV has itself been a censor, both to control its product and to reduce the attacks it receives as messenger.

When videos arrive at MTV to be considered for air, the channel requires that they be accompanied by a lyric sheet, both of which are then reviewed by MTV's Standards Department (created in 1984 in response to the criticism MTV was enduring). From 1984 until 1989, the Standards Department consisted of one person, who had complete control over every MTV video, promo, commercial, and imaging spot. In 1989, the Standards Department was expanded to include five people. Most of the additional staffers also served on the Acquisitions Committee, which forwards all submitted videos to the Standards Department after screening them for formatting considerations.

Guidelines used by the Standards Department, though inconsistently applied and completely open to subjectivity, rule out videos showing drug use; excessive alcohol consumption; explicit, graphic, or excessive sexual practices; gratuitous violence (such as knifings or physical restraint); or derogatory characterizations of ethnic or religious groups. In the words of one MTV exec, "naked women running around or throwing babies out of trucks would not be permitted." MTV has also tried to fend off criticism by airing some videos only late in the evening or through the late-night hours, as was the case with Cher's "If I Could Turn Back Time" and Sir Mix-A-Lot's "Baby Got Back." MTV itself recognizes the inconsistency inherent in its standards and practice guidelines. According to an MTV spokesperson, "Where it gets tricky is drawing the line. It's never a black-and-white issue. There's a lot of gray stuff. Is that too much of Cher's ass? Somebody has to decide."⁹

An additional duty of MTV's Standards Department is to police the appearance of product logos in videos. An MTV viewer can easily notice that logos are blurred out of videos and shows like *The Real World.* "The idea behind not having product endorsements is to differentiate the videos from the commercials," explained MTV's Tina Exarhos. However, MTV's true motives may be slightly different. With the costs of producing a major label video starting at about $100,000, it wouldn't take long before artists and their record companies began to consider the inclusion of product placement or endorsements to underwrite the expense—similar to product sponsorships of major concert tours or artists appearing in commercials. For example, it is not a coincidence that Apple's Macintosh computers seem to be the computer of choice in many motion pictures and television shows. Apple pays big money to put them there and would probably do the same with music videos if given the chance. In fact, many companies would.

Another way MTV controls music videos is by demanding re-edits. If MTV doesn't like something in a video or if it objects to lyrics, the entire clip is returned to the record company for another try. In 1984, MTV demanded edits to one out of every ten videos aired; by 1994, that number had grown to one in three, with some videos returned as many as six times for edits.

What's So Terrible About Condoms?

By 1989, the world was aware of AIDS, and educational efforts were in full swing to halt the spread of the disease. Also that year, a little-known garage-punk band, the Fuzztones, released their first American album, *In Heat.* The group's label, Beggar's Banquet (distributed by BMG), commissioned a video for the group's song "Nine Months Later." Upon review by the MTV Standards Department, the video was rejected for unacceptable sexual innuendos in the song's lyrics. Specifically, they objected to the third verse:

Listen boys, to these words of wit.
I said it's not attached to you, you're
  attached to it.
Well if you don't wanna live this life of
  shame,
Be sure to wear your rubbers when it rains.
And when it rains it pours!

According to the band's frontman, Rudi Protrudi, "The message of the song was quite
clear: 'Hey, kids, wear condoms!' We were the
first and only band to promote condom use."

MTV said that it would air the video, but only
if the lyrics were changed to something more
acceptable, like "raincoats" instead of "rubbers." Protrudi feels that the song's rejection
was intended to make an example of the Fuzztones. "It was a smokescreen," says Protrudi.

The Fuzztones—their video
for "Nine Months Later"
was rejected by MTV in
1989 because it contained
a reference to condoms.

"MTV was getting a lot of pressure from conservatives to remove all sex
from videos. At the time, no one in the U.S. had heard of the Fuzztones—
so we were an easy target. They never would have asked Madonna to
change that lyric."

Protrudi felt that MTV used a double standard in its judgment of the
video. "Safe sex is pretty much what MTV is about. They have commercials for condoms, specials about safe sex—so what's so bad about the
word 'rubbers'?

"I don't think there was any moral decision involved at all; whoever has
the most money gets the loudest voice. This is a 'funny' song, not a 'dirty'
one—that's the last thing I ever thought it would be. But somebody did."

After receiving intense pressure from their record label, Protrudi and
the group relented and rerecorded the lyric. MTV approved the revised
video but aired it only once.

The list of videos that MTV has returned for edits might surprise
some viewers (see "Videos Edited for MTV," p. 95). For example,
Culture Club's video clip for "Do You Really Want to Hurt Me?"
aired in Britain with its featured jury of black-faced minstrels.
MTV demanded the scene be cut before it was aired. The reedited

clip ignited the band's career in the United States—sans the Jolson-esque jurors. Before MTV added David Bowie's clip for "China Girl" to its rotation, a nude beach scene was replaced. The clip for Frankie Goes to Hollywood's "Relax" was returned four times by MTV before the video was aired. Even the Christian rock band DeGarmo & Key, one of few Christian acts featured on MTV, failed to make it past the Standards Department. Their video for "Six, Six, Six" featured a scene in which the Antichrist burst into flames.

MTV has asked for edits based on lyrics also. It insisted that the Fuzztones change the lyrics for their song "Nine Months Later" from "Well if you don't wanna live this life of shame, Be sure to wear your rubbers when it rains" to "wear your raincoat."

A smaller category are the videos that are so far gone with imagery or lyrics that MTV flat-out refuses to air them. Probably the most famous example of this type of deletion is Madonna's video for "Justify My Love." The black-and-white video caused quite a stir when it was released: nudity, gay and lesbian foreplay, sadomasochism, cross-dressing, and group sex. The video was originally scheduled to debut as part of an MTV "Madonnathon" in November of 1990. Once MTV viewed the finished product, they refused to air the clip. In a statement to the press, Madonna called attention to the media's double standard: "Why is it that people are willing to go to a movie and watch someone get blown to bits for no reason and nobody wants to see two girls kissing or two men snuggling?"[10] The incident wasn't all bad for Madonna; following the controversy's coverage in the press (including an airing of the unedited video on ABC's *Nightline*), her record company released the video in the consumer market and sold half a million copies the first month. Madonna refused to edit the video, and it still does not appear on MTV.

Other artists who refused to edit videos have seen their clips end up in the circular file: The Rolling Stones' video for "Under Cover of Night" was refused because it depicted violence (after being aired on MTV for two weeks), Public Enemy's "Hazy Shade of Criminal" was passed over for including a riot scene, and "Taste It" by INXS was turned down as well. On only one occasion has MTV reversed a ruling by its Standards Department: Neil Young's "This Note's for You."

Videos Edited for MTV

You might be surprised at the list of popular videos that were initially rejected by MTV for lyrics and imagery. Here's a sample:

Berlin	"Sex"
Bon Jovi	"Living in Sin"
Cars	"Hello Again"
Culture Club	"Do You Really Want to Hurt Me?"
David Bowie	"China Girl"
Duran Duran	"Girls on Film"
Frankie Goes to Hollywood	"Relax"
Golden Earring	"Twilight Zone"
Joan Jett	"Bad Reputation"
John Cougar Mellencamp	"Let It All Hang Out"
Queen	"Body Language"
Ramones	"Psychotherapy"
Rolling Stones	"Neighbors" and "She Was Hot"
Serious-Lee-Fine	"Nothing Can Stop Us Now"

Young's song and the accompanying video were meant to parody the ever-increasing number of product endorsements by musical celebrities. The video contained impersonators of Michael Jackson and Whitney Houston hawking Pepsi and Coke, and it was based partially on an Eric Clapton commercial for Michelob. The lyrics read, "Ain't singin' for Miller, don't sing for Bud, I won't sing for politicians, ain't singin' for Spuds. This note's for you." After scheduling the sight-unseen video for a MTV world premier on July 1, 1988, MTV pulled the plug when the Standards Department saw it. MTV explained that the video violated its policies regarding product placement because the clip

Even such uncontroversial acts as pop rockers Bon Jovi found themelves editing their videos to meet MTV's standards.

showed the logos of the products it was parodying. Young wrote a terse letter to MTV, calling them "spineless" and asked, "What does the 'M' in MTV stand for—music or money?"[11] MTV eventually relented, and Young's video went on to win the MTV Award for Best Video of the Year.

As it is for many institutions choosing to censor, the biggest problem with MTV's use of "standards" in videos is its lack of consistency in implementing these policies. While MTV will censor a Culture Club video because it might offend African-Americans, it does not censor Dire Straits' "Money for Nothing," which repeatedly refers to homosexuals derogatorily as "faggots." And speaking of homosexuality, Madonna's video for "Justify My Love" is censored for depicting same-sex cuddling and kissing—yet MTV displays heterosexual couples engaged in the same activities. Neil Young is banned from MTV for showing product logos, yet videos by DJ Jazzy Jeff and Fresh Prince have displayed product logos with no attempts made to cover or remove them. Although MTV confined Sir Mix-A-Lot's "Baby Got Back" to evenings only, the network had aired a similarly themed "Big Old Butt" by L.L. Cool J during daytime hours just two years earlier. MTV is also more likely to request edits from unknown artists than from established ones.

According to MTV spokesperson Carole Robinson, "our guidelines are fluid and open to interpretation so that each video can be reviewed on a case-by-case basis."

Some industry analysts suggest that a new artist's sales can increase by as much as half a million copies if he or she gains exposure on MTV. With numbers like that, it's no wonder that artists and labels are anxious to please MTV and that MTV easily wields near-complete control over the music video industry.

However, it should be noted that MTV does not hold a clear monopoly over the censorship of videos. In 1991, both Country Music Television and its parent company, The Nashville Network, banned Garth Brooks's video for "The Thunder Rolls." Although the networks had been airing the video in heavy rotation, the clip was pulled because executives felt that the themes of domestic violence, revenge, and murder were not up to network standards. Brooks eventually edited the video, claiming he had intended to release an edited version all along.

MTV and Race

There is one area in which MTV can be found guilty of shortsightedness rather than of censorship: race. During the early eighties, many artists, record companies, and industry insiders declared MTV racist for refusing to play videos by black artists. "God forbid people should be exposed to blacks on cable," joked A&M Records' Jeff Ayeroff.[12] But in this instance, MTV was neither racist nor censorious, it was simply late in realizing the crossover potential of artists such as Michael Jackson, Prince, and Lionel Richie. Not to say that there is no racism in music or music videos (for example, producers of Donna Summer's video for "She Works Hard for the Money" were told by label execs to include a white family in the clip's plot), but rather that MTV's programming *policies* are not racist.

From its inception, MTV adopted many principles common to commercial radio, especially a concept that gained a huge amount of radio programming popularity in the eighties: "narrowcasting." Narrowcasting is the idea that a radio station (or video music channel) should program itself to appeal to one specific music genre, thus strictly aligning to the demographic most associated with that blend of music. Radio fragmented into R&B, country, oldies, alternative, AOR (album-oriented rock), CHR (contemporary hits radio), AC (adult contemporary), and others. In the nineties, the concept was further refined when these categories were broken into several subcategories, each of which targeted a unique listener demographic.

When MTV began, it had its eye firmly fixed on fifteen- to thirty-five-year-old whites with high disposable income. The safest bet to hit that demographic was straight-ahead AOR—Rock with a capital R. Artists such as Lionel Richie and Rick James did not fit this mold. To claim that MTV was racist is like criticizing The Nashville Network for failing to air the New York Philharmonic or blasting Black Entertainment Television for refusing to play Jim Nabors.

Regardless, Rick James spoke about the absence of black artists on MTV in 1983, when he told the *Los Angeles Times:*

> I'm just tired of the bullshit. I have sold over 10 million records in a four-year period . . . and I can't get on the channel. I watch

all these fluffed up groups who don't even sell four records on a program that I'm being excluded from. Me and every one of my peers. It's like taking black people back 400 years.[13]

MTV countered that while James's music was indeed popular, it was not popular with MTV's bread-and-butter demo: the rock music fan. The MTV viewer didn't see Rick James as rock, so MTV was not going to play his videos.

James's interest in MTV was simple: "I figure if they played my video I could sell hundreds of thousands more records than I do now." According to Manny Sanchez, marketing director for Franklin Music, "Forget this black/white thing. The issue is 'green.' " And that's true. The real issue of black artists on MTV was money, wrapped in the banner of civil rights and race.

Well-intentioned artists such as David Bowie and Bob Seger chastised the music channel for failing to play more black artists. During an MTV interview, Bowie suddenly started quizzing veejay Mark Goodman about MTV's programming policies.

Black artists truly crossed over into MTV with the huge success of Michael Jackson's *Thriller*. When *Thriller*'s first single, "Billie Jean," was released in early 1983, it quickly jumped to the top of the *Billboard* pop singles charts. Still, MTV would not air the video. It is rumored that CBS Records officials became so frustrated with MTV's refusal to play the song that they threatened to pull all CBS videos from MTV (including such staple artists as Billy Joel, Journey, and Pink Floyd) if MTV didn't add "Billie Jean." The pressure tactic, if it occurred, worked, and MTV began a long involvement with Jackson and his video catalog. Jackson's success on MTV finally sent the message that black artists had tremendous crossover potential, eventually paving the way for many others.

6

"EBONY AND IVORY"

Race

∎

**If a white man kills a negro, they hardly carry it to court.
If a negro kills a white man, they hang him like a goat.**
—from "All Coons Look Alike to Me"

n 1974, Eric Clapton released a single entitled "I Shot the Sheriff," written two years earlier by reggae great Bob Marley. The storyteller says that the sheriff never liked him and regularly harassed him. Following a street confrontation between the two, the storyteller's gun discharges and the sheriff is killed. The song ends with the storyteller accepting that the sheriff's deputy will come for him soon to punish him for his mistake.

According to Marley, "I Shot the Sheriff" is a plea for social justice. "I wanted to say 'I shot the police' but the government would have made a fuss so I said 'I shot the sheriff' instead . . . but it's the same idea: justice." The single was a huge hit for Clapton, eventually reaching number one on the American pop charts. Yet, despite its theme of vigilante justice against police, it created no controversy for Clapton.

Eighteen years later, rapper Ice-T released a song entitled "Cop Killer" with his rock band Body Count. The song's theme was similar to that of the Clapton hit: A storyteller seeks revenge against the police for brutality committed against innocent citizens: "I got my 12-gauge sawed off, I got my headlights turned off. Cop killer, better you than me. Cop killer, fuck police brutality." But the reception to Ice-T's song differed significantly from that given to Clapton. Dozens of special-interest groups lobbied retailers to remove the record from stores, threatening bans and boycotts of Ice-T and his record label, Time-Warner. President George Bush and Vice President Dan Quayle both advocated censorship of Ice-T. Charlton Heston and the National Rifle Association attacked Time-Warner and Ice-T for glorifying the killing of law enforcement officials. Conservative talk-show host, Iran-Contra star, and former U.S. Senate candidate Oliver North offered to pay the legal bills for any wounded police officer whose assailant admitted to listening to the song.

What is the difference between Eric Clapton's hit single and Ice-T's "Cop Killer"? There is none. Unless you want to count the fact that Clapton is white and Ice-T is black.

Historically, race has been a huge issue in music and in music censorship. Racial discrimination is so ingrained in music (as well as in the rest of society) that it is sometimes difficult to separate them. You could almost say that censorship is a "natural" manifestation of racism: The lack of knowledge and abundance of fear that breed racism also create an urge to suppress and constrain minority cultures. In fact, racism and music censorship based on racism have had an enormous effect on the history of popular music in the twentieth century. Despite the radical metamorphosis that race relations have undergone during the evolution of rock music, whenever white teenagers bring home music created by black musicians, trouble is close behind.

Racism in "Prerock" Popular Music

Just the way American popular music reflects American culture and societal values, so does it reflect attitudes toward race.

While the era between the Civil War and World War I included a great deal of popular "nonracist" music, some of the popular titles would probably make a Klansman blush. Songs like "Two Real Coons," "Hottest Coon in Dixie," and "The Wedding of the Chinee and the Coon" were very popular in the South and, indeed, throughout the United States. One song, "All Coons Look Alike to Me" sold more than one million copies of sheet music around the turn of the century. The song became so popular that whites taunted blacks by whistling the first few notes of the tune as they walked past.[1] Strangest of all, the song's author, Ernest Hogan, was black.

In the early twentieth century, the Harlem Renaissance developed the idea of black enlightenment and fostered creative expression in literature, poetry, and music (especially jazz and blues). In 1920, Mamie Smith was the first black to score a hit record with her song "Crazy Blues"—which, the week following its release, sold more than seventy-five hundred copies. Before the stock market crash in 1929, as many as ten million black jazz, blues, and gospel records were sold each year. By the late 1930s and early 1940s, swing and jazz music originated by blacks was being appropriated by white musicians. Bandleaders like Benny Goodman, Artie Shaw, and Glenn Miller purchased and then brought to the mainstream the musical arrangements of black composers and arrangers. The music industry encouraged the practice, realizing that it was much easier to sell a white band playing a hit song than to popularize a tune with its original black band. Thus, many white bands dominated the pop charts while black bandleaders like Cab Calloway, Count Basie, Louis Armstrong, and Duke Ellington experienced significantly less financial success and popularity. Often, black musicians were forced to play gigs in lower-paying segregated clubs.[2] This habit of coopting music from black artists in order to keep music segregated (and profitable) continued when popular culture introduced its newest craze: rock and roll.

The "Tribal Rhythms" of Rock and Roll

While America's attitudes toward race and the resulting suppression of black performers are very significant components in the development of early rock music, many other factors contributed to the advent of rock. First and foremost among these was the abundant number of young people born in the mid- to late 1940s.

Those early Baby Boomers entered their preteen and teenage years during the 1950s, creating a significant "youth culture" that yearned for its own identity. The economic prosperity of the post–World War II era—and the concept of an "allowance" becoming popular for the first time—provided teens with independent buying power that was not apparent in previous generations. Teenage allowances amounted to $9 billion in 1957, growing to $10.5 billion by 1963. According to a 1960 survey by *Seventeen* magazine, the average teenage girl had "a weekly income of $9.53, gets up at 7:43 A.M., and listens to the radio for two hours a day."[3]

Television also played a huge role in the birth of rock music. By the late forties and early fifties, it was obvious that mass entertainment's big money rested with television, and program producers flocked to the new medium. Between 1948 and 1952, more than 38 percent of all network programs migrated from radio to television.[4] Although it was thought that television would lead to the death of radio, naysayers failed to predict the importance of transistor radios. With this new invention, portable and car radios were readily available at affordable prices. Between 1955 and 1960, the number of radios used increased more than 30 percent. The radio went from being the centerpiece of family evenings to a companion as you drove around town or sat in the park. Yet the depletion of talent and simultaneous increase in audience left the radio industry in a scramble to create "replacement" programming. Relying heavily on music formats, radio-station owners hired the talent that was available. The new pool of deejays consisted largely of music geeks, and many were fans of rhythm and blues music (a term coined in the late 1940s by Jerry Wexler at *Billboard* to replace the phrase "race music"). Of course, that's exactly what they wanted to play.

What drew R&B out of late-night radio and into the mainstream was the music industry's realization that there was money to be made from transforming black R&B into predominantly white rock and roll. Because early rock and R&B artists usually began their careers by recording for independent music labels, the larger music companies found themselves virtually locked out of the game when teenagers started to buy records. To get a piece of the action, record labels hired white musicians to "cover" popular R&B songs, often reworking the lyrics to remove racy or controversial phrases or themes. This also allowed the music industry to weasel out of the problem of promoting black artists to a leery public, thus reducing public exposure of black artists, with bad royalties and rights deals preventing them from receiving payment for their creative work. In 1952, labels grossed more than $15 million in sales from black R&B music; almost none of that money went into the hands of the people who created the music. Song composers were usually paid less than $10 (sometimes in an equivalent amount of whiskey), and they did not receive additional royalties or bonuses.

In some instances, the evolution of pop songs reflected a true melting pot. For example the song "Hound Dog" was originally written by two Jewish men and recorded in 1953 by black blues singer Big Mama Thornton. The song then was popularized by Elvis Presley in 1956.

More typical of white performers who made careers from rerecorded versions of R&B songs was Pat Boone. During his career, Boone recorded more than sixty sanitized cover songs (six of them became number-one hits), including material originally written and performed by Fats Domino, Big Joe Turner, the El Dorados, Ivory Joe Hunter, and Little Richard. Often Boone's versions included significantly different lyrics. When he covered "Tutti Fruitti" by Little Richard, the lyrics were changed from "Boys, don't you know what she do to me" to "Pretty little Susie is the girl for me." "I had to be selective and change some lyrics, but nobody cared," said Boone. "It made it more vanilla."[5]

The music industry produced white teen heartthrobs at such an alarming rate you might have thought they were mass-producing them on assembly lines. By doing so, the music industry curtailed the careers of dozens of black performers who sold their rights to songs (eventually worth millions of dollars). The net effect was a predominantly white version of R&B, known as rock and roll.

It's important to note that the whitewashing of rock was significant in its rise to popularity; however, there were many black performers (such as Little Richard, Fats Domino, and Chuck Berry) who broke through the race barriers to achieve popularity rivaling that of many white performers at the time. Thinking of rock as a bunch of white "impersonators" also discounts the importance of many early white rock pioneers such as Bill Haley, Buddy Holly, and Jerry Lee Lewis. Lewis, however, was also a victim of racially motivated censorship, even though he was white. When Lewis's "Whole Lotta Shakin' " was released in 1957, several radio stations refused to air the song because they thought Lewis was black.

Although the suppression of black music was an aftereffect of racial censorship in the music industry, it was not the primary motivator of rock music's censors. Many arguments against R&B and rock music were based on the fear that rock music's popularity would allow black culture to encroach into the American mainstream. By putting black music into a white context, conservatives cried that the resultant "race mixing" would "mongrelize" America.

In 1956, a spokesperson for the White Citizens Council of Birmingham, Alabama, called rock and roll "the basic, heavy-beat music of Negroes" that appealed to "the base in man," bringing "out animalism and vulgarity." The group's executive director, Asa Carter, wanted to outlaw jukeboxes because he felt they were tools of the National Association for the Advancement of Colored People. Carter reasoned that the NAACP loaded jukeboxes with black records to brainwash white teenagers with "vulgar music." During a Nat King Cole performance that same year, members of the council jumped onto the stage and beat the performer. They mistakenly believed that Cole was an R&B singer and wanted to discourage him from performing in Alabama in the future.

Asa Carter (*top, center*), head of the White Citizens Council of Birmingham, Alabama, addresses a group of students outside Clinton High School in Tennessee in September 1956. Carter's group was responsible for many protests and subversive activities against equal rights for blacks and desegregation, some resulting in censorship of black musicians and halting the distribution of "race" music.

In 1955 the Houston Juvenile Delinquency and Crime Commission blacklisted thirty songs, saying they were lewd and unfit for young ears. The list was almost entirely comprised of black artists such as the Drifters, Ray Charles, and the 5 Royales. Another critic of rock music testified before Congress in 1957 that the music "stirred the animal instinct in modern teenagers" with its "raw savage tone."[6] Radio stations across the country—such as Memphis's WDIA and WBAA of

Mobile, Alabama—banned lists of lewd and controversial artists, the lists often consisting entirely of black performers.

The Catholic Church entered the fray when several bishops declared that rock and R&B should be banned from Catholic schools and social gatherings because of their "hedonistic, tribal rhythms."

Fear went beyond simple integration of black music into mainstream culture with the widespread concern that rock's popularity would lead to interracial sexual relations. Record companies avoided promotional material that portrayed a mixture of races in the same photograph. Network censors forbade television programs to depict interracial mingling on popular dance shows. Alan Freed's television show, *Rock 'n' Roll Dance Party*, was canceled after a cameraman filmed a white girl dancing with black singer Frankie Lymon. According to industry veteran Russ Sanjek, "It was a time when many a mother ripped pictures of Fats Domino off her daughter's bedroom wall. She remembered what she felt toward her Bing Crosby pin-up, and she didn't want her daughter creaming for Fats."[7]

As the record industry manipulated black musicians to sell their music to white America, they also systematically abandoned the black record-buying public. Record companies continued to release "black music" exclusively on 78-RPM records until the late fifties, even though the vast majority of record players produced after the mid-forties could not play them. Their logic was that black record buyers couldn't afford to replace their equipment to play music on the current standard (45- and 33-RPM records, which stayed as the format of choice until the mid-eighties) preventing the majority of the American record-buying public from ever buying black titles. This practice started a segregation in the music industry that continues today; it created a "black music" (sometimes called "urban" or "urban contemporary") market segment secondary to and discrete from the "pop music" market.

Civil Rights, Integration, and Motown

The Civil Rights era of the mid-1960s had an indelible effect on American politics and culture. The Civil Rights Act of 1964, the Voting Rights Act of 1965, and the Economic Opportunities Act of 1964 were the beginnings of President Lyndon Johnson's vision of a "Great Society" in which, according to Johnson, "the city of man served not only the needs of the body and the demands of commerce but the desire for beauty and the hunger for community." The call from leaders such as Dr. Martin Luther King, Jr., was "integration"—allowing black Americans to become part of mainstream American life and culture, effectively ending the concept of "separate but equal."

Inspired by the work of Dr. King, Berry Gordy founded a record label called Motown Records, which eventually became the largest contributor to the R&B boom of the 1960s and the largest black-owned corporation in the world. Although Motown was staffed largely by blacks, Gordy understood that the white-dominated recording industry demanded whites in certain positions of authority. As a result, most of its legal and financial counsel were Caucasian.

Though Motown was started by Berry Gordy with a loan of eight hundred dollars from his family in 1958, things didn't start to click until the early 1960s. Gordy understood the potential of applying Dr. King's integrationist principles to the music business. According to Motown producer Mickey Stevenson, "Berry felt that our job was to make blacks aware of their culture, of the problems and some of the ways out of the problems."[8] Gordy worked hard to make his artists "presentable" to the general record-buying public. Motown employed an etiquette coach and a choreographer on the label's full-time staff because Gordy wanted to groom talent to be photogenic, television-savvy, and disciplined during performances. Posture, clothing, and speech were as important to Motown as were songwriting and musical ability. Gordy understood the social and business significance of having a stable of artists who would not create controversial situations, as the black R&B and rock performers of the 1950s had. The result was that Motown became a huge success, selling more records in the mid-1960s than any other record label.

Black music continued to evolve, but it was an evolution that occurred mostly outside the pop music mainstream. Black artists received significantly less promotional support and visibility than did mainstream artists. Even the most popular black artists were rarely considered mainstream successes unless they crossed over and onto the pop charts. As black music was pushed further from the spotlight, the success of its market segment became less important to the bottom line of the recording industry. Except during the disco era, predominantly black music continued to take a backseat to white pop music until the early nineties, when rap pushed black music and culture to America's center stage.

The Revolution Will Not Be Televised

Examined from a sociological perspective, rap music's development and importance to black culture (and the resistance to rap that was—and to some extent still is—demonstrated by the mainstream) is no surprise. By the time rap emerged in the late seventies and early eighties, things weren't looking good for many blacks in America.

In 1986, more than 30 percent of black families had yearly incomes of less than $10,000, and 14 percent had incomes of less than $5,000. In 1992, 59 percent of African-American households were headed by single females. The number of African-American males under age twenty-four who had never held a job rose from 9.9 percent in 1966 to almost 24 percent in 1992. Although black Americans comprise only 15 percent of the nation's drug users, close to 50 percent of the individuals arrested on drug charges are black.[9]

According to Census Bureau statistics for 1992, the poverty rate for black Americans was 32.7 percent, compared to 28.7 percent for Hispanics, 13.8 percent for Asians, and 11.3 percent for whites. According to the Children's Defense Fund, more than two-thirds of minority children lived in poverty during that same time period.

Also at that time, homicide was the leading cause of death among black teens, and one in three black males was involved at some level in the penal system. "The other day I was looking at an old picture from back when I used to play football," observed rapper Snoop Dogg, "and like of twenty-eight homies on the team, twelve are dead, seven are in the penitentiary, and three of them are smoked out."

Public Enemy's Chuck D: "I don't believe in boycotts. The best way to boycott is to build your own."

Black people have never been the players. We've always been the victims. We've been pimped, whored, played, and macked for the last

five hundred years in this land. The 1990s have been filled with black men being systematically ripped down and overexposed in the media like we're the worst criminals on the planet. There is a subliminal message that stated, 'If you're not a ballplayer, or entertainer, and you're not living a lavish lifestyle then you ain't shit.' "[10]

"My job is to build five thousand potential black leaders through my means of communication in America. A black leader is just someone who takes responsibility."[11]

Public Enemy's Chuck D

The abundance of free time and a lack of stable family life and community environments led many inner-city black youths to become involved in drugs and gangs. "There's a lot of admirable qualities to gang membership," says rapper and former gang member Ice-T. "A guy could look at you and say, 'If something happens to you I'll be the first one to die.' There's a lot of love."[12]

Rap itself grew out of the desire of club DJs to distinguish themselves from other DJs by adding turntable tricks and unique musical mixing to their performances. Eventually, some of the DJs promoted themselves by speaking, or "rapping," while mixing records. Many engaged in "call and response" dialogues with the audience. The competitive aspects of rap were born from a street game called "snap," where players used rhymes and street slang to outwit opponents.

As rapping evolved to become even more intricate, DJs added emcees (commonly known by the moniker "MC") to handle the rapping while devoting themselves to mixing the music. Eventually, the power roles reversed, and the rapping MCs became the main attraction.

Oral performance was not new to black culture. Oral traditions gave rise to the political and social commentaries of black leaders like Martin Luther King, Jr., and Malcolm X; the verbal artistry of the Last Poets ("Niggers Are Scared of Revolution") and Gil Scott-Heron ("The Revolution Will Not Be Televised") built on that existing foundation. Use of rap as an expressive art form—a soap-box from which to make political and social commentary—came quickly and easily to rap pioneers such as Grandmaster Flash, Afrika Bambaataa, and the Sugarhill Gang. Although each had some mainstream success with rap music, it wasn't until the emergence of Run-D.M.C. that rap showed its commercial teeth. Run-D.M.C.'s debut album became the first rap record to reach gold status, and they were the first rap act to secure airplay on MTV. After Run-D.M.C.'s success in the mid-eighties, the doors blew open for rap, which took over the music industry in a few short years. By the early nineties, rap outsold mainstream rock records; in 1991, rap records brought in $700 million a year (a $100 million increase over the previous year).

Many of the newer rap artists no longer sang about girls, cars, and tennis shoes. Having come from the poverty-ridden inner-city, they rapped about the life they saw every day. Rap began to threaten the status quo when it took inner-city problems and communicated, politicized, and validated them to a large audience. But the spark that really ignited the interest of censors wasn't blacks rapping to blacks—it was the fact that rap was leaving the inner city and heading for the suburbs. By 1992, 74 percent of rap records sold in the United States were being purchased by whites.

Hard-core or "gangsta" rap, as it became known, was an angry form of musical expression that openly discussed elements of the black inner city about which most Americans were not prepared to hear: guns, drugs, broken homes, injustice, gangs, murder, the breakdown of community, and police brutality. These rappers were not just complaining, they were critiquing mainstream culture.

According to black cultural scholar and author Clarence Lusane:

> Unlike the moralistic preaching, escapism or sentimentality that defines most popular music, hard-core rappers detail the unemployment, mis-education, discrimination, homicides, gang life, class oppression, police brutality, and regressive gender politics that dominate the lives of many black youth. Living in a post-industrial, Reagan-molded, increasingly-racist, anti-immigrant,

less tolerant, more sexist, Jesse-dissing, King-beating, Quayle-spelling, Clarence Thomas–serving America, too many young blacks find too little hope in the current society.[13]

It wasn't long before rap created a great deal of controversy. By the early 1990s, groups that supported music-labeling efforts (such as the PMRC and Focus on the Family) stopped targeting heavy metal and punk music and started to focus almost exclusively on rap. They thought that rap music themes were misogynistic, pro-drug, pro-gang, pro-violence, and they were unable to accept a distinction between *singing about* an issue and *endorsing* that issue. The media, in their attempts to show the American public a "magic bullet" to inner-city problems, offered rap as a culprit. As a result, Americans became very sensitive to the themes of hardcore rap, and people often subjected rap to a scrutiny that was absent for similar themes in other musical genres.

In 1994, the House Energy and Commerce Subcommittee held a hearing about the necessity of rating gangsta rap records. Despite attempts to provide an objective forum on the issue, the hearings were mostly filled with anti-rap advocates who claimed that there were clear connections between rap music, youth violence, and drugs. One of the few rap supporters permitted to address the committee was female rapper Yo-Yo (aka Yolande Whitaker) who testified, "Being from the 'hood, I can tell you that violence didn't start from a cassette tape that might have been popped into a home or car stereo system. We are a product of America."[14] That same month, then–House Speaker Newt Gingrich called for boycotts of radio stations that played any type of rap music, encouraging advertisers to pull ads from the stations. Feeling the pressure, record labels started to talk about adopting different labeling standards for rap releases.

Conservative William Bennett and National Political Congress of Black Women Chairwoman C. Delores Tucker began a four-year campaign to rid the country of rap music they found to be "blatantly pro-drug" and/or "obscene." "The original intent of the First Amendment was to protect one to have freedom of religion and freedom to address their government," said Tucker, "not to carry filthy, harmful messages or do anything harmful to people." Bennett rationalized the campaign by saying, "When people are confronted by what they have done, maybe they will stop."[15] Eventually some elected officials worked for their cause, including U.S. Senators Joseph Lieberman and Sam Nunn.

Radio became particularly sensitive to the baggage attached to rap music. Claiming that the level of profanity and violent themes prevented them from playing most rap records, urban contemporary radio stations abandoned most rap records, featuring only the blandest and most benign rap artists on radio. Rap also was subjected to excessive editing for radio, television, and retail.

Members of the group N.W.A (Niggaz With Attitude). The popularity of the group's single "Fuck Tha Police" resulted in a threatening letter from the FBI

One of the early breakthrough gangsta rap groups was N.W.A (Niggaz With Attitude). On their second album, *Straight Outta Compton*, the group included a single entitled "Fuck Tha Police," a direct call to action against the injustice, brutality, and double standards they saw in the justice system. At the urging of Focus on the Family, the FBI wrote a letter to the group protesting the song and its theme. Other law enforcement interest groups also boycotted the group and threatened arrest if N.W.A performed the song in public, under the guise of concern about potential riots.

Professor Griff (aka Richard Griff), an on-and-off member of the group Public Enemy, found his solo album banned by several record chains because the retailers felt that the album's themes (thought to be anti-Semitic and violently black-separatist) were too strong for their stores. The record was called "totally obscene," even though it contained little swearing and no sexual references.

Ice-T's "Cop Killer," discussed earlier in this chapter, caused an incredible amount of controversy when it was released in

Rap group Public Enemy

1992. Almost immediately after the *Body Count* album was released, police groups and conservative organizations across the country called for boycotts against Ice-T and Time-Warner Records. The media picked up on the controversy, igniting debates on both sides of the issue. The African-American Peace Officer Association called the boycotts "another act of police brutality." Ron Hampton, executive director of the National Black Police Association, said, "This vocal expression by Ice-T is no more than his personal frustration with the conditions facing oppressed people." Hampton also pointed out that the groups denouncing Ice-T had not shown "the same level of outrage when Rodney King was brutally beaten by four Los Angeles police officers."[16] After two months, Ice-T asked Time-Warner to remove the song from the album. The label immediately complied and recalled all copies of *Body Count*, reissuing the album without the controversial track. But the groups that had organized the boycotts said they would continue to protest until Ice-T apologized to them, which he refused to do.

Ice-T: "Every fucking thing I write is going to be analyzed by somebody white."

Many people are unaware that the song "Cop Killer" was actually recorded by a band called Body Count, not Ice-T as a solo rap artist. Body Count (which was led by Ice-T but was comprised primarily of white musicians) was an experiment by Ice-T in expanding the horizons of rap music by hybridizing it with heavy metal. However, when the controversy started, the mob targeted only Ice-T, the black rapper.

Ice-T had a critically and commercially successful career as a rap artist for almost a decade before "Cop Killer." He took his name from Iceberg Slim, a pimp who wrote novels and poetry about ghetto life. Ice-T is often credited as being one of the first gangsta rappers to use his raps to describe life in the inner-city ghetto poetically. His rhymes were clever, powerful, and always controversial.

Among Ice-T's many "accomplishments": He was the first rap artist to have his album carry a parental warning sticker. He came to censors' attention for his 1987 album *Rhyme Pays*, which included the song "Girls L.G.B.N.A.F.," which the PMRC learned stood for "Let's Get Butt Naked and Fuck." Several of his albums, including *Power, The Iceberg/Freedom of Speech . . . Just Watch What You Say*, and *O.G.: Original Gangsta*, are heralded as being among the most powerful rap albums ever produced.

Rapper Ice-T

Following the controversy surrounding "Cop Killer," Ice-T's career began to slip. Time-Warner refused to release his next rap album, *Home Invasion*, because label executives feared that its cover art and themes of retaliation against whites would create more controversy for the company (one of the album's songs contained the lyric, "I'm takin' your kids' brains—you ain't getting them back. I'm gonna fill 'em with hard drugs, big guns, bitches, hoes, and death"). Ice-T eventually released Home Invasion (and several later albums) on an independent record label. None of them achieved the levels of critical or commercial success of his previous albums.

Former N.W.A member Ice Cube became the target of boycotts and bans following the release of his album *Death Certificate* in 1991. In 1991, the Simon Wiesenthal Center, a Jewish human-rights group, lobbied several record retailers to remove the album from their shelves because of the anti-Semitic themes contained in some of the songs. A spokesperson for the center called the record a "cultural Molotov cocktail"[17] and identified other racist hate messages in *Death Certificate* that were directed at Koreans and homosexuals. One song in particular, "Black Korea," contained the lyric "Oriental one-penny-counting motherfuckers . . . don't follow me, up and down your market or your little chop suey ass will be a target." At the time, Ice Cube was a spokesperson for St. Ides, a malt liquor sold in many inner-city grocery stores. The National Korean Grocers Association asked its three thousand members to pull St. Ides from their shelves in protest. St. Ides immediately tried to stop the boycott by dropping Ice Cube as a

Ice Cube's 1992 album *Death Certificate*. The album's controversial themes led critics to label Ice Cube a racist and to call for boycotts and bans of the album.

This photo of Ice Cube would have been illegal to show in an Oregon retail store in 1992.

spokesperson. During the controversy, legislators in Oregon passed a bill that made it illegal to display Ice Cube's image in any retail store. Despite the controversy (or perhaps because of it), *Death Certificate* debuted at number two on the *Billboard* album charts and went on to become one of the hottest-selling rap albums of the year.

In October 1993, two urban contemporary radio stations, WBLS-FM in New York and KACE-FM in Los Angeles, began an "Enjoyability with Responsibility" campaign. The stations eliminated most rap music from their playlists and screened all new material to meet their newly established standards. Primary among their concerns were the violent and indecent portrayals of black culture; therefore, mentions of gangs, drugs, violence, or other controversial subject matter are no longer permitted.

Despite claims that its raps are meant to be comedic, the group 2 Live Crew fought battles for almost five years over its album *As Nasty as They Wanna Be*. The album's sexual themes led to declarations in more than half a dozen states that the album was legally obscene. The band was arrested for performing the material in Florida, and many municipalities attempted to pass legislation blocking the group from performing in their cities (see chapter 18 for more on the plight of *As Nasty as They Wanna Be*).

For the most part, those who call for the censorship of rap music do not understand the important subtext of rap, nor do they understand rap as a teaching instrument, as cultural history, or as comedy. Rap is a wake-up call to mainstream America. Rap was calling it like it was before the Rodney King beating, before the Los Angeles riots, and before all the issues embedded in the O. J. Simpson trial. Rap offered a resounding call to action; however, some of America was too busy worrying that their children might hear the words "bitches and hoes" to listen.

7

"DEAR GOD"

Religion

■

**You like to compose songs, as David did,
and play them on harps.
So you will be the first to go into exile.
Your feasts and banquets will come to an end.**
—Amos 6:5,7

Perhaps you have read Goethe's *Faust*.

In the legend, Faust is a learned man of science—a man in pursuit of truth and enlightenment. Although Faust yearns to understand the wonders of God's world, his devotion to his quest leaves him frustrated and lonely. Mephistopheles (the devil) bets God that he can corrupt Faust and make him renounce God. Shortly thereafter, Faust is visited by Mephistopheles, who comes to him in the form of a musician. Mephistopheles does not reveal his true identity to Faust; instead, he simply says that he has taken the form of someone Faust can understand and trust. He then shows Faust a beautiful young maiden. Faust immediately becomes entranced by the girl's beauty, strikes a deal with Mephistopheles and trades his soul for the girl's affections.

As the story progresses, Mephistopheles leads Faust further and further away from his true quest for enlightenment, convincing him to succumb to his feelings of lust and desires for carnal pleasure. When the first book of *Faust* ends, Faust has allowed himself to devolve into a creature who is completely devoid of his original purpose. Faust realizes the error of his ways only after the girl dies, and he also clearly sees the depths to which he has sunk as a result of Mephistopheles' trickery.

Since the birth of rock music in the 1950s, some religious leaders have equated popular music with Mephistopheles as a musician. They believe that it draws eager young fans away from more reverent pursuits into a world of decidedly un-Christian behavior that includes lewdness, blasphemy, promiscuity, profanity, and even devil worship. And they feel that popular music takes good, normal kids and leads them away from the high moral values taught by their families, churches, and communities. It encourages them to dress in nonconformist fashions, disrespect their elders, and behave in unconventional ways.

In many instances, parents and community leaders think they can solve these problems by eliminating sacrilegious and blasphemous rock music. Their logic is simple: If rock music causes fans to stray

Angry San Francisco residents protest against rock music during the summer of 1966.

from their Christian roots, then eliminating it will result in these same fans flocking back to Jesus. But the truth is not that simple.

Religious symbolism (like that found in the Faust legend) is an important part of American culture. Yet although the United States is a decidedly religious nation—if not a decidedly Christian nation—little non-Christian heritage has permeated American life. However, regardless of origin, religious symbols and the institutions and values they represent are taken very seriously in America. When someone shows disrespect toward those symbols and what they represent, it is called blasphemy.

Blasphemy is defined as showing irreverence, disrespect, or contempt toward God or anything held as divine by a group or religion. In the colonial days of what eventually became the United States, blasphemy was considered a crime. The Puritan colonies (such as Massachusetts, New Hampshire, and Connecticut) were run as theocracies (where religious leaders also served as political leaders, and their religious beliefs became law). There was little room for religious dissent. In Massachusetts in 1646, the colony's General Court adopted the Act Against Heresy, in which it was stated that the governing authority was responsible for ensuring that "the people be fed with wholesome and sound doctrine." The court felt that "damnable heresies . . . ought to be duly restrained." In Southern colonies (where the Church of England was the official religious entity), lawmakers made death the appropriate punishment for speaking "impiously of the Trinity . . . or against the known articles of Christian faith" or for "blaspheming God's holy name." However, the governor of Virginia was a much more "understanding" fellow: Rather than sentencing an offender to death, he simply insisted that a large needle be thrust through the tongue of a person who cursed. Public whippings were his recommendations for those who spoke out against a minister.

Thankfully, today we don't need to be too concerned about skewered tongues. Our Constitution's First Amendment provides some protection against religious persecution and even prevents the government from establishing a sanctioned religion. Under the First Amendment, the government cannot show religious favoritism or preference, nor can it punish someone for making a statement that involves religion. The United States Supreme Court reinforced this interpretation when it struck down a statute that banned "sacrilegious" motion pictures in the 1962 case *Burstyn* v. *Wilson*.

However, as noted previously, the First Amendment applies only to government action and not to the actions of private citizens, community groups, and/or religious orders. Those groups are free to "punish" whomever they choose.

Blasphemy in music can take several forms. The most common involves the Third Commandment in the Old Testament's Book of Exodus: "Thou shalt not take the name of the Lord thy God in vain." Although there is significant debate among modern biblical scholars regarding the meaning of this commandment, it is generally interpreted as an injunction against the use of expletive phrases such as "God," "Jesus Christ," "goddamn it," and the like. Use of expletive phrases is no more prevalent in music than in the rest of society. They are often deleted when the songs are broadcast, and rarely are they at the root of controversy.

However, other acts of "blasphemy" have caused Christians considerable consternation. Rather than centering on songs, the controversy usually focuses on the associated music videos or the on- and offstage antics of the performers themselves.

By comparison (and despite the claims of religious conservatives) only a small percentage of musical works (including music videos) contain *any* religious symbolism or imagery. A 1985 study of songs and videos appearing on MTV found that 17.7 percent of songs contained any element of religion, while 59.7 percent contained sexual references.[1] A 1995 study revealed that only 10.6 percent of the music videos on MTV showed any religious imagery, and 27.5 percent of those videos showed religious imagery and sexual imagery in the same video.[2] Interestingly, neither study found evidence of "alternative" religious imagery or any presence of satanic imagery in the songs studied.

Several well-known musicians have gotten into trouble over blasphemous statements. Perennial troublemaker Marilyn Manson also has generated considerable consternation by regularly tearing apart Bibles during his band's concerts and by admitting to membership in the Church of Satan.

During a 1992 performance on *Saturday Night Live,* Irish singer Sinéad O'Connor ripped in half a photograph of Pope John Paul II. Her protest against the policies of the Catholic Church sparked widespread condemnation of her music. There were protests in the press and calls for boycotts of all her music, resulting in considerable damage to her career.

Madonna also has been the center of controversy for religious imagery associated with her lyrics and music videos. Her 1989 video for "Like a Prayer" caused such a stir that Pepsi dropped the song from advertisements for its products. The video, set in a church, contains dozens of religious symbols and icons. In the video's story line, Madonna sees a black religious icon brought to life, saves him from a lynch mob, makes love to him, and celebrates afterward by dancing suggestively in the midst of a church

Say What?!?

The proponents of backmasking's existence agree that the grand-daddy of subliminal messages is contained in Led Zeppelin's "Stairway to Heaven," but they don't seem to agree on the message's context. In the second verse of "Stairway to Heaven," the lyric is:

> Yes, there are two paths you can go by, but in the long run,
> There's still time to change the road you're on.

However, as you see below, understanding of the alleged "subliminal message" (revealed when playing that section of the record backward on a turntable) is not as universal:

From *Why Knock Rock?* By Dan and Steve Peters:

> Here's to my sweet Satan, no other made a path.
> For it makes me sad.
> Whose power is Satan?

From *The Occult in Rock Music* by Eric Barger:

> Oh, here's to my sweet Satan.
> The One whose little path has made me sad.
> Whose power is Satan?
> Oh, my number, 666.

From *The Devil's Disciples* by Jeff Godwin:

> I sing because I live with Satan.
> The Lord turns me off, there's no escaping it.
> Here's to my sweet Satan.
> He'll give you six, six, six.
> I Live for Satan.

choir surrounded by burning crosses. The backlash against the video was started by the Reverend Donald Wildmon, head of the American Family Association of Tupelo, Mississippi, who called for boycotts against Pepsi for licensing the song for their advertisements. During a corporate press conference, Pepsi allowed Wildmon, an accused anti-Semite and ultraconservative, to announce Pepsi's decision to end their relationship with Madonna.

In 1966, Beatle John Lennon was widely misquoted when discussing what he perceived to be a decline in the popularity of Christianity. During an interview with a reporter from the London *Evening Standard,* Lennon said that he had been reading quite a bit about religion and that "Christianity will go. It will vanish and shrink. I needn't argue with that; I'm right and I will be proved right. We're more popular than Jesus now."[3]

While it is clear when reading the original quote that Lennon was not suggesting that the significance of the Beatles superseded that of Jesus, the popular press widely reported that Lennon had made the assertion

Sign posted along Route 93 in Beaver Meadows, Pennsylvania, in August of 1966

that his band was more important than Christianity.

The entire interview was printed in England shortly after it took place; however, it didn't appear in the United States for another five months. Once syndicated in the States, Lennon's quote was somehow altered to "I don't know which will go first—rock 'n roll or Christianity."[4] During the next several months, Americans seized on the comments, and Christians across the country (especially Christian youth) demonstrated against the Beatles during their fourteen-city concert tour that summer.

Young churchgoers in San Francisco protest a Beatles concert at Candlestick Park, August 30, 1966.

Led by a radio station in Birmingham, Alabama, twenty-two other stations across the South vowed never to play another Beatles song again (several of the stations had never broadcast them in the first place and were simply jumping on the anti-Beatles bandwagon). Numerous church and community groups sponsored burnings of Beatle-related records and merchandise. The Reverend Thurman H. Babbs, pastor at the New Haven Baptist Church in Cleveland, vowed to excommunicate any church member who listened to Beatles records or attended a Beatles concert. Legislation was introduced in Pennsylvania to prevent the Beatles from performing in the state. The Ku Klux Klan nailed Beatles albums to burning crosses in South Carolina and protested a Beatles concert in Washington, D.C. Band members even received threats that one of them would be shot during one of two performances in Memphis. And, in fact, during one of the concerts, someone threw a firecracker onstage and frightened the band members into thinking one of them had indeed been shot.

A Beatles record burning during the summer of 1966

Lennon was confused by the controversy surrounding the comment, saying, "In England, they take what we say with a pinch of salt." He added that he felt that the anti-Beatles protesters in the United States were a bunch of "middle-aged DJs and 12-year-olds burning a pile of LP covers."[5]

Moral Values

In his book *What Is Secular Humanism?* James Hitchcock wrote, "They [the Beatles], more than perhaps anyone else, were responsible for elevating narcissistic self-absorption to the level of a cult, deifying personal and subjective feelings, and establishing self-satisfaction as the principle goal of existence."[6] Hitchcock and other religious leaders did not limit their criticisms to the Beatles or even just to rock music. Jazz, rhythm and blues, and rap music have all been targeted by religious censors as denigratory to youth and lacking in virtue or Christian moral value.

In 1954, the Boston Catholic Youth Organization (CYO) demanded that record-hop deejays cease playing sexually explicit or otherwise obscene songs. The CYO was concerned that such records might stir the hormones of young Catholics attending dances. The group sent representatives to dances to monitor the disc jockeys' selections. After some initial success, it expanded its efforts to include local radio stations.

While censorship of music was not new at this point, it was the first time a religious entity had taken action as a result of the conflict between popular rock music and moral virtue. Since that time, several others have adopted similar measures against rock musicians in order to protect Christian values.

Worried that listening to pop songs might spur youngsters to commit such sins as "going steady," the Catholic Youth Center in Minneapolis began a campaign to ban "obscene" records such as "Secretly" and "Wear My Ring Around Your Neck."

In 1962, Bishop Burke of New York forbade young Catholics to dance "The Twist," fearing that its lewd gestures would lead to loose morals. In September of 1969, the Catholic Diocese of Seattle ran a two-page ad in the *Seattle Post-Intelligencer* calling for the criminal prosecution of rock musicians and for bans against "rock festivals and their drug-sex-rock-squalor culture."[7]

In 1970, a writer for the *Methodist Recorder* claimed that rock music creates "states of mind frequently stronger than man's will." The writer, Charles Cleall, thought that rock music was too obscene for Christian youth, that the "thrusting movement of the hips" was far too similar to sexual acts or masturbation.

In 1975, inspired by a biblical passage from the book of Deuteronomy—"The graven images of their gods shall ye burn with fire"—Baptist minister Charles Boykin of Tallahassee, Florida, started a trend of record burnings among Christian groups. Although censors had burned records for more than twenty years, such burnings now became a vogue activity among Christian youth groups across America that lasted for more than five years. Although the practice is still followed today, it is a rarity.

During the 1970s, a "cottage industry" emerged in the Christian antirock movement. Dozens of preachers established ministries based on exposing rock music as corrupt, evil, and anti-Christian.

They lectured to church groups across the country, published books, and presented "educational" films and slide shows. Most proclaimed that rock was the devil's music (more about that later in this chapter), while others professed that sin was so deeply engrained in rock music that it was nearly impossible to separate the two. Initially considered fringe kooks, as rock music (especially heavy metal) became more defiant and rebellious, these crusaders were taken more and more seriously. Most of these ministers filled their books and presentations with outrageous allegations and misinterpreted scientific findings, hoping to scare young people and their parents into fearing rock music's potential influence.

One of the most notable antirock ministers was Bob Larson, a self-styled expert on all things related to rock music. In his 1984 book, *Rock,* Larson described several examples of the rampant "pornography" that disguises itself as musical entertainment, and he lambasted dozens of musical artists as smut peddlers, hedonists, and drug pushers.

Larson claimed that record companies conduct research studies to test the degree of sexual arousal teens experience when listening to new releases. He presented no proof for this allegation.

Larson also offered his readers a lexicon of insider rock lingo. According to Larson, " 'Funk' refers to sexual odors; 'gig' is a reference to sex orgies; 'groovy' is a description of the physical position of intercourse; 'groupies' are prostitutes who ply their wares in the company of rock stars; 'get off' signifies the goal of love-making."[8]

Fornicators, Blasphemers, and Druggies

While you can understand how groups such as W.A.S.P., Black Sabbath, and AC/DC could ruffle some fundamentalist feathers, religious conservatives have called for boycotts of many artists. Below is a selection of some of the less-obvious artists to whom antirock crusaders Bob Larson and Jacob Aranza objected—plus the reasons the two ministers give that these albums should be immediately tossed into your fireplace.

ABBA While their music seems harmless enough, Larson points out that two of the members live together without the benefit of marriage. Listening to ABBA music is "a subsidy of public promiscuity."

Captain and Tennille Aranza suggests staying away from the seventies sugar-pop couple because they endorse vegetarianism, belief in reincarnation, and other aspects of Eastern religions.

Hall and Oates The pop duo wore women's makeup on the cover of their debut album. Daryl Hall professes an interest in dressing in women's clothing.

Olivia Newton-John Although claiming to be exercising, both ministers allege she is actually masturbating on the cover of her *Physical* album.

Adam and the Ants According to Aranza, singer Adam Ant "represents rebellion, absurd fashion, and bisexuality."

The Bee Gees According to Larson, "Though their public image exudes wholesomeness, interviews on their private lives revealed them to be less than paragons of virtue. Robin confesses to a hobby of pornographic drawings and all three lace their comments with obscenities."

The Beach Boys Group members are yoga practitioners.

Elton John Song themes include references to homosexuality and drugs. Larson asserts that Elton is interested in being a rock star only because he wants the money to support his sexual fetishes.

Pat Benatar Although she lives a "non-drug, domesticated lifestyle" off-stage, Pat has a "sassy and brazen" stage presence meant to stir the passions of the male members of her audience.

The Pretenders Chrissie Hynde's disheveled look, heavy eye makeup, and lyrics all endorse sadomasochism and sexual perversions. Also, she once was involved in an adulterous affair.

Bruce Springsteen "The Boss" encourages youth to substitute his concerts for going to church by creating a high-energy atmosphere, and his performances are akin to "attending the church of rock and roll."

Blondie Aranza points out that lead sing Debbie Harry admits to having had multiple sexual partners and once "living in sin" with guitarist Chris Stein.

Earth, Wind, and Fire Singer Maurice White is a practicing Buddhist and follower of "Eastern occult mysticism."

Bette Midler Exposed her breasts during a 1978 concert and supports audience member choices to smoke marijuana during her performances

Patti Smith Her song subjects include feminism, lust, and lesbianism.

Dr. John A licensed witch and supporter of voodoo

In another book, entitled *Rock and Roll: The Devil's Diversion,* Larson offered the reader this path to righteousness:

Antirock Pledge: CONFESSING my faith in Christ and desiring to communicate his love and truth to my generation, and RECOGNIZING that many of the songs and singers of rock music express and promote a morality and life-style contrary to the highest of Christian principles, I HEREBY PLEDGE MYSELF TO THE FOLLOWING: 1. I will abstain from voluntarily listening to rock music so that I may adhere to the admonition of the Apostle Paul to "Think upon those things which are pure, honest, just, lovely, and of good report!" (Philippians 4:8) 2. I will destroy all rock records and tapes in my possession as an outward, symbolic act of signifying my inner dedication to conscientiously discriminate as to the records I buy and listen to.

Another well-known antirock crusader was Jeff Godwin, who gained notoriety during the PMRC's heyday in the mid-eighties. Godwin declared that the Beatles were solely responsible for the rise of drug use among teenagers during the 1960s: "Many millions of young lives world-wide have been utterly ruined as a result." Godwin also blamed David Bowie for homosexuality: "He okayed the rebellion against God's law for the natural use of the man and woman."[9]

Godwin called Little Richard a "homosexual, peeping Tom, drug addict, jailbird, and would-be pimp."[10] Tina Turner didn't rate much higher in Godwin's estimation. He said that her image had always been "that of a heavy breathing, steamy sexual lust baby barely under control."[11]

As the mainstream press gave increasing attention to ministers like Godwin and Larson, they found more and more material to shock those willing to listen. Some of these ministers supported their ministries and themselves almost exclusively with income derived from their lectures and products relating to rock music.

Other antirock crusaders don't view rock music as simply condoning hedonism and narcissism. They believe that its intentions are much darker and more sinister. Instead of glorifying the self, rockers glorify Satan.

Beelzebub Is Everywhere

Some of the more extreme conservative antirock critics are convinced that a vast majority of, if not all, of the musicians playing pop music are in league with the devil and practice the occult. The word "occult" comes from the Latin root *occultus,* which means "things secret, hidden, and mysterious."[12] From a fundamentalist Christian perspective, "occult" can refer to many things in addition to satanism—including voodoo, Eastern religions, mysticism, witchcraft, or other non-Christian spiritual practice. To some conservative Christians, if it isn't worshipping Jesus, it might as well be devil worship. While some limit their criticism to heavy metal performers, others feel that rock is rock is rock: Any music that features a dominant beat is a tribal call to worship Satan.

Marilyn Manson: To Hell in a Handbasket

Marilyn Manson is the rock equivalent of a tough kid cruising the playground looking for a fight. Born out of the South Florida death metal scene, Marilyn Manson as a band was founded to push the threshold of acceptability. The band broke into the charts with a cover of the Eurhythmics' "Sweet Dreams," and for a time they were blamed for nearly every bad thing that has happened to teenagers.

The band centers on singer Marilyn Manson, born Brian Warner in Canton, Ohio. Manson blames much of his resentment toward society on his early years in Ohio, where he endured teasing from other children, a grandfather who liked hard-core pornography and women's clothes, and the poisoning of his family dog. "People are stupid," says Manson, "and fewer things bear this out better than war, organized religion, bureaucracy, and high school—where the majority mercilessly rules."[13] He became rebellious at school, actively trying to get expelled for his antics. Young Warner turned to writing as a way to express himself. His early creations were mostly horror and sci-fi short stories and poetry.

As an adolescent (by then living in Florida), Warner discovered heavy metal and drugs. After a brief stint in college, he decided that he needed to start a rock and roll band, and he became Marilyn Manson.

The band was originally called Marilyn Manson and the Spooky Kids. Each member of the band adopted a stage name containing a combination of the names of famous actresses and serial killers—Twiggy Ramirez, Madonna Wayne Gacy, Gidget Gein, and the like. They quickly became known for their onstage antics (orchestrated, according to Manson, to distract attention from the band members, some of whom didn't know how to play their instruments), which included throwing rotten meat into the crowd, committing sadomasochistic acts, cross-dressing, and displaying religious symbols. On one occasion, Manson tossed Ziploc baggies into the crowd. Some bags contained chocolate chip cookies, others contained cat feces.

As the group's popularity grew, so did their reputation. Marilyn Manson, the band and the singer, both revel in controversy. An avowed satanist and drug user, Manson enjoys telling stories simply to elicit a response from critics. Repeatedly, Manson has acknowledged his role as a showman, attempting to exploit controversy to further his artistic vision. The band became known as troublemakers and hedonists, a distinction they wore with pride and actively worked to develop. After protests began against them by animal rights activists for rumors of animal abuse during concerts, they began to incorporate fake or dead animals into their act to further rile the protesters.

Since Marilyn Manson became a major success, their albums and concert tours have been magnets for fundamentalist protesters. Additionally, the band has been subjected to political pressure, death threats, and bribes to *not* perform in some towns. After officials canceled a performance in Salt Lake City, Manson appeared onstage with Nine Inch Nails. During the appearance, he slowly ripped pages out of the Book of Mormon while repeating, "He loves me, he loves me not." In December of 1994, Manson himself was arrested in Jacksonville, Florida, following a performance. During the show, police had mistaken some of his costume accessories for artificial penises, which

Brian "Marilyn Manson" Warner

they claimed he inserted into his rectum. Later in the performance, Manson was doused by buckets of water, which he shook off into the crowd. Police interpreted this as Manson urinating into the crowd. Although bail was immediately offered at Manson's arrest, the singer was detained for more than sixteen hours, subjected to cavity searches, and (he claims) beaten by the police officers.

In his testimony before the Senate hearings on record labeling in 1985, Dr. Joe Stuessy claimed, "Most of the successful heavy metal projects one or more of the following basic themes: extreme rebellion, extreme violence, substance abuse, sexual promiscuity/perversion—including homosexuality, bisexuality, sadomasochism, necrophilia, etc.—and Satanism."[14] However, a study focusing on the top one hundred heavy metal songs of the 1980s, as determined by Hit Parader magazine, found that song themes actually contained quite different messages:

Assertion of or longing for intensity: 27

Lust: 17

Loneliness, victimization, self-pity: 17

Love: 14 (affirmation, 8; regret or longing, 6)

Anger, rebellion, madness: 8

Didactic or critical (anti-drug, anti-Devil, anti-TV evangelism, critique of the subversion of justice by wealth): 5[15]

According to Carl Raschke in his book on the evils of heavy metal, *Painted Black,* the message of music is

> religious—in the sense that it proclaims a higher power overseeing the universe. The higher power, however, is not God or even fate. It is *violence*—often the most irrational and uncontrollable violence engineered by the Archfiend himself, whom unsophisticated minds have a hard time identifying as "psychodrama" or "symbol."[16]

For mainstream society, the idea of Satan has changed considerably since the mid-twentieth century. While a majority of Americans still believe in purgatory, or some element of damnation, fewer than a quarter of Americans believe in the existence of Satan or the devil as an evil force actively involved in human life. The Catholic Church has also softened its rhetoric on Satan. Following Vatican II (a revision in the 1960s of the Catholic Church's canons and policies), candidates for Catholic service no longer are required to pass through the minor order of "exorcist" before becoming priests. Also, the official Catholic baptism no longer references potential demonic possession of the unbaptized, dropping the phrase "Accursed devil, come forward and acknowledge your condemnation." The Catholic Church prefers to remain silent about things like the presence of Satan, exorcism, and the like. It is church policy not to comment on exorcism, but church officials have confirmed that a handful of the rituals, which must be approved by a presiding bishop, are performed each year.

Critics of rock and heavy metal music point to a few examples to justify their position that these genres are the devil's music. A favorite is Ricardo "Richard" Ramirez. Ramirez, dubbed the "Night Stalker" by the press, was responsible for more than fourteen murders and twenty assaults. When caught, Ramirez told investigators that he worshipped Satan and had commited the crimes as offerings to Beelzebub. Ramirez claimed he was first introduced to satanism by listening to AC/DC's 1979 album, *Highway to Hell.*

Similar claims have been made concerning other act of violence. Teenagers Thomas Sullivan, Steve Boucher, and John McCollum committed deadly acts of violence against others or themselves, presumably as a result of their contact with satanic messages in heavy metal music. In a 1999 newsletter to his followers, minister Bob Larson claimed that Eric Harris and Dylan Klebold were possessed by demons before killing themselves and thirteen others at Columbine High School in Littleton, Colorado.

The problem lies in the ways in which critics utilize an incredible amount of selective thinking and literalism when drawing their conclusions. Rarely will any antirock critics mention that Ramirez suffered from mental, emotional, and drug-related problems throughout his tormented life and was found to be insane. Other examples of youth violence cited by activists involve people who are troubled by demons other than Lucifer, such as broken homes, depression, socialization problems, or mental illness. Many had become alienated from their parents and society long before they began to listen to heavy metal music.

Some critics point to a variety of popular metal groups who demonstrate their allegiance to Satan through the acronyms hidden in their band names, citing acts such as KISS (*K*nights *I*n *S*atan's *S*ervice), W.A.S.P. (*W*e *A*re *S*atan's *P*eople), and AC/DC (*A*nti-*C*hrist/*D*evil's *C*hildren). Conservative minister J. Brent Bill even points to guitarist Carlos Santana's name as evidence that he worships the Dark Prince. According to Bill, "Drop the first *n* and the last *a* and what have you got? Together now—SATAN!"[17]

Many Christian rock critics point to the common use of *il cornuto* as a rock salute as testament to Satan worship. The hand gesture (made by raising your index finger and pinky while using your thumb to hold down the two other fingers) has been a salute among rock fans since the 1960s. Rockers claim that it was derived from the American sign language symbol for "I love you"; antirock crusaders claim that the pointed fingers are meant to represent the horns of Satan.

Jeff Godwin claimed that Jimi Hendrix used voodoo rituals, rhythms, and dancing—both in the studio and in performance—to turn his music into voodoo ceremonies praising Satan. As proof,

Godwin cited that Hendrix had titled a song "Voodoo Child" and hired African musicians.

Godwin also accused pioneering rappers Run-D.M.C. of being delivery boys for the devil's music. As evidence, he pointed to the cover of the group's debut album, which includes band member Joseph Simmons's outstretched hand in an *il cornuto*–like gesture. According to Godwin, the photograph of Simmons's hand was deliberately blurred because "Run-D.M.C., obviously servants of Satan, were trying to obscure the proof just enough to throw Christians off the track."[18]

Run-D.M.C.—Satanists!

Minister Jacob Aranza authored several books exposing all the artists who used subliminal messages to conduct Satan's business. According to Aranza, Led Zeppelin, Judas Priest, Styx, David Bowie, ELO, Queen, and the Beatles regularly included hidden messages in their songs. These messages were intended to accomplish a variety of tasks, ranging from encouraging youth to purchase more records to urging them to commit suicide or kill others.

Some antirock crusaders point to other groups as indications of how deeply rooted Mephistopheles is in popular music. For example, Jeff Godwin said that the eighties new wave pop group Bananarama was, in fact, in league with Lucifer. He said that their hit song "Venus" referred to a secret occult meaning of "Venus" or "bright morning star," which Godwin claimed is another name for Satan.

Almost universally, the only people to claim any satanic presence in rock music are ministers and antirock activists. Outside this circle of crusaders, there is not a single shred of evidence demonstrating that any of these claims are valid.

In reality, there are four types of groups commonly referred to as "Satan worshippers." There are organized religions like the Church of Satan and the more mystically oriented Church of Set. They are both registered, tax-exempt churches—just as legitimate in the eyes of the government as the Catholic or Baptist churches. Both adamantly deny any connection to devil worship, are decidedly atheistic, and have a humanist bent. (The Church of Satan believes that there is no such thing as God, and members contend that there is no such thing as Satan.) They also deny the existence of any secret, underground satanic activity. (For more information on the Church of Satan, see "Counterpoint," p. 134–37.)

Another type of "Satan worshipper" is the underground pagan or witchcraft coven that recognizes Satan as a powerful force to be feared. Then, there are teenage dabblers who engage in quasi-religious rituals because they want to see what happens. Their activities are usually born out of boredom and are limited to getting drunk or high and spray-painting pentagrams and inverted crosses in graveyards, on highway overpasses, or on some institutional structure that represents authority, like a school or church. The group that receives the most attention are the mentally or emotionally disturbed, who create their own homegrown satanic practices.[19]

In any case, it is quite a stretch to assume that any—or all—of these groups carry enough power or influence to coopt the whole entertainment industry. There are record labels whose entire artist roster contains more people than any of the previously mentioned groups. According to Peter Gilmore, a spokesperson for the Church of Satan, "I challenge anyone to find me a 'devil-worshipper' who is not mentally ill in some way. Thinking that there is a connection between Satan and the music industry is absurd. Just take a look at who is making the accusations and what they have to gain from their claims."

False Prophets

When it comes to tangible evidence regarding the presence of Satan in the music industry, things get pretty thin. Why? Because, quite simply, there is no proof.

Should parents worry if their child is a good kid, knows right from wrong, and would be smart enough to understand when he or she was being asked to do something wrong or sinful? According to antirock ministers, all parents should separate their children from pop music. They contend that some of the music is so oblique in its satanic work that the evil messages and themes are transmitted subconsciously and can be understood only by the brain's innermost workings. Yet AC/DC, Ozzy Osbourne, Led Zeppelin, and Judas Priest all have sold tens of millions of records. At best, only a handful of possible examples of the effect satanism has on young fans have been produced. Even if someone could produce a dozen tangible examples, that breaks down to just .00001 incidents per million albums sold. Hardly an effective message delivery and hardly cause for mass concern. Furthermore, there were more than a million violent crimes committed during the mainstream heyday of heavy metal—1986 to 1991—yet only 60 had satanic overtones (that is .00006 of these crimes).

In 1987, a group of Missouri teens murdered one of their friends and then blamed the crime on the influence of heavy metal. Those using this as an example of the Hoofed One's influence fail to mention that several members of the group had histories of trouble that dated to early childhood. All the boys were either heavy drug users or drug dealers. One had been convicted of abusing animals before he was in his teens. The ministers also don't say that the jury trying the case disagreed with the boys' claim and found them all guilty of murder.

Counterpoint: The Church of Satan

After reading more than a dozen books written by Christians about the whole "Satan thing" in music, I wanted to hear an opposing perspective. Where better to go than the Church of Satan? Like many curious people, I had borrowed and read a copy of *The Satanic Bible* when I was younger, afraid that I might rot in hell for even touching it. The book was written by the founder of the Church of Satan, the "Black Pope," Anton Szandor La Vey. La Vey died in 1998, and since then the church has come under the guidance of his successor, the High Priestess Barton, and the Council of Nine (kind of a board of directors for the Church of Satan). In speaking with Magistrate Peter Gilmore, a member of the Council of Nine, I was shocked to learn that the Church of Satan doesn't believe there is, or ever was, a Satan.

"We see human beings—especially those who have been influenced by Christian thinking when they are young—as damaged," says Gilmore. "We think that oppression actually changes the brain—changes how one thinks and perceives reality. We think that people who follow the Christian spiritual, Ghost-in-the-machine kind of thinking actually have damaged brains that are actually nonnatural. They don't have the integration of reason, emotion, instinct, and higher thinking that we think is natural to mankind.

"We have a completely different premise than the Christians," Gilmore continued. "We don't believe in their Jesus or their devil. Satanism is an approach to life that acknowledges man as the carnal animal that he is. We are very materialistic. We are not spiritual at all. We see Satan abstractly—as a grounds for existence—the dark force that permeates all forces of nature.

"Christians think of God and a devil that He created that opposes him. We don't see how that is valid or makes any sense. It is a myth system for self-hating people. We feel, as satanists, that there is nothing in us that needs forgiveness. We feel we are part of nature and enjoy and embrace that. Rejoicing in the fleshly life."

EN: Then why call yourselves satanists, if you don't believe there is any such thing as Satan?

Gilmore: Because we reject their point of view—then we are satanists. We do not believe in a savior, we do not believe there is anything wrong with man. And, by accepting that, we are considered evil and satanic.

EN: Then aren't you allowing someone else to define you?

Gilmore: We feel that Satan is an important archetype for us. The word itself means "adversary," "opposer," or "accuser"—and we are the adversaries, opposers, and accusers of all spiritual doctrines—not just Christians.

EN: If you don't believe in spirituality, why do you organize yourselves as a church?

Gilmore: We believe man is a perceptual being. We create metaphors and symbols to grasp a large range of concepts. Symbol is important to us, therefore ritual is important to us.

I mentioned to Gilmore that many conservative Christians think *The Satanic Bible* and the philosophies shared by satanists amount to nothing more than intellectual humanist trickery. That while satanists *say* they are simply ultrahumanists, they are, in fact, devil worshippers in sheep's clothing.

EN: What is the difference between a satanist and a devil worshipper?

Gilmore: A devil worshipper believes there is a devil—a Christian heretic. They believe in a God and a devil, and they opt to go for the bad guy. For our system, neither exists.

EN: Are there people out there who are devil worshippers?

Gilmore: There is no organized group out there. While you will find some disturbed individuals, you will basically find handfuls of those people at best.

EN: What about Marilyn Manson? He palled around with Anton La Vey, is a member of the Church of Satan, and refers to himself as a devil worshipper?

Gilmore: Marilyn Manson is a showman. Basically, whatever persona he puts out there is going to be the one that he feels is going to sell the most records. It's the showman aspect that makes him a real satanist, not whatever blather he is spouting at the moment to get people to buy his albums. Marilyn Manson is a showman, so was Anton La Vey.

EN: What is so evil about Marilyn Manson?

Gilmore: There is nothing evil about him.

EN: I think a lot of people would disagree with you.

Gilmore: That depends on what you mean by good and evil. We believe good and evil are subjective. What is good for you is good, and what's bad for you is bad. We don't believe there is any such thing as a universal good or evil.

EN: But what if Marilyn Manson falls into someone's definition of bad or evil? And in order to protect what they feel is good, they need to oppress it?

Gilmore: Then that person, by my personal definition, is evil. They are an oppressor who is trying to destroy someone else's freedom.

Gilmore and I discussed the alleged link between satanism and music. Backstage rituals, praying over stacks of records and CDs, backmasking, curses, symbols, and the like. I asked Magistrate Gilmore if there was any basis in fact for this.

Gilmore: No. None whatsoever. That is something I know Christians like to tell people to scare them into giving their ministries money, but actually in the rock industry there are very few people who are actual satanists. Most people who are supposedly linked with satanism will tell you that they do it for show, to gain attention.

The main thing that Christians need to know about satanists is that we don't want them. We are not interested in converting anybody. We wouldn't even try to influence them, because we think, by birth and genetics, they can't be one of us. We aren't out there trying to convince people they are Satanist if they feel that they naturally aren't.

Anton La Vey himself understood the struggle between satanism and Christianity, and though neither side will readily admit it, each needs the other to legitimize itself. La Vey once wrote, "One hates what one fears. I have acquired power without conscious effort, by simply being."

Those looking for a scapegoat are quick to point to popular music. According to FBI Behavioral Sciences Unit agent Kenneth Lanning, "If police look in a teen murderer's room, besides Judas Priest music, they'd probably find a Bible, too. But no one would write that down in his notebook."[20] Lanning also points out that far more crimes have been committed in the name of God than in the name of Satan. Many thousands have died in holy wars, inquisitions and witch trials, yet no one tries to ban Christian music.

Be it heavy metal music, Elvis, or integrated schools, fear about rapid social change has always been challenged under the guise of protecting the innocence and sanctity of children. Many parents, ministers, and community members mistakenly believe that kids become involved in crime, drugs, alcohol, and antisocial behavior *because* of rock music. They refuse to accept rock as anything other than a disease, when it would be better categorized as a symptom. The real question for parents is not whether music has a negative effect on their child, but what draws their child to intense music in the first place.

One thing almost everyone, including the antirock ministers, agrees upon is that communication is an important step toward understanding and helping a potentially troubled teen. Ministers also support the idea of establishing a strong sense of spirituality in everyday home life, with parents letting children know what they feel is right or wrong, then asking for and accepting the children's opinions. Most instances of teen violence, drug abuse, and suicide that are blamed on satanic influences in rock music are actually the result of other problems a child is having: fitting in at school, self-image, depression. A caring, supportive parent or friend can have significantly more effect on a young person's attitudes and actions than any CD can.

It reminds me again of the Faust legend. After he strayed from all his values, Faust realized his mistake and renounced sin. Despite Mephistopheles' attempt to corrupt him, Faust's inner sense of right and wrong triumphed in the end. Faith and virtue, a belief in the true power of God, and the good nature of the world persevered.

God knew this all along. As a cursing Mephistopheles returned to the underworld, God looked down on Faust and smiled.

8

"COMFORTABLY NUMB"

Drugs

■

**At the heart of liberty is the right to define
one's own concept of existence, of meaning,
of the universe, and of the mystery of human life.**
—Supreme Court Justice Sandra Day O'Connor

In his book *Painted Black*, antirock crusader Carl Raschke claims that rock music is to drugs what lotteries are to compulsive gamblers. While Raschke admits that proving a drug/rock connection is difficult, he has observed that "the chemically dependent adolescent adopts a lifestyle of swagger, brutality, theft, and sexual excess, all of which is reinforced by the yowling and bellowing of the [rock] groups." Raschke isn't the only person who sees a connection between rock music and drug use; the notion that listening to popular music leads impressionable children to drug experimentation has been a common complaint for more than thirty years.

Although drugs have been a widely publicized component of the rock music scene since the late sixties, drug use among musicians has been recorded as far back as the 1800s. At that time, several classical composers experimented with drugs like opium, thinking it would stimulate their creativity. Hector Berlioz admit-

Jeremy Lyle breaks three dozen record albums in front of the First Baptist Church in Salinas, California, in June of 1980. He blames rock music for his past drug use, before he became a born-again Christian.

ted that he composed his *Symphonie Fantastique* after experimenting with opium. Composers Schumann, Schubert, Mozart, Michael Haydn, Glazunoff, and Mussorgsky all abused alcohol or drugs during their careers. Many other composers were suspected of such behavior, but musical whitewashing has led to convenient memory lapses when it comes to such unflattering details.

Certainly, mentions of drug use in rock music differ from Berlioz's oblique references to opium. Pop music is direct and rarely subtle. Since the late sixties, when drugs became a large part of the youth culture, pop music did not stop with simple references to drugs—songwriters placed drugs front and center. Songs extolling marijuana ("Hits from the Bong" by Cypress Hill, Steppenwolf's "Don't Step on the Grass, Sam," and "Rainy Day Woman #12 & 35" by Bob Dylan), heroin ("The Needle and the Damage Done" by Neil Young, "Sister Morphine" by the Rolling Stones, and "Berkshire Poppies" by Traffic), and cocaine ("Casey Jones" by the Grateful Dead, the Eagles' "Life in the Fast Lane," and "Cocaine" by Eric Clapton) have been huge hits. While there has been plenty of rock music condoning drug use, there also are many rock musicians who have adamantly opposed drug use, such as Frank Zappa, Dee Snider of Twisted Sister, Henry Rollins, Public Enemy's Chuck D, Madonna, and Janet Jackson. Those artists are not mentioned in Raschke's book.

Unfortunately for Mr. Raschke, there is no scientific evidence that links rock music to drug experimentation, use, or abuse. However, you could probably prove that drug use, drug abuse, and drug-related deaths are more prevelant among rock musicians than they are among people in other careers, such as accountants, clergypersons, or grocery clerks.

Drug use and rock music do have something in common: Both are used as coping mechanisms, releases from the pressures of an overbearing society, and ways of dealing with social circumstances. While someone who enjoys rock music *may* use drugs and others *may* choose to use one to enjoy the other, drugs are not necessary to enjoy rock music. Drug users among music fans are an obvious minority; the numbers of drug abusers and drug-related deaths are not even statistically significant. Drug use didn't start with rock and roll, and it doesn't end there either.

Despite these facts, drugs have been used as an excuse to control music since the 1960s. Censors, in trying to suppress music *they* find offensive and objectionable, regardless of the presence of or connection to drugs, use supposed or real connections with drug use as convenient justifications.

Everybody Must Get Stoned

When drug use came into vogue with the emerging youth counter-culture of the late 1960s, mainstream Americans considered it a big problem. As usual, politicians and civic leaders started coming out of the woodwork to save the country's youth from the evils of drugs. Just like many of their solutions to civil rights, welfare, and economic problems, the quick-fix solutions offered for the nation's drug issues either didn't work or didn't address the root problem. In their search for the magic bullet that would end drug problems, many community leaders assumed that music must have been the cause of drug use and abuse. As public pressure mounted against the entertainment industry, record-company executives made some lame attempts to control music that mentioned drugs or drug use. In doing so, the companies regularly glossed over their big-selling acts and concentrated on "problem" acts. The Velvet Underground's debut album was delayed for nine months in part because the label was concerned that the group's references to drugs (and its relatively small fan base) would kill any chances of success. Earlier, in September of 1967, producers of *The Ed Sullivan Show* worried about the lyric "Girl we couldn't get much higher" from the Doors classic "Light My Fire," and asked the band to substitute a different line in its place. After initially agreeing to the request, singer Jim Morrison sang the original lyric directly into the camera.

In 1970, President Richard Nixon decided to lead the charge against the infestation of drugs among helpless American youth, and he was quick to reinforce the alleged connection between rock music and drug experimentation. Following a meeting on rock music and lyrics between Nixon and the governors of forty states (the politicians had the lyrics projected on slides so they could understand what they were listening to), the president asked radio broadcasters to screen lyrics and suggested they ban songs containing drug references. Joining the fray, Vice President Spiro Agnew promoted the notion that rock music was a brainwashing tool employed to convince young Americans to use drugs, and he called for government censorship. Agnew offered examples—"With a Little Help from My Friends" by the Beatles, "Eight Miles High" by the Byrds, and "White Rabbit" by Jefferson Airplane—as proof that rock music meant to recruit young people to the world of drugs.

In March of 1971, the Federal Communications Commission (FCC) joined the game, offering a policy statement that eventually was telegraphed to more than eight hundred radio stations around the country. In the statement, the FCC said it had received a number of complaints about "the lyrics of records played on broadcasting stations relate [sic] to a subject of current and pressing concern: the use of language tending to promote or glorify the use of illegal drugs as marijuana, LSD, 'speed,' etc."[1] The FCC further explained that the determination as to whether or not a song promotes or condones drug use is the duty and responsibility of the individual licensee (radio-station owner). However, the commission warned licensees that knowingly airing such songs could result in trouble:

Such a pattern of operation is clearly a violation of the basic principle of the licensee's responsibility for, and duty to exercise adequate control over, the broadcast material presented over his station. It raises serious questions as to whether continued operation of the station is in the public interest.

Several statements by individual commissioners were appended to the policy statement, including the remarks of Commissioner H. Rex Lee, who felt that the warning should extend to all advertising aired by the station (promoting either outside businesses or the station itself). The sole dissenting opinion was offered by Commissioner Nicholas Johnson.

Johnson saw potential danger, saying, "This public notice is an unsuccessfully disguised effort by the Federal Communications Commission to censor song lyrics that the majority disapproves of."[2] Johnson questioned why the policy was limited to illegal drugs, pointing out that alcohol abuse was a much larger problem in America. Alcohol was not included in the FCC statement. He also questioned the lack of guidelines provided by the commission, asking if "Up, Up, and Away," sung by the Mormon Tabernacle Choir, could be interpreted to glorify the virtues of "being high."

Johnson felt that the policy was an attempt by the establishment to control what the country's youth could say and hear on the radio. He alleged that then-President Nixon's "war on drugs" was meant to distract the American public from problems like the war in Southeast Asia, racial prejudice, inflation, unemployment, and education. Johnson also questioned the constitutionality of the policy. Although Johnson was the only commissioner to step forward with questions, he was not the only critic of the policy.

Broadcasters, record companies, and special-interest groups such as the National Association of Broadcasters and the Recording Industry Association of America were quick and direct in their vilification of the FCC policy. There were also threats of lawsuits from the American Civil Liberties Union. ACLU Executive Director Aryeh Neier warned that broadcasters would tend to ban every controversial song rather than risk losing their licenses. He also warned that private pressure groups might use the same rationale to attempt to convince the FCC to "blacklist" other forms of objectionable material.

Media and broadcast industry pressures prompted the FCC to issue a clarification of the March policy five weeks later, which confused the matter even more. The commission wrote in the April clarification that the March policy statement contained no threat, directly or indirectly, that suggested that licensees were barred from presenting "a particular type of record." The commission said that the "selection of records was a matter for the licensee's judgement."[3] However, three paragraphs later, the "clarification" stated that "the broadcaster could jeopardize his license by failing to exercise licensee responsibility in this area."[4] The commission also acknowledged that it had received a list of songs from the Department of the Army that would meet its unspecified standards for objectionable lyrics, but refused to release the contents of that list to the public. By acknowledging the presence of the list and its originator, however, the FCC confirmed allegations that other government agencies had pressured to the FCC to adopt the new policy.

Even though the FCC would not release a list of objectionable drug-related songs, the Illinois Crime Commission did just that. The same month that the FCC's "clarification" was released (sans a list of songs), the Illinois group released a list of drug-related songs that it felt should be banned from retail sale and broadcast. The list included Peter, Paul & Mary's "Puff the Magic Dragon," Procol Harum's "A Whiter Shade of Pale," Carla Thomas's "Hi De Ho (That Old Sweet Roll)" and the Beatles' "Yellow Submarine."

Following the FCC clarification, a group of radio broadcasters and legal advocates filed a petition with the FCC and a lawsuit in federal court, calling the policy and its clarification vague, contradictory, and inconsistent. The petitioners suggested that if screening lyrics before broadcast was required to assure license renewal, the FCC should say so and establish appropriate policy and guidelines. Also included was a request from Yale Broadcasting, which asked the commission to review the playlist for its station WYBC-FM in New Haven, Connecticut, to see if it complied with the commission's directive. Affidavits from fourteen Virginia radio stations (all petitioners in both actions) stated that they perceived the FCC ruling as either a "Big Brother nudge" or outright censorship.

Finding itself under increasing pressure, the commission released a third clarification of the policy in August. This final edict stated that the commission did not believe that the matter warranted any further consideration. It also refused to hear the petition from Yale Broadcasting to review the station's playlist, saying, "We loathe to embark upon individual rulings for individual licensees concerning their proposed handling of specific types of programming upon the basis of general policy statements not fleshed out by the licensee's actual operation."[5] Again Commissioner Johnson was the sole dissenter on the commission. His statement, appended to the decision, said that the vagueness mentioned by the petitioners "can have an inhibiting effect on the licensee's full freedom to choose his programming without the threat of government censorship."[6]

Although the FCC petition was dead in the water, the group of radio broadcasters continued with their civil action against the commission. In the meantime, the RIAA attempted to stave off criticism by producing a series of anti-drug commercials for broadcast during Drug Abuse Prevention Week the following October.

After a three-judge panel initially agreed with the FCC's right to make the policy decision, a federal appeals court judge ruled in 1973 that the FCC policy was unacceptable because it would lead to government-sanctioned censorship. The judge found that the later clarifications amounted to nothing more than restating the commission's "basic threat" against broadcasters. He said that even though drugs are illegal, *talking* about drugs is free speech, protected by the First Amendment.

But the FCC war against drug lyrics took a few casualties before being put to rest. WNBC in New York City immediately pulled several questionable songs, including the Brewer and Shipley hit "One Toke Over the Line." Radio stations across the country dropped "Rocky Mountain High" by John Denver. Denver later clarified that he was referring to the sense of peace and elation one feels when experiencing the beauty and magnificence of the Rocky Mountains. WFAA in Dallas received a petition with six hundred signatures asking for the station to drop all pro-drug songs.

Inspired by the anti-drug furor ignited by federal get-tough policies, Indiana attorney general Theodore Sendak proposed legislation in 1973 that would similarly get tough on large outdoor rock concerts, which Sendak referred to as "drug supermarkets." Shortly after Indiana legislators adopted the proposal, they realized that they had also mistakenly outlawed the popular Indianapolis 500 motorcar race (as well as many other large outdoor gatherings). They quickly began to revise the legislation.

The same year, New York Senator James Buckley released a report to Congress that attempted to link rock music and the drug culture. The Buckley report is one of the most articulate arguments ever made against rock music. Buckley blasted the music industry for being completely unconcerned with the alleged influence that drug use and abuse among its artists had on young people. Buckley quoted Sly Stone, who said, "This business is amoral. If Hitler put together a combo, all the top executives would catch the next plane to Argentina to sign him up."[7] Buckley felt the music industry had routinely abandoned any sense of corporate responsibility or ethics in pursuit of higher sales and profits.

Buckley quoted extensively from a United Nations report on the link between rock music and drug use, which said, "Sooner or later, when an urban child, who lives in the ordinary world, not in the pop world where a drug conviction can be shrugged off, is offered a marijuana cigarette or a dose of LSD, he will remember them not as something his health and hygiene teacher spoke warningly about, but as something Mick Jagger, or John Lennon, or Paul McCartney had used and enjoyed."[8]

In his conclusion, Buckley summarized rock music's defense against his charges:

1. People do not take drugs solely because they listen to rock music.

2. Drug taking has underlying causes; get rid of those causes and kids will stop taking drugs. Kids are alienated and bored because of great injustices in society. Don't blame rock for society's faults.

3. Rock music reflects society. It is, in Clive Davis's phrase, "a footnote to the events within society."

4. Jazz stars take drugs. Movie stars take drugs. Why single out the rock music for criticism? Besides, what a star does in private is his or her own affair. The companies have no responsibility to tell rock stars how to live.

5. Stop picking on the record companies. They cannot control the lives of their artists. How is a record executive to know about drug usage by his company's record stars?[9]

Buckley conceded that there was no sound, clinical proof that there was a link between rock music and drug usage among children, but he also believed there was no reason to discard that notion. "It is hard to believe that the net effect has not been at the very least to lower the threshold of resistance among the more susceptible."[10] Buckley concluded that there was every reason to believe the music industry was responsible for policing its artists and their music, to ensure that their lifestyles and songs did not condone or promote drug use. He also hinted that the federal government might be compelled to take further action if the industry did not meet its responsibility.

Unfortunately for Senator Buckley, his report and the resulting Senate hearing did not receive much attention. His efforts came on the heels of the big story of 1973: the Watergate hearings, which completely monopolized the attention of both Congress and the American public.

Though drugs had dominated music censorship through the early years of the 1970s, following the Buckley report and the demise of the FCC ruling, drugs slipped off the censors' agenda for the next decade. An exception was a proposal by Julio Martinez, director of the New York State Division of Substance Abuse Services, who in 1980 suggested that a one-dollar tax be imposed on any artist whose songs endorsed drug use. The money would go to pay for the drug rehabilitation services the agency provided.

While drugs continued to be a problem in America, and the role of popular music in drug use continued to be a topic of debate, it wasn't until the emergence of the PMRC in 1985 that anyone again proposed censorship as an alternative.

Standing in Front of a Charging Rhino
In addition to campaigning against sex, violence, profanity, and satanism, Tipper Gore and the Parents Music Resource Center also attacked drug-related music. Compared to the other PMRC topics, drugs were almost the ugly half sister. By the mid-1980s, drugs had clearly lost their vogue status in the mainstream. Musicians were routinely entering rehab facilities like the Betty Ford Clinic to clean up, Nancy Reagan's "Just Say No" campaign was in full bloom, the nation had its first "Drug Czar," and America seemed to be doing a good job of stopping the evils of drugs from spreading to the nation's youth. Despite their generation's experimentation with drugs just a short fifteen or twenty years earlier, America's parents were, by and large, united behind the war on drugs.

However, the PMRC's list of demands to the recording industry included rating albums whose song lyrics "glorify drug or alcohol abuse." Tipper's own book, *Raising PG Kids in an X-Rated Society*, included a picture of the heavy metal group Mötley Crüe surrounded by mounds of white powder, presumably cocaine. The PMRC's original "Filthy Fifteen" listed only two artists (Def Leppard and Black Sabbath) for drug themes. Even though the PMRC's battle against drugs never took center stage, the group relegitimized the idea of suppressing music that appeared to glorify drugs.

Music today still refers to drugs, although usually not as openly as it did in the late sixties and early seventies. Over the past decade, most controversies involving drug-related music and drug use by performers have been anything but subtle. Following the resurgence in the popularity of the Grateful Dead in the early nineties, along with concerts by bands attracting similar followings (such as Phish, the HORDE festival, and others), many police officers targeted the fans and concerts for drug stings and arrests. The increase in heroin use in the nineties also has been met with widespread condemnation, although there have been few incidents in the way of censorship. A frightening exception occurred in 1995, when a group of fifteen state employees traveled in state vehicles to WBCN-FM in Boston to protest the station's airplay of selections from the *Hempilation* CD, which benefited the National Organization for the Reform of Marijuana Laws (see chapter 10).

In general, the nation's attempts to control drugs has turned away from music. In Oregon, parents can be arrested if their kids are caught with marijuana, Los Angeles school officials have considered rewarding student drug informants with concert tickets and CDs, and California has adopted state laws allowing alleged drug dealers to be arrested before they actually commit a crime.[11]

For argument's sake, assume that drugs and music *were* connected. Although drug use or possession is illegal, *talking* about drugs is not. While numerous people believe that drug use is wrong, it is not legal or ethical to suppress speech that refers to drugs—or to their use—simply because you or I or the majority of Americans don't think it's right. If a person or group censors music because it refers to drug use, it may not be long before that person or group will want to censor music that questions drug laws. That creates a true "slippery slope," where a cascade of semilegitimate reasons are used to control messages one at a time, until no permissible expression remains.

9

"I WANT YOUR SEX"

Sex

■

Censorship, like charity, should begin at home,
but unlike charity, it should end there.
—Clare Boothe Luce

You can't talk about rock and roll without mentioning sex. It's like movies without a screen, baseball without a field, potato chips without salt. Sex, or sexuality, is so engrained in popular music that the concept of the latter seems to fall apart without the presence of the former. The term "rock and roll" itself was derived by deejay Alan Freed from a black slang term for sexual intercourse.

Therefore, it really isn't any wonder that critics have often considered rock and roll the cause of loose morality, promiscuity, and degrading attitudes toward women. In the 1950s, worried parents and community leaders felt that rock lyrics portrayed stories of immorality, that the beat of the music caused listeners to mimic lewd and provocative dances, and that the on- and offstage antics of the performers presented dangerous role models for youth. The concerns voiced in the 1950s aren't much different from those we hear about today.

Concerns over sex in popular music started not with rock music but with recorded music. Once music was widely available in a recorded medium, censors have bewailed its content and themes.

The lyrics of Duke Ellington's hit "The Mooche" were considered so provocative in 1928 that protests were organized in order to ban the song. The protesters blamed the song for the increase in the number of rapes in the United States and feared that women would not be safe if it were allowed to be broadcast, recorded, and performed. Ellington also found himself on a list of performers banned from the NBC network in 1940, when the network banned 147 songs from airplay over concerns about sexual content, including such titles as "Lavender Cowboy," "Dirty Lady," "Keep Your Skirt Down, Mary Ann," and "I'm a Virgin, But I'm on the Verge." Other notable artists included in the ban were Cole Porter, Billie Holiday, and Bessie Smith.

In 1956, Holiday and Porter ran into some other trouble when the ABC network refused to play Holiday's version of the Porter classic "Love for Sale," fearing that the lyrics were an endorsement of prostitution and glorified the life of prostitutes.

Beginning in the early 1930s, *Variety* magazine made it an ongoing practice to exclude bawdy songs from the magazine's record charts, such as the blues classic "Hoochie Coochie Man" and one of the sexiest songs ever recorded, "I'm Gonna Shave You Close." The policy also barred hit songs by country legends Gene Autry and Jimmy Rodgers because *Variety*'s editors were unfamiliar with the artists' material.

Contemporary critics will quickly point out that while some of the complaints about the presence of sex in modern music and music videos are similar to those heard decades ago, the music itself has changed. While the rock songs of the fifties dealt with themes of love and romance, music of later decades deals more with gratuitous sex and promiscuity. While hits of the 1950s were more concerned with holding hands or kissing under the moonlight, studies of more modern music have demonstrated that sexual themes in music have progressed from slightly suggestive to explicit, aggressive, and violent.

The reasons for concern seem obvious: Sex issues shoot straight to the core of any cultural standard of morality. Many feel that if the cultural standards that apply to relationships, love, sexual relations, and gender roles are compromised, society will be like a house of cards in a stiff breeze, scattered for lack of a solid foundation and structure. They have good reason for placing sex so high on the moral food chain—a few bad decisions about sexual activity can permanently alter your life, if not end it. Some of the contemporary statistics are quite alarming. By the age of twenty, 80 percent of young men and 70 percent of young women have had sexual intercourse, and one in seven has contracted a sexually transmitted disease. The United States leads developed nations in teenage pregnancy, with teenage mothers giving birth to one out of five white firstborns, one out of three Hispanic firstborns, and one out of two black firstborns.[1]

Why is sex such a dominant issue in music? Two reasons. First, sex (or lack of sex) and rock music have a lot in common. A person "comes of age" sexually—and in musical taste—during his or her preteen and teen years. Both are expressions of attitude, feeling, and emotion. Second, sex sells.

A lot of the claims that rock music affects attitudes concerning sex and morality are rooted in "third-person effect"—while "I" am not susceptible to influence by music, "others" can and will be influenced by the acts, lyrics, and themes of musicians and their music. This can fuel a great many more "isms"—such as stereotyping music's influence on morality based on racism, genderism, economic status, and fandom of a particular artist or musical genre. While different musical genres do contain more or fewer references to sex, and while different genres do tend to attract different demographic types of listeners, there is no validity to any hard-and-fast analysis of music's influences on sexual mores. But this has never stopped anyone from attempting to suppress music because it expressed how much the singer wanted to get naked, slap his woman on her ass, or simply hold her hand.

Immoral, Amoral, and Depraved

When rock and roll music came to the mainstream's attention in the mid-fifties, the reactions of fans were unlike anything America had ever experienced. Rock fans seemed manic and out of control in their appreciation of the new music. It was an uncomfortable and confusing period for parents. For the first time, young white fans swooned over young black singers, and performers looked and acted much differently than the crooners parents had grown up listening to. They saw their children adopt different hairstyles, clothing, dances, and slang vocabulary. Primary among the complaints of parents were the role models these performers provided for kids. According to a 1955 article in *Variety*, "We are talking about rock and roll, and 'hug' and 'squeeze' and kindred euphemisms which are attempting a total breakdown of all reticences about sex."[2]

Some of the early rock stars—such as Elvis Presley, Gene Vincent, Little Richard, Chuck Berry, and Jerry Lee Lewis—presented very sexy images, along with song lyrics and themes to match. Presley's "black" singing style and gyrations caused a great deal of consternation among adults convinced that he, his music, and his performances were obscene. Numerous radio stations and concert promoters washed their hands of the young "King of Rock and Roll," fearing the repercussions of presenting the singer and his music. Gene Vincent's breakthrough hit "Be-Bop-A-Lula" was actually the B-side to another song called "Woman Love," which was deemed too risqué by American deejays. Little Richard, concerned about the ramifications of being a black teen idol, created an outrageous image and performance style so that parents would think of him as a clown—harmless and benign.

The presence of sexual themes in rock music, like rock itself, has its roots in black R&B music. Open discussions of sex were much more common in black music than in the pop mainstream. When "blue" black music crossed over into white culture, censors were usually there to slam the door closed. An example of such a song is "Sixty Minute Man" popularized by the Dominoes in 1951, in which the storyteller expounds upon his virtues as a lover. The lyrics are far from discreet: "There'll be fifteen minutes of kissin', then you'll holler, 'Please don't stop.' There'll be fifteen minutes of teasin', and fifteen minutes of pleasin', and fifteen minutes of blowin' my top."

Hank Ballard and the Midnighters experienced a run-in with censors over their classic songs "Work with Me, Annie" and "Annie Had a Baby," which were considered far too explicit for radio broadcast. The same occurred with the Drifters' hit "Honey Love."

Little Richard's "Tutti Fruitti" raised eyebrows even before it was recorded. When Richard was hired to record the song, record executives hired a second lyric writer to clean it up. The writer dropped the line "Tutti fruitti good booty, if it don't fit don't force it."

Many of these controversial songs were rerecorded, sans controversial themes and lyrics, by white teen idols. When Pat Boone covered "Tutti Fruitti," he substituted several lines to remove sexual innuendo. Remembers Boone, "I had to change some of the words, because they seemed too raw for me." The Midnighters' song "Work with Me, Annie" was morphed into the more acceptable Georgia Gibbs hit "Dance with Me, Henry," featuring the same music and melody, just with different lyrics.

Some were so concerned about possible sexual content in songs that when the Kingsmen released their classic "Louie, Louie" in 1963, critics claimed it *had* to contain obscene and pornographic lyrics, or why else would the singer sing so unintelligibly? Following encouragement from radio stations and interest groups (including the governor of Indiana), the FCC conducted a study of the song. The FCC listened to it forward and backward at more than a half dozen different speeds in an attempt to discern the lyrics. Eventually the agency ruled that "the song is unintelligible at any speed"—and therefore posed no threat.

Years earlier, several civic and religious organizations took up the cause of ridding popular music of sexual content. Many lobbied successfully to prevent rock concerts from coming to their towns, claiming that the music influenced the young people to break into lewd dancing, acts of violence, and other manifestations of moral and civil decay.

The Catholic Church stepped up to the antirock plate early in the game. As early as 1954, Catholic groups and officials were protesting the depravity they saw in rock music (see chapters 3, 7, and 14).

Congress threw its hat into the ring on several occasions. Crusading Congresswoman Ruth Thompson introduced legislation to add music to the list of "pornographic" materials illegal to ship through the mail. If successful, this would have crippled the national distribution system for records.

In many instances, both in the past and closer to present times, the music has not been so much of an issue with potential censors as have the actions of performers on- and offstage, in music videos, and even in their personal lives.

Most famous of all these was Elvis Presley's early 1957 appearance on *The Ed Sullivan Show*, when cameramen were instructed to show Elvis only from the waist up. A similar incident occurred with Bo Diddley. When he was booked for his first television appearance in 1958, Diddley's contract for the appearance included a proviso that he stand completely still during the performance. During the show, Diddley forgot the restriction and began to sway, resulting in a forfeiture of his performance fee. A 1966 James Brown concert in Kansas City was stopped because police viewed Brown's dancing as lewd and obscene.

Despite their popularity, both Chuck Berry and Jerry Lee Lewis saw their careers permanently damaged by morality issues. Berry was arrested in Mississippi in 1959 for dating a twenty-year-old white woman. Later that same year, Berry was prosecuted under the Mann Act for transporting a minor across state lines for "immoral" purposes. The incident involved a fourteen-year-old prostitute Berry brought back with him from Mexico, had a relationship with, and employed in a club he owned in St. Louis. The controversy and resulting jail sentence ruined Berry's career as a hitmaker. Lewis's short reign at the top of the charts ended in 1958 when it was revealed that he had married his thirteen-year-old cousin a year earlier. The media had a field day with the revelation, calling Lewis a "baby snatcher" and "cradle robber."

In some instances, songs have been censored because their themes are considered too racy. In 1965, the Rolling Stones had trouble keeping their song "(I Can't Get No) Satisfaction" on radio playlists, because programmers feared that the song's suggestive title would alert censors to its partially sexual theme.

Many conservatives attributed the "love" themes of pop songs in the late sixties to the "free love" movement, promoting open and indiscriminate promiscuity. Songs inspired by the equal rights movement met with similar trepidation.

In 1975, the popularity of the birth control pill led some people to believe that reproductive control would lead to an explosion of promiscuity among young women. Such fears caused several radio stations to pass on Loretta Lynn's song "The Pill," which celebrated the newfound freedom and control for sexually active women.

Two radio stations in Salt Lake City, Utah, removed the Olivia Newton-John hit "Physical" from airplay because they feared that the city's heavily Mormon population would find the song offensive.

In 1985, the producers of *American Bandstand* refused to let Sheena Easton sing her then-current hit single, "Sugar Walls," because of its explicit lyrics and status as a PMRC target. Similarly, George Michael's breakthrough hit "I Want Your Sex" was banned from dozens of radio stations in 1987 because programmers felt that the song promoted casual sex. Sensibilities were running exceptionally high because of the exploding AIDS crisis.

Sometimes even the mere suggestion of sex has led to censorship. The popular 1953 tune "These Foolish Things" was altered because of a reference to a perfume-scented pillow, implying that the male singer had recently had a woman in his bed. The lyric "gardenia perfume lingering on a pillow" was changed to the innocuous "a seaplane rising from an ocean billow." Songs by other artists, such as Them (featuring Van Morrison) and the Swinging Medallions, had relatively minor suggestive lyrics removed, replaced by less controversial phrases. The title of one Marvin Gaye song, "Sanctified Pussy" was changed after the singer's death to "Sanctified Lady."

Such minor alterations have become less frequent as rock has evolved, in part because of increased levels of tolerance by the mainstream and in part because references to sex have grown more explicit. With increase in boldness by musicians, corresponding censorship movements have come to blossom.

Radio-station owner Gordon McLendon undertook a massive censorship campaign in the 1960s. One of the employees of McLendon's thirteen radio stations had found his young daughter listening to the Rolling Stones' "Let's Spend the Night Together" and immediately mutilated the record so it could not be played. Once McLendon heard of the incident, he felt compelled to act. All of McLendon's radio stations ceased playing songs the boss found offensive, such as the Beatles' "Penny Lane," "Try It" by the Standells, and Mitch Ryder's "Sock It to Me, Baby." McLendon eventually took his cause to the American Mothers' Committee convention in New York City, claiming that British musicians were to blame for the infestation of obscene music in the United States.

One of McLendon's proposals included assembling a committee of prostitutes and junkies to screen songs for hidden obscene lingo. The group quickly passed an ordinance supporting McLendon's campaign, promising to go home and inform their local radio stations they were behind the initiative.

In 1975, the Reverend Charles Boykin of Tallahassee, Florida, blamed rock music for teen promiscuity and teen pregnancy. Boykin

claimed to have conducted a local survey of 1,000 unwed mothers and found that 984 of them became pregnant while listening to rock music (ignoring the fact that they actually became pregnant while having sex). He used the survey results to justify several of his large record burnings. Among the "devil's music" destroyed by Boykin and his followers were records by Kitty Wells, Jackie Gleason, and Neil Diamond. After questioning by the local press, Boykin admitted that he did not conduct the survey himself, but found the data in a scientific report. Then he changed his story again, claiming he was given the data by a local college professor. Finally, after several more claimed sources, Boykin admitted he was uncertain of where the information had come from.

The Reverend Charles Boykin sits among his collection of "devil's music," which he blames for teenage pregnancy.

Time magazine weighed in later that same year with an article on "sex rock," which accounted for as much as 15 percent of the content on radio. Leading on the list of offending songs was Donna Summer's "Love to Love You Baby," which was "mostly five words repeated 28 times" and contained "a marathon of 22 orgasms" (a claim later seized upon by conservative Christians in their attacks against disco music). Two 1976 hits also came under criticism from the press and conservative activists: "Disco Lady" by Johnny Taylor and Rod Stewart's "Tonight's the Night"— which was eventually edited to remove the lyric "spread your wings and let me come inside."

Late in 1976, Jesse Jackson's civil rights organization, Operation PUSH, proclaimed that it would lead a campaign, initiated by Jackson, to rid the airwaves of "sexy songs" he believed affected children's minds and were at least partially to blame for teen pregnancy. Jackson hinted that if the music and radio industries did not yield with voluntary compliance, boycotts might become necessary. Jackson said he knew he had to do something after attending a rock concert, where he "heard kids in the audience singing 'get up off your ass, smoke some grass, shit goddamn.' This has gone too far and we must do something about it." The civil rights leader called for ethics review boards in major cities to create "no-play lists" and the establishment of a ratings system, similar to that used for movies.

Bitches and Hoes

While the presence of degrading images of women in popular music is not necessarily a sexual issue, it does involve gender and sex-role stereotypes. Critics of rock music that presented women as otherwise useless sexual objects, playthings, or vixens worried that not only did this teach young men that it was okay to disrespect women, but that it taught young women that they needed to act like sluts to be respected or desired. Some lyrics make an easy case: from 2 Live Crew's "S&M": "I turned her over, got it from behind. The pussy was sorry so the bitch got slapped." From Body Count's "Evil Dick": "Evil Dick likes warm, wet places; evil dick don't care about faces. Evil dick likes young, tiny places; evil dick leaves gooey, telltale traces."

As women stepped away from "traditional" gender roles in the 1960s and 1970s, potential censors became very critical of songs considered demeaning to women. In 1976, the group Women Against Violence Against Women called for boycotts of all Time-Warner products over a billboard campaign to promote the Rolling Stones album *Black and Blue*. The billboard featured a photograph of a bound and severely abused woman. The group called the billboard a "crime against women." In 1985, a group calling themselves Women Against Pornography began an educational campaign to "bring to the

According to writer Tama Janowitz, "Madonna is not selling sex, she is representing power."

public's attention the sexist and violent content of rock videos." The lecture program was adopted for use in high schools, colleges, and women's civic groups. Surgeon General C. Everett Koop addressed the topic in a speech in May of 1984, saying he was concerned that young people would not be able to form satisfying relationships because of their exposure to rock videos.

Since rap emerged in the late eighties, many have criticized hardcore rap for the genre's misogynistic treatment of women. Repeatedly referred to as "bitches" and "hoes" (short for "whores"), women are something that get in your bed and then in your way—a source of sexual fulfillment and constant frustration.

The rash of censorship centering on 2 Live Crew's *As Nasty as They Wanna Be* was a result of the sexual themes of the record. In an article titled "Polluting Our Popular Culture," *U.S. News & World Report* commentator John Leo said, "What we are discussing here is the wild popularity of a group that sings about forcing anal sex on a girl and then forcing her to lick excrement."[3] Leo further claimed that music like 2 Live Crew's was causing "10- to 12-year-old boys to walk down the street chanting about the joys of damaging a girl's vagina during sex." Furor over the group's music led to the album's dubious distinction of prompting the first federal court judgment that popular music can be obscene. Despite the group's eventual success in the court system, the victory was almost anticlimactic, considering that in the meantime more than half a dozen retailers were arrested on obscenity charges, and retailers across the country deemed the record "too hot to handle." Legislation had been introduced in more than a dozen states declaring the album either legally obscene, unfit for sale to minors, or illegal for sale to anyone.

Sex and gender roles in rap led to further criticism from politicians throughout the 1990s, even making it into the campaign rhetoric of both President Clinton and Senator Bob Dole during the 1996 presidential campaign.

Cause and Effect

Critics of rock music through the decades have claimed a connection between listening to rock and the apparent decay of sexual morals. While times have changed, the arguments used in the 1950s are similar to complaints heard today. Critics quickly point out that while the arguments may seem the same, the fact is that music is significantly racier than it was in its early days. While fifties rock fans found their thrill on Blueberry Hill, today's rock fans are told by their musical idols to fuck like beasts, party on pussies, and rock their lovers like a hurricane.

Surprisingly, and despite the contentions of critics, there are no more or fewer "love and sex" themes in music now than there were decades ago. Studies in both the 1960s and 1980s detail that roughly 60 to 70 percent of popular tunes feature sex, romance, or love themes (although "love and courtship" themes did account for more than 90 percent of songs on the ultra-pop *Hit Parader* charts in the 1950s). What has changed is the explicitness of these songs. While critics and censors claim that music has gotten more profane and vulgar, there is a more accurate way to describe the transition in pop themes concerning affairs of the heart: a move from "emotional" to "physical" descriptions of love, romance, and sex.[4]

But does that more explicit content have an effect? The PMRC thought so. A 1985 video released by the PMRC opens with a scene from *Sesame Street* featuring characters and children singing and dancing together. The narrator's voice informs us that years ago, *Sesame Street* proved that children learn from music, words, and images. The scene cuts to images from heavy metal videos showing sex, violence, and drug abuse, plus shots of a group of scantily dressed young girls mugging for the camera. The narrator asks, "At what age does a child cease to learn from music, words, and images?" The video and its producers make some rather broad assumptions. First, that words, music, and images in rock music and videos do indeed have an effect. Second, that negative messages in music produce negative effects in viewers. And finally, that the recipient of these messages is an empty vessel who is easily manipulated. Their claims are based on nothing more than their own "common sense" and conjecture.

A fascinating study conducted by social researchers J. D. Brown and L. Schulze in 1990 examined reactions to Madonna's "Papa Don't Preach" among college students to demonstrate how what appears to be a rather cut-and-dried song and video can be interpreted differently by diverse groups. The song and video tell the story of a young woman who falls in love, becomes pregnant, and copes with trying to tell her father she intends to keep the baby. The video was an especially interesting choice for the study because it had been the subject of some criticism from conservative groups who felt that the song and video promoted promiscuity and premarital sex and sent the message that teen pregnancy was acceptable and insignificant to a girl's life.

The video was shown to three hundred students at two Southern colleges, one group at a predominantly white school and another group at a predominantly black school. Following the viewing, the students were asked what the core themes of the video were and what they expected the outcome to be. More than half the white students felt the theme of "Papa Don't Preach" was teenage pregnancy. In fact, more than 85 percent of white males and 97 percent of white females mentioned pregnancy as at least one of the video's main themes. Black students had a much different reaction to the clip, feeling that the core theme was the father-daughter relationship. When listing the video's themes, 57 percent of black males and 27 percent of black females made no mention of pregnancy. When asked about the outcome, white males were the most likely group to predict that the young couple in the video would settle down together and marry, with black males being the least likely to agree with this outcome.

The study also helped put another canard to rest—that listeners are more likely to be influenced by the behaviors of their favorite musicians or role models. Respondents in the Brown and Shulze study were asked if they were fans of Madonna. While more than 10 percent of the respondents responded affirmatively, there was no statistical difference in their response to the video than from that of non-fans.[5]

Further studies into other media have yielded similar results. A study of elementary-age children found that if the children encountered themes in songs they did not understand (be whether about sex, violence, or other subject matter), the kids simply "invented" a theme or message that fit with their own understanding. An interesting perceptual study conducted in the 1980s found that when adult romance-novel fans were asked to detail the story line of a story they had read, they were very likely to leave out details that disagreed with their own belief systems. Numerous studies have repeatedly shown that music fans are more likely to reject or ignore songs that do not gel with their own belief structures, believing that songs that go against their own morals are nonsensical or devoid of meaning. These listeners become confused, disgusted, uncomfortable, or simply block out the song's meaning.

Over the past few decades, there has been a change in how researchers approach the effects of media on viewers and listeners. Instead of focusing on the media product as culprit, studies are now focusing more on the end user—moving from a "sender-centered" focus to a "receiver-centered" perspective.[6] Rather than considering end users as passive "empty vessels," they are now viewed as an intense structure of mores, values, and ethics through which any message must pass, be filtered, and then be processed. In other words, rather than try to prove that any media product has a universal negative effect (such as corrupting morals or encouraging promiscuity), it is more revealing to look at how this message fares once it processed by a child or adult with unique belief patterns. This paradigm shows the message recipient as an active participant in how the message is perceived, something that goes against allegations that music fans are helpless in the face of tribal beats and profane themes.

The bottom line: No piece of music, no matter how vulgar or obscene, can ruin a good kid—or a good adult for that matter. One thing that becomes crystal clear is that any influence music has over the morals of young people pales in comparison to the influences of other pillars in a young person's life, such as family, church, school, and peers. While parents may be concerned about the subject matter of the music their children encounter, the true lessons about morality begin in the home—and should end there as well.

10

"WHAT'S SO FUNNY 'BOUT PEACE, LOVE, AND UNDERSTANDING?"

Politics and Protest

■

The revolutionaries always take the radio station first. They get the presidential palace later.
—Cal Thomas, vice president of public relations for the Moral Majority

America. Land of the free, right? Not if you're Shawn Thomas.

On March 3, 1998, police officers entered the home of Shawn Thomas and arrested him. Shawn's crime wasn't murder, drug trafficking, or robbery. It wasn't even jaywalking. He was arrested for "rapping."

Thomas—better known as gansta rapper C-Bo—was paroled in early 1997 after serving nine months on a weapons conviction. C-Bo's troubles stemmed from the violation of a fairly common clause in his parole agreement: Thomas was not permitted "to engage in any behavior which promotes the gang lifestyle, criminal behavior and/or violence against law enforcement."

Several months after C-Bo's release, his parole officer read the lyrics to *Til My Casket Drops*, his first major-label release. To say the least, the parole officer was not amused. The song "Deadly Game" contained lyrics that criticized California's "three strikes

and you're out" law: "You better swing, batter, swing 'cause
once you get your third felony,
yeah, 50 years you gotta bring . . .
Fuck my P.O., I'm going
A.W.O.L. . . . bound for another
state, me and my crew . . . California and Pete Wilson can suck
my dick." Within days of the
album's release, Thomas was
arrested and charged with
parole violation. Fearing that
the parole violation charge
would not hold after the incident hit the press, corrections
authorities kept Thomas in jail
by adding nine more charges, including resisting arrest.

C-Bo's *Til My Casket Drops*. Its lyrics
landed the rapper in jail for parole violation.

C-Bo's run-in with the police can be considered both an exception and the norm. It is an "exception" in the sense that, while far
from rare, there has been significantly less music censorship resulting from political ideology than for reasons like violence or sex. It
is the "norm" in the sense that the incident involving C-Bo, like
most other political music censorship, falls under the guise of violating more "acceptable" motives, such as advocating drugs or violence.

Some of the earliest violations of free expression in music have
resulted from political speech. Following the defeat of the South
in the Civil War, reconstruction forces forbade Southerners to
sing pro-South anthems such as "I'm a Good Ol' Rebel" or
"Bonnie Blue Flag" in public. "I'm a Good Ol' Rebel" originally
was written as a parody but was adopted by Southerners as a
resentful and violent condemnation of Northern values and politics—and their new presence in the South. "Bonnie Blue Flag"
was a wildly popular tune in the South during the Civil War, considered by some to rival "Dixie" as a musical testament to the
"Southern" attitude toward the war and Southern culture. Its
lyrics, penned by Harry McCarthy to the traditional tune "The
Irish Jaunting Car," described the secession of Southern states in
the early 1860s:

We are a band of brothers, and native to the soil,
Fighting for the property we gained by honest toil;
And when our rights were threatened, the cry rose near and far:
"Hurrah for the Bonnie Blue Flag that bears a single star!"
Hurrah! Hurrah!
For Southern rights, hurrah!
Hurrah for the Bonnie Blue Flag that bears a single star.

Political protest songs seemed to reemerge following the turn of the century. Groups such as the International Workers of the World (IWW), known as the Wobblies, began using songs to document the plight of the underprivileged and poor, as well as to advance socialist political messages. IWW members Ralph Chaplin and Joe Hill compiled the *Little Red Songbook* in 1909, which included a Chaplin-penned song to the tune of "The Battle Hymn of the Republic" entitled "Solidarity Forever":

They have taken untold millions that they never toiled to earn,
But without our brains and muscle not a single wheel can turn.
We can break their haughty power, gain our freedom when we
learn
That the Union makes us strong.
Solidarity forever!

Less than ten years later, Hill had been murdered and the IWW office had been raided and closed by federal authorities, who feared that the group was linked to subversive Communism.

This Machine Kills Fascists

The phrase "This machine kills fascists" was written on the guitar of activist/songwriter Woody Guthrie, who adopted the legacy of protest songs following the demise of groups like the Wobblies. He rose to prominence in the late 1930s as a radio host in Los Angeles. During his show, he read from socialist newspapers and sang songs of the working class. By 1940, he had moved to New York and was beginning his recording career while writing columns for two Communist papers. By the end of his career, he had penned more than a thousand songs, including "This Land Is Your Land," "Tom Joad," and "Pastures of Plenty." Many of his songs were considered quite controversial and inflammatory, something that confused Guthrie. "I sing songs of the people that do all of the little jobs and the mean and dirty hard work in the world and of their wants and their hopes and their plans for a decent life."[1] The tradition of protest music that Guthrie fostered caused trouble not just for him but also for some of those whom he influenced, like Bob Dylan and Pete Seeger.

Pete Seeger

When I spoke with activist, folklorist, and singer/songwriter Pete Seeger about music censorship, he began the interview by asking me a question: "How do you draw the line between censorship and editorial control?"

EN: Well, a good editor finds the focus of something and helps bring clarity. Censorship is someone else taking unwelcome control over an act of expression.

Seeger: It's a bit more subtle than that. You know what A. J. Liebling said: "Freedom of the press belongs to the person who owns the press." Censorship has been in effect for not just decades but centuries. It could be press-titution, I don't know. I am leery of thinking we know exactly what the definition of censorship is. Censorship used to be a clear definition. Nowadays censorship doesn't really work at controlling the message.

Control of art has been a problem throughout the ages. There is an Arab proverb I often quote, "When the king puts the poet on his payroll, he cuts off the tongue of the poet."

Pete Seeger has never shied away from controversy or allowed himself to be put in a position where his voice is silenced. Whether it was playing for striking union workers in the 1940s or campaigning for the Clearwater Sloop project to clean up the Hudson River in New York, Seeger has always put principles first and consequences later.

Born to two Juilliard instructors in 1919 (his mother was a violinist, his father a musicologist), Seeger mastered the guitar, banjo, and ukulele by his early teens and embarked on his career as a folksinger at sixteen. He joined Woody Guthrie and Lee Hays to form the Almanac Singers in the 1940s; he later started the Weavers with Hays in 1948.

The Weavers were one of the first acts to popularize American folk music; many of their records appeared on popular music charts. Their single "Tzena, Tzena, Tzena" backed with a cover of Leadbelly's "Goodnight Irene" sold more than two million copies, which was unprecedented for a folk recording. Seeger eventually left the Weavers after the group decided to perform in a cigarette commercial (Seeger would have nothing to do with it) and went on to have a very successful solo career—releasing more than fifty albums. He was a vocal supporter of the antiwar effort during the Vietnam War and constantly campaigned on behalf of the environment and civil rights. His latest work was 1996's *Pete.* Now that Seeger is in his eighties, he feels that he "doesn't have much of a voice left for recording."

During the 1950s, the political affiliations of Seeger and other members of the Weavers' came under the scrutiny of the McCarthy-Era House Un-American Activities Committee. Although the concept of "blacklisting" an artist hadn't previously been applied to popular musicians, the Weavers found themselves widely censored because of their leftist political ideologies. Seeger said that he was never given proof that a "blacklist" existed or that his name appeared on it, but he did receive several confirmations of its existence from others. He also noted that, when Seeger was approached to appear on a CBS television show in the late 1950s, the producer informed him that whenever guests were booked, there was a phone extension the producers called to check an artist's "availability" according to the network's censors. During the 1950s and early 1960s, producers found that Seeger was rarely "available" to perform.

Folksinger Pete Seeger

Seeger is concerned that people have forgotten the importance and implications of the McCarthy era. "People have short memories and forget past lessons. The U.S.A. doesn't really need censorship anymore. The media can keep us distracted with sex and violence so that we are not concerned about the fact that huge numbers of children die in places where the powers that be decide to throw around some force. It's a way of distracting the American people from problems we really need to solve: problems of the underclass, education, prisons, and the drug problem."

I asked Seeger to define what is dangerous about music.

"No one can put their finger on it. Music brings people together. Churches have music, and wars have music, and the people have music that is not always so friendly to the persons in charge. They have satirical songs about hypocrisy and religion and being forced to go to war when they don't want to. Folklore is full of lamenting and voices of injustice."

Surprisingly, and despite his own personal history, Seeger doesn't necessarily view censorship as a bad thing. "I think that we have a younger generation that is entranced by violence and sex, and they should be a little more concerned with control." Seeger feels there are many ideas, expressions, and thoughts that should be controlled.

EN: Do you think that "control" is a good thing?

Seeger: Absolutely. Take scientific inquiry, for example. How can you research dangerous things without risking the end of the world? Should we persuade scientists throughout the world that we shouldn't be creating new bacteria, when we know that information could be used to wipe out every dark-skinned person in the world? Or every light-skinned person? Sometimes that information needs to be suppressed.

I censor myself every time I put on a concert. I have only a limited number of songs to sing, so I am going to concentrate on what matters.

Seeger thinks that by concentrating on the "evils" of censorship, we focus on the wrong side of the equation. Instead, we should worry about raising our collective moral consciousness: "In one hundred years, if we are still here in one hundred years, we will have to develop a higher moral consciousness in order to survive. Miracles happen of all sorts. I have a bumper sticker that reads, THERE'S NO HOPE . . . BUT I MAY BE WRONG."

Pete Seeger sang with Guthrie in a group called the Almanac Singers for many years, eventually striking out with fellow Almanac Singer Lee Hays to form the Weavers in 1948. The political and social messages of the Weavers' repertoire drew criticism from Joseph McCarthy during his relentless pursuit of "Communist sympathizers" in the early 1950s. Seeger and the other Weavers members were put on an unpublicized "blacklist" of entertainers who were too controversial to broadcast on radio or television or to book for concerts. This stigma followed Seeger into the late 1960s, when network censors canceled or edited his appearances because the singer performed anti–Vietnam War songs.

Bob Dylan also had trouble during television appearances in the 1960s. An appearance on *The Ed Sullivan Show* fell apart once

CBS producers learned that Dylan planned to perform his politically themed "Talkin' John Birch Paranoid Blues." Dylan again fell victim to censors in 1968. Fearing that his songs contained subversive political messages that were masked by his sometimes undecipherable diction, an El Paso, Texas, radio station refused to play any Dylan records. But the station continued to air Dylan compositions covered by other performers.

Fellow protest singer Phil Ochs was also the subject of controversy. Ochs was the target of an FBI investigation that lasted more than ten years, yielded a four-hundred-page file on the singer, and included the agency's advocacy of his

Singer Bob Dylan. His song themes, both when understood and undecipherable, caused him trouble with broadcasters.

arrest as a subversive. In a query into Ochs's involvement in several anti–Vietnam War protests, longtime FBI director J. Edgar Hoover said Ochs was "potentially dangerous; or has been identified as a member or participant in Communist movement; or has been under active investigation as member of other group or organization." Hoover also cited Ochs's past conduct and statements as showing a "propensity towards violence and antipathy toward good order and government."[2]

The newfound popularity of folk music in 1960, along with the American military presence in Vietnam a year later, helped to advance the careers of performers who used the genre as a means to promote social and political messages. Singers like Dylan, Joan Baez, Judy Collins, and Tom Paxton were as much activists as performers, promoting civil rights, equality, and peaceful resolution to conflict as both melody and mantra. Despite the themes of many of their songs, the songs created relatively little in the way of censorship or extreme controversy. The music of the sixties was only part of the protest lodged against the establishment of that decade. According to Jerry Rubin, head of the Youth International Party (Yippies), the youth culture "merged New Left politics with a psychedelic lifestyle. Our lifestyle—acid, long hair, freaky clothes, pot, music, sex—is the Revolution. Our very existence mocks America. The older order is dying."[3] However, by 1968 the number of American soldiers sent to fight the war in Vietnam had topped half a million, and it wasn't long before folksinger protests could not contain the anger and frustration that was bubbling over among the nation's young people. Larger actions and louder music were the new calls to action.

Revolution Is Everywhere

By the late 1960s, a new form of protest music had emerged to take its place beside folk music: wild, hard, bluesy, electric rock. Artists like Jimi Hendrix, Janis Joplin, and Jefferson Airplane created the soundtrack for a protest movement that was disenfranchised by the ineffectiveness of "flower power" and the pacifist nature of folk music and enraged by the establishment's war in Vietnam that was killing thousands of American boys each week.

The Democratic National Convention in Chicago during August of 1968 was a flash point of protest against the Vietnam War. Preceding the convention, Mayor Richard Daley called in more than twelve thousand military troops and National Guardsmen to augment the Chicago police force. Ostensibly available to keep the peace, they were armed with tanks, bazookas, and riot gear. Daley requested that radio stations stop playing the current Rolling Stones single, "Street Fightin' Man," in hopes of quelling any violence the song might stimulate. Despite the absence of the Stones, a great deal of violence erupted during the protests and gatherings centered on the three-day convention. Several large outdoor concerts were gassed by police to disperse crowds before they could riot. By the end of the convention, the armed forces "protecting" crowds of demonstrators had injured 198 and arrested 641 people. If Chicago marked a turning point in youth protest over the Vietnam War and the social establishment, it was a turning-away from a paradigm of social love, understanding, and community—and toward one of tearing down the establishment with revolutionary thought and action.

The spirit of this time was captured on an album by Jefferson Airplane entitled *Volunteers*. The antiestablishment, prorevolu-

tionary themes of the album's artwork and lyrics caused RCA to hold up release of the album for several months. The label claimed to be concerned about potential protests over drug themes in several of the album's songs, although the band openly opined that the suppression was part of a conspiracy to prevent entangling the label (and its parent company, RCA) in any political controversy.

Release of Jefferson Airplane's album *Volunteers* was delayed because the record company feared that the album's content would create problems. The delay spurred the group to create its own record label for future releases.

By the end of the 1960s, campus violence was widespread. Angry protests at colleges in Wisconsin, California, Minnesota, Maryland, and Mississippi resulted in injuries, arrests, and deaths. Most notable were the killings of four students when National Guardsmen opened fire on a group of protesters at Kent State University in Kent, Ohio, on May 4, 1970. At the time, there were pervasive fears across the country that more deadly violence would break out at any time. Neil Young was so moved by the tragedy that he penned the song "Ohio" for his group Crosby, Stills, Nash, and Young. The song was released ten days after the tragedy. Several radio stations in the state pulled the song from the air due to overwhelming public support for the actions of the Guardsmen. Sensitivity to violence remained high even a year later, when police in the District of Columbia dispersed a crowd assembled for a rock concert that was to take place later that day. Local officials (including future Supreme Court Chief Justice William H.

Rehnquist) feared that the concert would erupt into a violent and deadly antiwar protest.

Commie Bastards

Spawned by the McCarthy-Era Communist hearings, fear of Communism spread into criticism of music in the mid to late 1960s. In 1965, the Reverend David Noebel wrote a pamphlet titled *Communism, Hypnotism and The Beatles: An Analysis of the Communist Use of Music*. Noebel claimed that the Beatles' music is part of a Communist plot to jam the nervous systems of young people. He urged readers to "throw your Beatle and rock and roll records in the city dump. We have been unashamed of being labeled a Christian nation, let's make sure four mop-headed Anti-Christ beatniks don't destroy our children's emotional and mental stability and ultimately our nation."

In 1966 in Indiana, the John Birch Society set up a telephone system called "Let Freedom Ring" featuring a recorded message alleging that rock music was Communistic, claiming that Communist scientists had determined that rock music could cause the young to go into fits of hysteria.

In 1970, a former musician named Joseph R. Crow spoke at several rallies for the Movement to Restore Democracy. In his speeches, he accused bands such as the Doors, Jefferson Airplane, and the Beatles of being part of a large conspiracy to destroy American values through music. He claimed that rock music can cause "radical and social political change," by glorifying "drugs, destructiveness, revolution and sexual promiscuity."

After the Gold Rush

Between the end of the Vietnam era and the evolution of rap into a mainstream genre in the late eighties, very little censorship resulted from "unpopular" political ideologies expressed through music.

When Frank Zappa turned in his single "I Don't Wanna Get Drafted," his label, Mercury Records, refused to release the song. The event prompted Zappa to create his own label, Barking Pumpkin, on which he released all his recordings until his death.

Potential censors got a little "egg on the face" when they protested the breakthrough album from Bruce Springsteen, *Born in the U.S.A.,* because they thought he was desecrating the American flag. The cover photo shows hip-cocked Springsteen standing in front of an American flag, leading the protestors to believe he was relieving himself on Old Glory. Springsteen, surprised by the controversy, offered a less politically motivated explanation: "It just turned out that the picture of my butt looked better than the picture of my face."

However, not all incidents are quite so humorous. In December of 1995, a group of Massachusetts state employees, in the company of a Drug Enforcement Agency agent, drove their work vehicles to Boston radio station WBCN to demand that the station stop playing music by Blues Traveler, 311, Sublime, and others from the *Hempilation* CD. The group claimed to be concerned about possibly advocating drug use to the station's younger audience. However, the CD was issued as a fund-raiser for the National Organization for the Reform of Marijuana Laws (NORML)—a completely legal political action organization that was not much different from lobbies for the diary industry, environmental groups, or gun owners.

Fear of a Black Planet

Although rap music gained widespread popularity in the mid-1980s, it wasn't until later in the decade that rap created significant controversy for its political and social messages. Early in its evolution, rap music served as a mass-media pedestal for social commentary on black inner-city life. However, with the explosion of rap's popularity in the late eighties, the ghetto's message was regularly exported to the suburbs. But how does a white suburban teenager relate to a black inner-city rapper?

For the first time since the Vietnam era, mainstream teenagers found a powerful music that legitimized their dissatisfaction with the politics and social policy of the older generation. This empowerment transcended race, class, or culture. Rap made it cool for teens to question authority, disagree with the locus of power in our country, and explore the revolutionary nature of self-empowerment—empowerment taken by right or force. Rap was dangerous to the establishment, and the establishment rushed to judge it.

Rap music, especially "gangsta" rap, was criticized as violent, misogynist, and pro-drug. As mentioned in the chapter on Race, rap critics failed to recognize it as a cultural force that was intended to document, criticize, and parody the society in which we live. They felt that rappers needed to shoulder some responsibility for the plights they sang about.

The group Public Enemy gained attention for its rap themes, which critics considered to be violent, anti-Semitic, and militantly black-separatist. The group's leader, Chuck D, strongly disagreed that the group's message could be harmful. "You've got to know the rules of the game so we won't be falling into traps and keep coming back to places like these! Our goal in life is to get ourselves out of this mess and be responsible to our sons and daughters so they can lead a better life." Public Enemy remained a target of negative press through the 1990s for its political views.

Songs like N.W.A's "Fuck Tha Police" and Body Count's "Cop Killer"—both subject to censorship supported by the law enforcement community—served as much as political statements as they did chronicles of racial discrimination and violence. When critics quickly dismissed Ice Cube's *Death Certificate* as angry, racist rhetoric, they failed to acknowledge it as a political statement about how our society does not treat everyone with the equality promised by our laws and doctrines. The cover of *Death Certificate* even features Ice Cube standing next to a covered body on a mortuary gurney. The toe tag on the body reads simply "Uncle Sam."

The rap/rock hybrid group Rage Against the Machine has repeatedly found itself at the center of controversy for its support of death-row inmate Mumia Abu-Jamal. Shortly after the band organized a benefit concert for Abu-Jamal, police groups called for its cancellation. The concert also featured the Beastie Boys and Bad Religion (all three groups had track records of supporting political and social causes). Abu-Jamal was convicted of murdering a police officer in 1981, and attempts to prove his innocence have created considerable controversy. Despite the promoter's offer to refund tickets to fans who did not know of the concert's beneficiary, few purchasers returned their tickets, and the sold-out concert took place as scheduled. Police organizations and supporters have repeatedly targeted Rage Against the Machine for its support of unpopular political causes.

Of all the various reasons to justify censorship of musical expression, doing so on the basis of politics is the least convincing.

Whether the reason be radical or controversial political messages or protesting social and economic conditions, it is difficult for political censors to enforce their suppression. While freedom of speech is not always enforced in the United States, it is a concept that most Americans hold dear; we rarely tolerate its direct violation. As a result, censors attempt to divert attention to other controversial aspects of a performer's music or lifestyle. For the protest singers of the forties, fifties, and sixties, it was their involvement in subversive Communism; for Jefferson Airplane, it was their drug use; for rap, it was advocacy of violence and gang life. However, you can put a pig in a frilly dress, put red lipstick on it, and call it "Monique"—but it is still a pig. While violence, promiscuous sex, drug use, and alternative lifestyles may enjoy varying degrees of acceptability in society, talking about them is neither illegal nor immoral. Regardless of intent, content, or reason, the censorship of unpopular expression violates the most basic principles upon which our country was founded.

11

"I FOUGHT THE LAW
AND THE LAW WON"

Law

■

One man's vulgarity may be another's lyric.
—Supreme Court Justice John M. Harlan

In June of 1991, the sheriff of Butler County, Ohio, decided he'd had enough of the smut being peddled in video stores in his community. He met with the owners of every local video store and informed them that, together, they would review their inventories with the sheriff's department and negotiate which "adult" titles had to go. The sheriff informed the group that store owners who cooperated would not have to worry about the raids, arrests, and obscenity prosecutions that were being contemplated.

During negotiations, the sheriff told one store owner that the video *Doing It Debbie's Way* would have to be removed. The sheriff assumed that the video was part of the infamous series spawned by the film *Debbie Does Dallas*; however, he was wrong. It was actually an exercise tape featuring "golden oldie" Debbie Reynolds. Save for a group of bouncy, energetic seniors shakin' their groove things, nothing contained in the videotape would raise an eyebrow. The sheriff held fast, telling the store owner that it was an all-or-nothing prospect: Remove every "questionable tape" or face possible prosecution. After the store owners consulted their attorneys, they decided against resisting the sheriff's "friendly" suggestions. Quite simply, it would be too expensive and risky to fight the sheriff in the court system.

How does this incident pertain to music censorship? Because it illustrates several severe problems with constitutional protection of free speech and our ability to invoke that protection. Surprisingly, the sheriff's effort may have been completely legal. Even more surprising, unless store owners had been able to secure the help of a group like the American Civil Liberties Union—or an attorney willing to work for free—it would have been impossible to enforce their constitutional right to sell or rent a Debbie Reynolds exercise tape.

The lesson? Your ability to enforce your civil rights is limited to your access to resources (financial or otherwise) that can be used to protect them.

Back to the sheriff for a moment. How could these "friendly" negotiations and subsequent tape removals be legal? Because of the Supreme Court's current standard of obscenity: If local "community standards" (in this case, defined by the local sheriff) say something is "obscene," then it can legally be subject to government censorship. It doesn't matter if communities down the road, across the state, or anywhere else find the material to be acceptable. If the citizens of Butler County say something is obscene, then the person producing, distributing, or possessing those materials can legally be prosecuted as a felon, even though an identical item is legal elsewhere. This can create quite a problem, particularly with popular music.

If creating "bad" music were illegal, the Spice Girls, Jim Nabors, and Vanilla Ice would have been confined to shackles years ago. However, when music is outlawed, it is not legislated on the basis of its merit; it is restricted on whether or not it is "obscene." And "obscene" speech is not protected by the Constitution's free-speech provisions. Teenagers across the country can listen to a Marilyn Manson CD, but if a local community decides it is obscene, a young person could be arrested for listening to it in his or her hometown. Legal? Constitutionally correct? Absolutely. The Constitution asks average community members to apply a simple test—the SLAPS test—to any work in question. In the SLAPS test, the following question are asked: Does the work, according to your standards, have Serious Literary, Artistic, Political, or Scientific value? According to the Constitution, "obscenity" is anything a jury of twelve people thinks it is.

In this chapter, we'll review the First Amendment to the United States Constitution. We'll see how its free-speech provisions have been interpreted and enforced over the past two hundred–plus years. For good measure, we'll even look at how the First Amendment applies to music.

The Law of the Land

Many people mistakenly believe that the Declaration of Independence is the founding document of the United States. Not true. The Declaration's purpose was to inform the British Crown that the colonies intended to separate from the British Empire and function independently. The Declaration of Independence is not a legal document in the United States, and it has only symbolic and historical significance today. Our country's true founding document is the Constitution of the United States, created in September of 1787 and put into effect a year later. Soon after the Constitution's ratification, the Bill of Rights was proposed. That document, adopted several years later, in December of 1791, guaranteed the rights of citizens in the new country.

Our Constitution (and its attached Bill of Rights) is the legal framework for our country. It is our first and primary law, the contract between the government and the governed, the ultimate authority, a guidepost for the roles of federal, state, and local government.

The freedom of speech enjoyed by Americans (along with freedoms of religion and of the press) is found in the First Amendment to the Constitution, which reads:

> Congress shall make no law representing an establishment of religion, or prohibiting the free exercise thereof; or abridging the freedom of speech, or of the press; or the right of the people peaceably to assemble, and to petition the Government for a redress of grievances.

Notice that the First Amendment specifically mentions "the Government." The goal of the First Amendment is to ensure "uninhibited, robust, and wide-open" discussion about matters of government and governance. An important aspect of the Constitution is that it applies to the rights of citizens in relation to the government—not to each other. The rights granted in the Constitution are meant to protect individual liberty from a corrupt or ill-intentioned government or its agencies. The First Amendment does not protect us against implicit or direct censorship by businesses, community groups, or each other.

There also is a common misconception in the United States that citizens have a "constitutional right" to *not* be offended. While it is certainly unfortunate that people encounter music, art, or literature that they find offensive, there is no legal basis for applying restrictions because something might offend. Anyone who reads Thomas Jefferson's *Notes on the State of Virginia* can see that Jefferson, the author of the Declaration of Independence and third president of the United States, expected Americans to encounter material that they found to be offensive. He endorsed the idea of an ongoing revolution of authority so that those in power would not grow to abuse their authority or force their ways of thinking onto the mass populace.

The History of Obscenity

The evolution of our current free speech and obscenity standards stretches back more than 130 years to the late 1860s. Until then, the United States had made no clear distinction between those types of speech that were protected by the Constitution and those that were not.

In 1867, a young Civil War veteran named Anthony Comstock moved to New York City and began working in a dry goods store. Comstock was incensed by the smut that was passed around the break room, and he began to track down the publishers of sexually explicit materials and push for their prosecution. After having several early successes, Comstock became obsessed and embarked on a lifelong campaign against indecency. He almost single-handedly pushed Congress into adopting the Comstock Act of 1873, which outlawed the sending of "obscene" communications or any communication relating to birth control or abortion through the mail. Following the passage of the act, Comstock became a volunteer postal inspector and led the U.S. Postal Service and U.S. Customs

Office to ban hundreds of books and works of art. The act outlawed "obscene" materials; however, it provided no guidelines or definition for that designation.

The earliest working definition of "obscenity"—the Hicklin Rule—actually was adopted from the British, who developed it as their obscenity standard in 1866. It was first used in the United States during a Supreme Court review of an 1896 court case involving New York publisher Lew Rosen (who had been convicted of selling nude girlie pictures). The ruling stated that "the test of obscenity is this, whether the tendency of the matter charged as obscenity is to deprave and corrupt those whose minds are open to such immoral influences, and into whose hands a publication of this sort may fall."[1] This stuck as our constitutional definition of obscenity for more than fifty years.

In 1942, the Supreme Court heard the case of *Chaplinsky* v. *New Hampshire,* which led them to establish the difference between *worthwhile* speech and *worthless* speech. Walter Chaplinsky was a Jehovah's Witness who was arrested for creating a disturbance while distributing religious pamphlets. Chaplinsky, who declared that organized religion was a "racket," had verbally assaulted people on the street as well as the arresting officers, whom he called "Fascists" and "God-damned racketeers." Although, the Supreme Court let Chaplinsky's conviction stand, it drew a distinction between *worthwhile* speech (speech that has social value) and *worthless* speech (that which does not). The court viewed Chaplinsky's statements as "fighting words" (a concept discussed later in this chapter), rather than social or political commentary.

In 1957, the Supreme Court made another important distinction in evaluating obscenity. The case involved Samuel Roth (*Roth* v. *United States*), a publisher who had been arrested and convicted of publishing and selling obscene books, magazines, and photographs. In their decision to uphold Roth's conviction, the Court used the case to further refine the definition of obscenity in what became known as the Roth test. In part, the Roth test asks "whether the average person, applying contemporary community standards [finds] the dominant theme of material, taken as a whole, appeals to prurient interest."[2] Therefore, if a film contains a nude scene or a book describes a murder in detail, the entire work cannot be ruled obscene. This is a very important distinction, particularly when considering that many films, record albums, and books (even the Bible) contain something that someone might find obscene and is, therefore, illegal. This decision also marked the beginning of the nebulous "average" person applying "community standards"—a factor that, even today, remains a central component in defining obscenity.

The final refinement to the Supreme Court's current definition of obscenity came in 1973. In *Miller* v. *California,* the Supreme Court reviewed the conviction of Marvin Miller, who had sold advertising brochures that contained sexually explicit illustrations. The Court used the case to create a new standard for measuring obscenity, known as the Miller Test, which is the standard used in our court system today:

> (1) Whether the average person, applying contemporary standards of the state or local community, would find that the work, taken as a whole, appeals to the prurient interest; (2) whether the work depicts or describes in a patently offensive way sexual conduct specifically defined by the applicable state law; and (3) whether the work lacks serious literary, artistic, political, or scientific value.[3]

The third segment of this definition is the SLAPS test described earlier, and it is the most applicable to controversial musical works.

How Do You Solve a Problem Like Obscenity?

The concept of obscenity is unique in criminal law because it requires a subjective decision of guilt or innocence. If someone says that the sky is blue or that he or she stole a car, that person is making a statement of fact. The same is not true for obscenity. Obscenity is strictly a matter of opinion, with little or no fact required to prove guilt. A conviction for obscenity is unique because it cannot be tested against facts. In the words of censorship expert Dr. Harry White, "the practical question has always been not *what* defines obscenity, but *who* defines it."[4] Supreme Court Justice Potter Stewart (in his written opinion for the obscenity case *Jacobellis* v. *Ohio*) said that even though he could not satisfactorily define pornography, "I know it when I see it."

A work's status as "obscene" also depends upon a community's moral standards and its interpretation of the work's social value. While a group of community citizens might find the Butthole Surfers to be obscene because the group shows films of automobile accidents during its performances, another group of citizens might see the display as a commentary on society's attitudes and our "numbness" to extreme violence. Who is correct? Which reflects the "community standard"? No matter which side you choose, it is impossible to judge this example simply based on a single perform-ance by the group. Other factors—time, place, and manner of the performance—weigh heavily on the judgment.

With those details in mind, exactly what are obscenity laws and provisions supposed to prevent? Are they designed to stop authors from writing controversial books, to discourage painters and pho-tographers from creating provocative imagery, to prevent musi-cians from performing controversial songs?

If you listen to the censors, you will notice copious justifications and arguments offered against "obscenity." There are numerous references to protecting children, aiding parents, and preventing controversial music from being sold or performed. Censors rarely think they are trying to suppress an artist; however, they don't want their children, families, friends, or community to come into contact with controversial subjects. The censors are more inter-ested in protecting those whom they fear may be influenced by the work and are much less interested in protecting the work's creator. In short, Joe Censor doesn't care about Prince, but he also doesn't want his thirteen-year-old son to start dressing like him. Those who want to censor don't really care what happens in the rest of the country, but their own lives are sacrosanct. According to Dr. White, "Obscenity and pornography are terms that ultimately serve to define people more than expression. What the censor ultimately seeks to discover and control are not works that are typically obscene, but people, who, it is believed, are typically cor-rupted by works of literature."[5]

Existing in the first segment of the Miller test is another problem with applying obscenity provisions to music: Works must be judged as a whole. Contemporary songs can consist of several "components," such as vocal (lyrical), instrumental, thematic, etc. If the lyrics are judged to be indecent, is the entire song *as a whole* obscene? If one song on an album is obscene, does the entire album deserve that judgment? The answer to both questions is no. Making that distinction would ignore the "work as a whole" principle of the Miller test.

The Miller test also calls a work obscene if it appeals to "prurient interests." Is the intent of the work to stimulate the listener sexually? First, how many songs are capable of sexually stimulating the listener? Is sexual stimulation the song's focused intention? Second, while many songs contain *references* to sex, few contain graphic *depictions* of sex (which would make the work legally obscene). Finally, could the work fail the third part of the Miller test—the SLAPS test? Musical preferences aside, can one come up with a piece of music that is completely lacking in social, political, or artistic value? Music, by nature, is an artistic expression.

What Is "Prurient"?

If you see the word "prurient" in this chapter and are unclear about its meaning, don't feel bad. When Supreme Court Justice William Brennan first used the word in his definition of obscenity in *Roth* v. *United States* (1957), several other justices admitted that they scrambled for their dictionaries. Materials that appeal to the prurient interests are, basically, things that "turn you on"—or provide sexual stimulation. Various dictionaries describe the word as "causing sexual lewdness" or "lustful thoughts." Like many aspects of obscenity law, prurient interests involve an end result (or reaction) rather than an action. If someone does not "react" to your work, it is legal; however, if they become sexually stimulated (if it appeals to their "prurient interest"), you've committed a crime.

Other Applicable Constitutional Standards

There are three other First Amendment issues that have greatly influenced music: access by children to controversial material, ability to provoke anger, and regulation of the public airwaves.

An important caveat to the definition of obscenity is how it applies to contact children have with material best suited for adults. In the Supreme Court case *Ginsberg* v. *New York,* the

Court stated that the government had the power to adjust obscenity standards, as applied to minors, to restrict children's access to adult materials. For example, it is legal to restrict the sale of *Playboy* magazine to minors; however, it is not permissible to restrict access of that magazine to everyone simply because it is inappropriate for children.

"Provocation to anger" questions whether or not speech can be constitutionally protected if it incites violence or other lawless activity among those who hear it. Is free speech protected if it condones or incites violence or lawless action? A Supreme Court case discussed earlier, *Chaplinsky* v. *New Hampshire,* defined the concept of "fighting words." The Chaplinsky decision affects lewd, profane, and obscene language, and it also affects words that might provoke a fight. In the Chaplinsky decision, the Court stated that "fighting words" were *worthless* speech that tend "to incite an immediate breach of the peace."[6] Applied to music, if a performer encourages concertgoers to flip over their seats and trash the performance venue, then that performer might be subject to prosecution. Because his or her words *may* lead to imminent lawless action, the person loses his or her First Amendment protection. The issue becomes very fuzzy in situations such as the events surrounding Ice-T's song "Cop Killer." Does the song advocate violence against police officers? The answer to that depends upon whom you speak with; some people feel that Ice-T in fact does promote violence against police. Ice-T, on the other hand, considers the song to be a social (and political) protest against the treatment of black Americans by white police officers. But here's the critical question: Does the song incite an immediate breach of the peace? The answer is no. Censors of Ice-T's song should expect to *prove* that a person hearing the song will immediately pick up a weapon, hunt down a police officer, and end the officer's life on the spot. Obviously, you won't find many examples of that type of reaction.

Regardless of the speaker's intention, use of profane language on the radio is exempt from free-speech privileges. Since 1927, all federal regulations of the broadcast spectrum have recognized that broadcasting is unique because it is an invasive medium. While a person must make a conscious decision to read a book, listen to a CD, or attend a political rally, broadcast media are delivered into the home without the recipient's discretion. Radio, in particular, is easily accessed by children, and that fact is used to justify broadcast content regulation.

Indecency was directly addressed in the groundbreaking Radio Act of 1927, which stated, "No person within the jurisdiction of the United States shall utter any obscene, indecent, or profane language by means of radio communication." This regulation was later reinforced in the Communications Act of 1934, and it was added to Section 1464 of the Federal Criminal Code in 1948.

The Federal Communications Commission (the federal agency charged with regulating the broadcast spectrums) never applied the indecency provisions until 1970, when it fined a Philadelphia radio station for the excrement and sex references that were contained in an interview with the Grateful Dead's Jerry Garcia. The reason the FCC sat on the proverbial sideline until 1970? The FCC, by law, is not meant or required to "monitor" the airwaves, but simply to act upon complaints it receives from citizens. It apparently took censors until 1970 to understand the utility of calling in the FCC's calvary.

The landmark regulation of radio indecency came in 1975 when the FCC sued the Pacifica Foundation over the content aired on its New York station. The Pacifica Foundation is a nonprofit organization that owns and operates a small group of public radio stations across the country. Pacifica stations, largely volunteer-staffed, feature a broad range of political, ethnic, and cultural programs targeted at a variety of audiences. During a midday program, the New York City Pacifica station, WBAI-FM, aired a sketch by comedian George Carlin called "Filthy Words." The monologue's theme was the seven words you cannot say over the airwaves: "shit, piss, fuck, cunt, cocksucker, motherfucker, and tits." The FCC brought suit against Pacifica after it received a single complaint from a man who had heard the broadcast as he was driving through the city with his young child. The complainant was a member of the New York chapter of the pro-censorship group Morality in Media, and the "young child" who heard the broadcast was fifteen years old. The Supreme Court, which heard the case in 1978, sided with the FCC's right to restrict indecency during hours that children were likely to listen to radio. In turn, the

FCC determined that indecent programming, like the Carlin monologue, could be broadcast only after midnight.

During the 1980s, the FCC significantly stepped up its role as regulator of indecency on the airwaves. Following several policy statements (such as the Indecency Policy Reconsideration Order in 1987) and lawsuits, the "blackout" period for indecent material swung from as lenient as 6 A.M. to 10 P.M. to as strict as a twenty-four-hour-a-day ban. Blackout times changed every few years, as the FCC and different interest groups fought the issue through the court system. In January of 1996, things seemed finally to settle when the Supreme Court refused to hear an appeal of the current standard—which forbids indecent material from 6 A.M. to 10 P.M.

Of course, the most obvious implementation of indecent language pertains to indecent lyrics. According to FCC regulations, stations are required to remove or "bleep out" indecent language during blackout time—even though it would be okay to air those words during late-night hours (broadcasters rarely take this step, however, because it involves the logistical nightmare of keeping two different versions of the same song in rotation). This becomes censorship when the indecency standards are irregularly applied or are applied to material that is not indecent or obscene.

Often, rap songs are heavily edited for broadcast to remove indecent language. However, Top 40 songs by artists such as Green Day, Marilyn Manson, and the Clash contain a great deal of uncensored, indecent language that seems to go unnoticed and cause little turmoil. Why the difference? Is it because rap music is a more controversial medium than pop tunes, or is it because the majority of artists usually involved in rap are black and come from urban areas? Could this degree of editing also be attributed to song themes? Green Day and Marilyn Manson use profane language to describe their dissatisfaction with society, but the specific targets of their complaints are vague. Many popular rap artists, especially "gangsta" rappers targeted by censors in the early 1990s, also express dissatisfaction with society. The difference is that rappers are very specific about the problems they and their communities face, and they are quick to point fingers at the sources of their problems.

In 1969, more than half the Top 40 stations in the country either refused to air or edited the Beatles song "The Ballad of John and

Yoko" because of the lyric "Christ, you know it ain't easy . . . they're gonna crucify me." Although station managers may have found the song's references to Christ and crucifixion offensive, those lyrics certainly are not indecent. Therefore, the song doesn't fall under the FCC's regulation of indecent speech in broadcasts. Such speech may be considered blasphemy (speech condemning the church or religion); however, blasphemous speech is protected by the First Amendment. The FCC can outlaw obscenity and regulate indecency, but it cannot regulate constitutionally protected speech just because it is potentially offensive.

Things Fall Apart

Indiscriminate use of indecency and obscenity laws are not confined to the broadcast spectrum. For example, the Miller test was used in the prosecution of Jello Biafra, leader of the Dead Kennedys, on charges of distribution of harmful matter to minors.[7] The case involved a poster that was included in the band's album *Frankenchrist* and that offended a mother in suburban Los Angeles whose child purchased the album. In order to win a conviction, prosecutors had to: (1) prove that the poster appealed to prurient interests; (2) prove that the average Californian adult would deem it offensive to minors; and (3) prove that it was utterly without redeeming value. You can easily see how this mimics the three standards in the Miller test. In order to substantiate their innocence, the defendants disproved these three points by demonstrating that the poster passed the SLAPS test and was directly linked to the political and social themes of the album's lyrics (more on this case can be found in chapter 17).

In the case of Luther Campbell and 2 Live Crew (also discussed at length in the Chronology), the performers filed suit because they wanted a judge to determine if the album's content was legally obscene (as was asserted by a county sheriff).

2 Live Crew had been the victim of the censors' wrath for several years before Broward County, Florida, sheriff Nick Navarro blew a gasket over their controversial album *As Nasty as They Wanna Be*, which contained the word "fuck" 226 times, 87 mentions of oral sex, 163 references to women as "bitches" and "whores," and 1 mention of incest. Following the release of the album, the local circuit court judge found that there was probable

cause to rule the album obscene. This provided the sheriff's office with all the ammunition it needed to pressure local record stores to remove the album from their shelves. In March of 1990, retailers started to comply with the sheriff's "suggestion." The band's label, Skyywalker Records, immediately filed suit seeking a declaratory judgment that the sheriff's prior restraint actions violated 2 Live Crew's First Amendment rights. In a separate

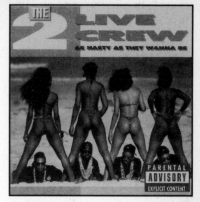

2 Live Crew's *As Nasty As They Wanna Be*

action, Sheriff Navarro asked the court to declare the record obscene under Florida's obscenity law.

In May, Federal Judge Jose Gonzalez, Jr., found *As Nasty as They Wanna Be* to be obscene. Gonzalez stated in his decision that he saw little artistic merit in 2 Live Crew's music and felt that rap music in general (a predominantly black art form) was not on the same level of artistic sophistication as "melodic" music (a predominantly white art form). Despite an injunction (and eventual reversal) secured by 2 Live Crew to prevent criminal prosecution while the case was under appeal, Sheriff Navarro promptly arrested a local retailer on pornography charges because he continued to sell *As Nasty as They Wanna Be.* Navarro also arrested three members of the band when they performed material from the album in a local nightclub.

During the entire process, the sheriff did not try to censor the album because he didn't like it (although I think it's safe to say he didn't); instead, he focused on establishing content obscenity by claiming that it failed the Miller test (content that lacks any redeeming social value). However, it took several trips through the court system to establish 2 Live Crew's right to perform and sell its music.

While our Constitution gives citizens the luxury of freedom of speech, that luxury can be very expensive. Regardless of the amount (or lack) of common sense, the legal merit, or the constitutionality of a law, it is never wise simply to ignore or disobey any

Broward County, Florida, sheriff Nick Navarro and 2 Live Crew's Luther Campbell on the *Geraldo* show in June of 1990, one day after Campbell's arrest for obscenity for performing material from *As Nasty as They Wanna Be.* Navarro's pursuit of 2 Live Crew would land more than half a dozen people in jail, close three record stores, and eventually cost him reelection to office.

law. The Supreme Court has said that the battles for truth and justice should be fought in the courtroom. Therefore, although legislation that forbids dancing in public or listening to a certain CD may obviously violate your civil rights, participating in any forbidden act can still get you into a lot of trouble. It is sometimes a hard concept to grasp, but the Supreme Court (and many other appellate courts) do not deal with matters of guilt or innocence—those issues are decided entirely in the lower courts. Appellate courts are concerned only with enforcing your civil and legal rights. While a higher court might find the law you violated to be unconstitutional, that doesn't necessarily mean you get off scot-free. You still broke a law, and it is not considered unjust to punish someone who deliberately violates the law.

The rules are pretty simple: You aren't supposed to take action on your own; you are supposed to appeal to the courts for protection. These are relatively simple concepts to grasp; however, unless you have bags of money sitting around, or can appeal to a legal nonprofit like the ACLU, or can find a lawyer who is willing to represent you pro bono, your chances of successfully protecting your rights are slim. While the American justice system is one of the fairest in the world, it still requires an advocate to get anything done; those advocates (lawyers) cost money. Lawyers charge by the hour (often hundreds of dollars per hour), and civil rights cases can be very expensive (in time and, thus, money) to bring before a court. And there still is no guarantee of success. You are certainly free to exercise your right to expression, but you'd better have the resources to cover your butt in case you run into some trouble. This is a concept that does not escape the censors.

After Jello Biafra's obscenity case was finally thrown out of court, it was widely speculated that Assistant Los Angeles City Attorney Michael Guarino prosecuted the case for political reasons and because the defendants would lack the savvy and financial resources to fight the charges. Although the trial would have allowed Guarino to establish legal precedent against "controversial" music, many critics cited the weak case and the prosecution's weak courtroom presentation as testament to Guarino's complete lack of preparedness to actually take it to trial. Even the *Los Angeles Times* called the prosecution's case "highly unusual." But Guarino was not alone in mistakenly believing that musicians were too inept to navigate the legal system.

During the late 1980s, antirock legislation was passed in more than a dozen states, including Pennsylvania, Arizona, Delaware, Florida, Illinois, Iowa, Kansas, Maryland, Missouri, New Mexico, Oklahoma, and Virginia. Each state legislature acted on the assumption that all controversial music was legally obscene and had no redeeming social value. Judith Toth, the antirock crusader who served in Maryland's legislature, echoed those sentiments in defending her actions. Toth stated that while her legislation's intention was to help parents protect their children, the real purpose was to rid the country of the undesirable elements of rock and rap music. Said Toth, "I say [the recording industry] is going to go broke defending themselves. Wait until we start court cases under existing laws. The purpose isn't to win; the purpose is to keep them so tied up that they don't know what hit them."[8] Toth's sentiments were the norm among antirock legislation's proponents. According to Toth and many other labeling supporters in the 1980s, if questionable constitutional legislation is passed that censors a group that can't legally defend itself—who cares?

Several organizations have fought battles against music censorship. In response to the PMRC's campaign in the 1980s,

Former President Ronald Reagan spoke out against music in 1985, saying, "I don't believe that our Founding Fathers ever intended to create a nation where the rights of pornographers would take precedence over the rights of parents, and the violent and malevolent would be given free rein to prey upon our children."

record-industry executive Danny Goldberg founded the Musical Majority. The group, which consisted of concerned recording-industry insiders and performers, attempted to draw attention to the vagueness and constitutional inappropriateness of measures proposed by Tipper Gore and the PMRC. The American Civil Liberties Union has also responded to civil rights cases involving anti-rock legislation, the cancellation of controversial concerts, and groups of high school students who were suspended for wearing T-shirts featuring their favorite musicians.

Several grassroots organizations also have led efforts to educate music fans and the general public about legal and social issues surrounding controversial music. Rock Out Censorship, *Rock and Rap Confidential*, the Massachusetts Music Industry Coalition (run by Nina Crowley—one of the most dedicated and passionate advocates for free-speech issues involving popular music), and JAMPAC (founded by former Nirvana bassist Krist Novoselic) are just a few of the organizations working to ensure First Amendment protection for musicians and fans.

12

"CENSORSHIT"

From the Mouths of the Censors

**A censor is a man who knows more
than he thinks you ought to.**
—Granville Hicks

Whether rock music represents a fall from grace, a lure to impressionable youth, or a force of evil, its critics have never been underrepresented in the dialogue concerning controversial music. Yet how many, among those critics, would argue for the importance and intrinsic value of understanding the opinions and perspectives of those who believe differently?

This chapter chronicles my efforts to contact some of the people and institutions who have been involved in censoring music. It also serves as a "where are they now?" for those whose fifteen minutes of fame have expired.

Washington Wives

The Parents Music Resource Center has remained in existence from the time of its founding in the spring of 1985. Since its heyday, the four primary players have gone their separate ways. Tipper Gore resigned from the group in the early nineties, Susan Baker retired and returned to Texas with her husband, and Pam Howar and Sally Nevius both lost their husbands to cancer. In 1995, long-time supporter and board member Barbara Wyatt took over the reins and is now the organization's president. The PMRC is now known as PMRC International because, as Wyatt says, "so many other countries are alarmed by what is coming in from the United States." The PMRC has consulted with groups in Malaysia, Russia, and Greece as well as with Muslim communities in other countries. Marching into battle with no paid staff (Wyatt is a volunteer), the PMRC has virtually no budget. When the PMRC phone rings, it rings directly into Mrs. Wyatt's home.

When we spoke, Mrs. Wyatt and I discussed the role the PMRC has played in our country's cultural history and how that affects her and the organization today.

"I received a few death threats when I first took over the organization, but all that negativity has gone away," said Mrs. Wyatt. "Mostly because the young people who were around in our beginning are now parents, and they have a whole different feeling about things now."

Wyatt—still confused by the negative attention and animosity expressed toward the PMRC's efforts—said that the group's mission has always been to educate and not to censor or endorse legislation or regulation. She said, "The majority of people have no idea what is in there [the music], and everything else— whether you are buying food or a crib—you know what it is made of and you have a return policy on it. However, with the music it is not so.

"And we feel very strongly that music is one of the most influential items that children listen to or are involved in. When you want to learn a language, you listen to it again and again. If you want to get something in your head, repetition is the way to do it. Music isn't the same as movies or television; music is listened to over and over. Whether it is 'Suicide Solution' or the garbage of Marilyn Manson, music is a powerful tool."

EN: I have trouble understanding how you qualify your claims. I just can't find evidence that supports your assertion that music influences children the way you say it does.

Wyatt: You never know what is going to push a child over the edge. Take, for instance, the parents of those two boys at Columbine—they had no idea. You don't know what is going on in that brain. So if you don't know what's going on and you are putting material in that *could* tilt them in the wrong direction, then you have a problem. If you were listening to *The Sound of Music,* you probably won't go over the edge; if you were listening to "Suicide Solution," you might. The brain recalls the most violent and explicit, so it is very strong in the brain. There was a study from Case Western, that showed that the more violent the person, the more violent the music.

EN: In that case, are you so sure that the music is the disease itself, or is it a symptom of something else?

Wyatt: Well, it's chickens and eggs. If we don't know what the situation is with the child, why chance it? I have never said that the music is the cause; I am saying that they are more vulnerable—so why chance it?

EN: When you are talking about "children at risk," what percentage of children are you talking about?

Wyatt: I don't know.

EN: Ten percent? Two percent?

Wyatt: I would have to make a guess. Having raised three sons, they were all fine, but I was very cautious about what they saw and heard. I had to be careful what I put in their brains.

EN: Regardless of the exact percentage, are you saying that "good kids" shouldn't have access to materials because a small percentage may be "at risk"?

Wyatt: Why risk it? You never know if the other children, maybe as young as age eight, will get a hold of a Walkman with this stuff in it, and no one would know.

When I asked Mrs. Wyatt if she felt that the PMRC/RIAA sticker, now in use longer than a decade, could be considered a success, she said it was. However, she added a big qualifier to that success: "The problem is, there is no consistency. Parents can't rely on it. We know more about what is in a jar of pickles than we know is in some of these albums. We need to have it standardized."

EN: Do you think that retailers like Wal-Mart are doing a good thing by not selling CDs and tapes with the warning sticker?

Wyatt: I applaud them. They are a family-oriented company, and I think they are doing the right thing.

EN: Do you think not selling these stickered or controversial albums is a good solution?

Wyatt: What I think they should do is take all these stickered and objectionable CDs, either because of lyrics or their covers, and put them in a separate area of the store that you have to be eighteen to enter. So that way, there is a protection.

EN: A lot of the critics of your efforts feel that if we rid all sex and violence from music now, soon we'll try to eliminate all political messages or other things we don't agree with.

Wyatt: I don't think that will happen—not if we have any sense, it won't. There are things that have been right and wrong since time began. But you can't find one plus in exposing children to this stuff. Some of this music tells people to rape, kill, necrophilia [*sic*], and all kinds of other stuff.

EN: By your estimates, how much of the music that gets stickered actually condones bizarre sex, murder, or rape?

Wyatt: I believe it is about 60 percent. That varies. If you went through the Top 40 this week, it may be 40 percent. Maybe next week it's 70 percent.

I was curious about how Wyatt and the PMRC felt about the Littleton, Colorado, incident. Quite a few people pointed out that the two perpetrators were fans of KMFDM and Marilyn Manson, and even that the boys quoted lyrics on their Web pages with threats of violence. Did the PMRC see a connection between the music and the violence committed at Columbine High School?
"I spoke with one of the teachers, and there was no doubt in her mind that the music played a very key role," said Wyatt. "We have

no definite [*sic*]—but killing is definitely something in those musical recordings—so who knows? It would be impossible to say for sure, because I don't know how much time they spent listening to music."

If the percentage of time spent listening was high, I asked if that would indicate a connection. She refused to speculate, but on several occasions cited the incident as evidence to support the need for further restriction of popular music.

We talked about the PMRC's future: Did the group intend to continue fighting against popular music the group finds offensive? Well, yes and no.

The PMRC has big plans. By partnering with a group called the National Center for the Preservation of Traditional American Family Values (TAFV), the PMRC will expand its efforts to include all aspects of the entertainment industry. "We have been getting calls about the Internet, video games, movies, television—you name it," said Wyatt. The partnership also will give the new organization a "broad base of support," allowing them to dip into other concerns, like family values issues and teaching patriotism. "There will always be a PMRC, just as part of the TAFV." According to Wyatt, "It is a nice little package."

The God Squad

I contacted two of the most infamous of the Christian crusaders against rock from the 1980s: Bob Larson (author of the book *Rock*) and the Peters brothers (authors of the PMRC-era *Why Knock Rock?*)

Dan and Steve Peters are still ministering to the masses about the evils of popular music. They travel often and sell a wide variety of pamphlets, books, cassettes, and videotapes. During our initial phone conversation, Steve Peters was very enthusiastic and receptive to the idea of an interview, assuring me that we could talk after he returned from two weeks of ministry in Hawaii. I called him once a week for three months, but he never returned my calls.

Bob Larson had moved away from the anti-rock component of his ministry (although audio- and videotapes of his sermons and lectures can still be purchased for $24.95 to $59.95). Mr. Larson's ministry now focuses on spiritual healing and freedom from demonic influence and possession. Larson can be seen and heard on his daily radio talk show (broadcast in a hundred U.S. cities and over the Internet), on two weekly syndicated television shows, and on his frequent lectures around the world (usual admission price is about $49, discounts apply for multiple members of the same family).

After I'd had several dialogues via telephone and e-mail with his staff, Larson agreed to talk to me about his feelings on popular music.

I asked Mr. Larson why he had changed the focus of his ministry so it had significantly less emphasis on rock music.

"It's a natural and evolving thing. I still have concerns in that area and address them from time to time, but I have an emphasis that resonates more with my radio and television audience. It's a little more about where they are and what they want me to talk about. The music scene is much different than it was when I was addressing those issues."

EN: You mean less heavy metal, right? Rap music is still pretty popular.

Larson: Yeah. Rap music is still popular, but you don't have that intense heavy metal subculture that you did some years ago.

EN: To what do you attribute that change? If this music was so overwhelmingly powerful in its appeal to and control over kids, then how come it fell from popularity?

Larson: I think a lot of it is an evolving of our culture. In some ways, it's mellowed out.

EN: Do you think there is still music out there for parents to be concerned about?

Larson: Sure. You can pick up a copy of the charts, and seven, eight, nine, or ten of the top albums would be by heavy metal bands that were misogynistic, immoral, and so on. Now you look at the top ten and you see Mariah Carey, Celine Dion, and Whitney Houston up there.

EN: Do you have any problems with those artists you just mentioned?

ner side of the coin is that the parent isn't around
ur hours a day. And so the culture does bear some
We all should be our brother's keeper. We have lost
ety.

on't want Bob Larson, or anyone else, being my
ildren's keeper?

t it this way: Not many people think what these
it; some of the producers and directors—big peo-
awful what the entertainment industry does with
es. These people should be shamed. We no longer
ocks in this society, but I think it's time we got
ss of shaming the directors, the producers, the
duce this stuff. They need to be held up to some
ontempt.

y main concerns with that line of thinking is
vrong person. In the Columbine situation, critics
finger at Marilyn Manson almost immediately. It
that Harris and Klebold weren't even Manson
were already lined up to "shame" Marilyn Man-
in their eagerness to see justice, the lynch mob
wrong guy.

of the other shootings, the killers were big Man-
ink you are right in what you say about this par-
ut that is the way culture is. It tends to
simplicity. Yeah, we could have lynched the
he should have been lynched a long time ago.
t to Columbine.

ent of Larson's ministry, in his antirock heyday
ic possession and influence. I asked Mr. Larson
hts on the influence of demons in our lives.
see indications in our society of extreme acts of
outrageousness for which there is no explana-
. "If you read below the surface, you find the
rk. The kid who shot kids in Mississippi admit-
t of a satanic cult and the demons entered into
se instances, people will describe being out of

Larson: No, if we are speaking in very broad terms. That element
of very hard-core, angry, rebellious, immoral cult following that
you found earlier isn't there. It's more fragmented than that now.

EN: It surprises me that you say that. In your book *Rock*, you
wrote about artists like Hall and Oates, Captain and Tennille,
and ABBA as examples of the immorality you felt plagued rock
and roll. I have trouble seeing how Mariah Carey or Celine Dion
is any different from those artists.

Larson: Well, except that Celine Dion is a happily married
woman, singing love ballads. Plus, let's face it, the boundaries of
culture have moved so far . . .

EN: In what direction?

Larson: In a bad direction. What it takes to shock or offend
today requires something so much more extreme. A lot of the
stuff today isn't so much the sex and drugs things, but, like,
gangsta rap for example. With its guns and violence. You can't be
quite as simplistic and categorical about it as you were ten years
ago. If you are going to express a moral concern about where
pop music is, it's kinda all over the place. Of course I have concerns. Do I like the fact that Lauryn Hill has the popularity she
has with her very sexually explicit lyrics, and her lifestyle? No.
But when you have Snoop Dogg and some of those guys, it's not
who's sleeping with who, it's who's shooting who. Now you've
got guys like Tupac and Biggie who are dead. It's who's putting a
bullet through who today.

As our conversation moved more toward music censorship and
freedom-of-speech issues, I asked Mr. Larson what he thought censorship was or wasn't.

"That's tough. At the fundamental core of decency, we have to
know what's right when we see it. Obviously, that is a highly subjective way to deal with matters. I think people know when something is too far out of line, that is where the force of public opinion
comes into play. I have always believed that censorship is a very
poor way to deal with these issues, because it doesn't really solve
the problem. Everything is market-based in our economy, and if
you don't have a buyer for the product, it won't sell. At the buyer

level, at the consumer level, is where the change needs to be made. The old-fashioned boycott, and speaking out. I find it so ironic when people like Bill Bennett come along, and they are just exercising old-fashioned free speech. If they are saying 'We don't think you should buy this,' what is wrong with that? I don't think that is censorship."

EN: Maybe not in the legal sense, but wouldn't you agree that if someone goes beyond protesting and not purchasing that material themselves and moves on to trying to force a retailer to stop carrying an album so that *no one* can purchase it—wouldn't you agree that those actions amount to censorship?

Larson: Again, I don't see that as censorship. I think that if the community believes that their children should not access a Tupac album, fine—let the parents put the pressure on the local retailer. Tell them, "We aren't going to shop here anymore, we are going to protest outside, because we don't want that album in our community."

EN: Well, what about those who don't mind their kids listening to Tupac or Snoop Dogg? What if they appreciate the artistic merit of these artists?

Larson: If anyone thinks anything Snoop Dogg has to say has "artistic merit," they are crazy. This is screwed-up people screwing up other people. I think we in this society have the right to say, "Look, if you want to live your life like an animal, go live your life like a animal. But don't tell my kids to live it like an animal. Don't infest them with attitudes that the answer is in the barrel of a gun. And I am going to do everything in my community to see that you don't do that."

After the spring 1999 shootings at Columbine High School in Littleton, Colorado, however, Larson felt called to examine music and violent media once again. He was offered a book contract to fast-track a volume on Satan's role in the tragedy. Larson mentioned the incident in his June 1999 newsletter to his followers, saying, "The answer is obvious, if we'll admit it. The two shooters were spiritually neglected youth whose desire for revenge opened

them up to demons. It was demon[...] Larson pointed out that on many [...] demons and exorcised them from h[...] was willing to take the heat to stop o[...]

I'm determined to stop it. First, I'l[...] Democrats and Republicans, aren't [...] ger of blame to shame those who ar[...] afraid to go on national radio and [...] those who took Bible reading and [...] schools have blood on their hands! [...] violence in films like *Matrix* and rec[...] music like Marilyn Manson are acco[...] should be thrown in jail. I'll also inte[...] the demons of murder that are lurking[...]

Larson asked his readers for the fifty[...] needed to fight similar demons that m[...] defenseless Christians. Donors didn't [...] rather if a thousand would each contrib[...] son's ministry stay afloat to fight Satan[...] there are no more Columbines. No m[...] reach them before it's too late," wrote [...]

I asked how he qualified linking the[...] music and media.

"It seems obvious to me," said Mr. [...] shot were Christians. The kids who sh[...] It's like—duh, excuse me, there is a m[...] got shot were not listening to Marilyn [...] The kids who shot them were."

EN: How do you propose protecting [...]

Larson: You tell parents, "You just d[...] concert—you know something abou[...] You don't just drop them off at a m[...] about what they are watching."

EN: Are you saying that this boil[...] supervision and responsibility?

control, or hearing voices. People who see them describe an evil look in their eyes."

EN: You don't think that was just a guilty person looking for an excuse or something to share blame?

Larson: If you trace how these people did what they did, you either have to say there is absolute utter insanity, or an unimaginable evil, or both. And I believe there is a deep level of evil in our society that is demonic in nature and that it is demons that finally push these people over the edge.

EN: Have you encountered someone faking demonic possession?

Larson: Well . . . yes I have. But not someone who I didn't know right away was faking. These are people who are severely emotionally disturbed and are hoping that "demons" will be an answer for them. They don't want to work on their problems, they just want a quick fix, and they act like they have a demon.

EN: Speaking of demons, I have noticed that you sell videos of exorcisms you've performed. And maybe I'm just cheap, but it seems like you are charging a lot of money for those tapes.

Larson: Not all of them.

EN: You sell a tape featuring two exorcisms for a hundred dollars. You don't think that is a lot?

Larson: We have other tapes available at workshops for fifteen dollars apiece.

EN: Yes, but if you pay forty-nine to get in the door . . .

Larson: The reason some videos have a higher price tag is they were so much more expensive to produce them. To amortize that and get our costs back—which were extraordinary—we had to put the price up that high. Plus you add the cost of television, radio, and traveling every weekend—our expenses are high. Plus the hotel or church auditorium we visit costs money to rent. We have expenses of sometimes five thousand to ten thousand dollars a night that has to be met. So there are a lot of factors in there that the average person doesn't think about.

Sam's Choice

Ever since an article detailing the music-merchandising policies of Wal-Mart stores appeared on the front page of the *New York Times* in 1996, the retailing giant has been considered a "demon" by many music fans. Regardless, the chain maintains its position as the world's largest music retailer, selling as many as one out of every ten CDs sold in the United States.

Despite the bad will and press on the issue, I was surprised when one of Wal-Mart's music buyers telephoned me within a week after receiving my interview request. The gentleman started off our talk with a request for anonymity. Nothing sneaky here, according to Mr. Wal-Mart Music Buyer: "One of the characteristics of Wal-Mart is we try to do everything as a team." Mr. Music Buyer didn't want his name used so that you, the reader, would understand that he was speaking on behalf of the company and not offering his own personal opinion. "We don't have anything to hide. We just want to sell a lot of stuff and do what our customers want us to do."

I began by asking for clarification on what Wal-Mart will and won't stock in its stores. According to Mr. Music Buyer, "We have a blanket policy that we won't buy stickered product. With non-stickered product, we buy only what we believe our customers would be interested in."

EN: What criteria do you use to make that decision?

Mr. Wal-Mart Music Buyer: Whatever we believe will sell. You see, in movies, there is a regulated national ratings system. Well, not really regulated, but everyone kinda understands how it works. As a company, we rely on the industry to accurately rate video product. If it's NC-17, we don't buy it. We don't make a judgment call; we rely on the industry. We make buying decisions based on the industry standard.

EN: Do you consider the RIAA universal warning sticker to be the equivalent to the movie ratings system?

Mr. Wal-Mart Music Buyer: (*pauses*) Yes. It is not as organized or as regulated—to be blunt, the music industry doesn't have its act together like the movie industry. Our policy is real simple: If it's stickered—we don't buy it; if it's not stickered, we purchase it based on its sales merit.

Mr. Music Buyer stressed that Wal-Mart is not involved with editing CD artwork or lyrics. Instead, he passed the buck to the music industry.

"We do not review edited product. We do not ask for edited product. We do not participate in the editing of product in any way. Let's say Joe Smith has a CD coming out. Typically, the label will try to solicit or sell us the CD ten to fourteen weeks out. They come in and say, 'Joe Smith has a stickered CD.' We say we are not interested in that. Then they say they are coming out with an edited version."

EN: The record company comes to you and tells you there is a choice.

Mr. Wal-Mart Music Buyer: Yes. Then we'll buy it—if we think it will sell. Then the product goes into the item-review process just like any other product. I don't listen to it, I don't try to make a determination if their editing was adequate. I rely on them to do it and do it right. Sometimes they don't.

EN: That is an awful lot of power and control. Do you realize the tremendous influence that has on the industry? Their largest customer, the largest retailer in your industry—in fact, the largest retailer in any category in the entire country—they aren't telling you what to do, but they *are* telling you what doesn't meet their criteria. Don't you think that comes with a proverbial "wink, wink"?

Mr. Wal-Mart Music Buyer: If you just want to back up for a moment, we have a saying around here, that the customer votes every day. We are the clear market leader in the music industry. Everything we do may not be perfect, but the customer seems to like it.

Our conversation turned to albums that Wal-Mart had agreed to sell but then pulled for various reasons, such as Prodigy's *The Fat of the Land*. Mr. Music Buyer explained some of Wal-Mart's retail policies: "We authorize every store manager in every store with ability and the right to alter his merchandise mix to fit his customer base. So if we buy a piece of edited music, or we buy something unedited, and a store manager has a number of customer complaints, that manager has the autonomy to pull that merchandise from the floor and not sell it anymore. Because his job is to have the merchandise mix in his store that services his customer base. What happened with Prodigy was a groundswell among stores, starting in Los Angeles, that because of implied abuse of women, we were getting customer complaints. So we pulled the item. The decision to pull that CD went to the highest level of management here at Wal-Mart.

Bizzy Bone's *Heaven'z Movie* was removed from the shelves of many Wal-Mart stores following customer complaints that the rapper was advocating violence in schools. Store officials pulled the album even though they knew that the allegations were not true.

"There was another album that we pulled because of customer sensitivity: Bizzy Bone. The album cut in question was quite . . . busy, if you'll excuse the pun. It was difficult to understand. It was about the whole 'children shooting each other at school' thing going on. If you really listen to the lyric, the song was *condemning* the whole 'kids shooting kids' thing. If you listen to it once, and you have the right attitude, it sounds like he was promoting it. Some of our stores went nuts; they wanted to pull the product and did. In reality, the piece of music had nothing to do with promoting violence, but it was perceived as promoting violence."

EN: And the corporation has no input on that, even when it is something that obviously isn't true—simply a perception problem?

Mr. Wal-Mart Music Buyer: Well, marketing is perception. When I am called by stores about these issues, I say, "It is your store, and you have to judge your customer base. If you think the perception is so strong, be it factual or not, it would be better for you to pull this one item."

EN: Let's say a bunch of people—PETA members—decide they are going to protest that Wal-Mart sells leather. They demonstrate against your selling leather jackets, wallets, or shoes—perhaps even a record album that features a band dressed in leather. Their protests get all kinds of press, and the store manager calls headquarters and says they're going to pull all the leather from the store, which means no one gets anything made of leather—what would the corporation do?

Mr. Wal-Mart Music Buyer: That's a real good question. I don't know.

EN: Can you imagine that same thing happening with music? If Bizzy Bone is pulled because of a small percentage of customers complaining—now no one can have access to that record from Wal-Mart.

Mr. Wal-Mart Music Buyer: I am not saying it's right or wrong, I am just telling you what we do. At one point our company decided not to carry controversial music, and it was the single most positive marketing thing we have ever done in home entertainment. We get customer letters and comments that say they are glad we don't sell stickered stuff. Compared to the people who are upset we don't sell it, it is a hundred to one.

EN: When you purchase edited music, do you feel the need or responsibility to sticker that as well? To make sure people know they are buying an altered product?

Mr. Wal-Mart Music Buyer: Our policy is that if the *content* of the CD—the music—is edited, it should be indicated on the product-identification code with the word "edited." We have moved away from using the word "clean" because it is too subjective. We are rolling out a sticker that will say the word "Edited" on it, and across the top it will say who edits it and warn that it may still not be suitable.

Cover art is another kind of thing. We don't ask about it, we don't participate in it. What happens is the label usually perceives that we won't like it, and they come up with two versions. One for record stores and one for retailers like Kmart and Wal-Mart. A lot of times they do it and we don't even know they are doing it. We do not encourage them to do it.

EN: But they could sell hundreds of thousands of copies if they do it, right? You won't sell it otherwise.

Mr. Wal-Mart Music Buyer: I don't even look at the covers. You have to look at this like bar soap. You are the bar-soap buyer at Wal-Mart. Do you take all the bar soap home and use it? No, you can't—there are hundreds. Do you review all the packages? No. You buy it based on who is bringing it to you, what is their past history of success, how much money are they willing to invest in marketing, what is the customer interest in this kind of bar soap, and what you think the potential is. Bar soap is not music, but they both are products.

I asked Mr. Music Buyer about the decision to not sell Sheryl Crow's second album because it contained a negative reference to Wal-Mart's gun-sales policy. The chain had sold more than half a million copies of Crow's debut album. Mr. Music Buyer said that the decision was an example of how the chain will go beyond its stated business practices when provoked. "That decision came from the absolute highest officer in this company. We believe that the most valuable thing we have is our name. Frankly, we just got upset. That was a time when child violence was at a peak, and she took our name and used it in a bad way, and the decision was made to pull the album. That wasn't an editing decision; that was a 'we don't like what you did' decision. It was an emotional response. Would that same decision be made today? I don't know. That was an interesting moment in Wal-Mart's life."

EN: I can see that your market position is a source of pride for Wal-Mart. If you started to lose that market share if people didn't want to patronize a retailer that refused to sell stickered or controversial titles, would you reexamine your policy?

Mr. Wal-Mart Music Buyer: Sure. Would there be a different decision made? I don't know. The decision not to carry stickered product is "beyond business."

I asked him to explain what "beyond business" meant. He felt it was a moral distinction. "It's like the magazines that featured explicit photos of Princess Diana's death—we pulled those from our shelves. The amount of money we lost because of that was unbelievable, because we didn't have that product. That, too, was a 'beyond business' decision."

EN: Now, wait a minute. Just a few minutes ago you were trying to get my thinking away from those kinds of thoughts, comparing the morals and ethics of music to soap, leather, and other things.

Mr. Wal-Mart Music Buyer: You're right, you are absolutely right. But there are times when we step outside the box, because we are a bunch of people here trying to run a business to the best of our ability. With Sheryl Crow, and those magazines, we made a decision to step outside of the box.

Corporate Policy

Following is the Wal-Mart "Statement on Stocking Entertainment Merchandise":

Wal-Mart stores has worked hard to create and protect its unique identity. That identity, one of low-price, quality merchandise; fast and friendly service; and community involvement has helped make Wal-Mart the most successful retailer in history.

To sustain our "family-friendly" identity Wal-Mart attempts to exclude from its shelves merchandise that is sexually explicit and extremely violent. This is accomplished, in large part, by following the ratings systems of the entertainment industries. Wal-Mart does not stock X-rated movies, music with parental guidance stickers, or "adults-only" video games or magazines. Occasionally Wal-Mart may refuse to stock additional merchandise that may not seem appropriate; this is done by 1) understanding our customers, 2) requiring our suppliers and distributors to control the types of merchandise delivered to Wal-Mart, and 3) empowering merchandise buyers and store managers to make common sense decisions and enforce our policies.

While Wal-Mart sets high standards, it would not be possible to eliminate every image, word, or topic that an individual might find objectionable. Our goal is not to eliminate the need for parents to review merchandise that their children purchase.

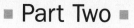

Part Two

THE

CHRONOLOGY

OF MUSIC

CENSORSHIP

IN THE

UNITED STATES

13

BEFORE THE 1950s

■

1865

Following the Civil War, Southerners are forbidden from publicly singing pro-Confederate songs. Songs like "I'm a Good Ol' Rebel" (with its open and violent disdain for the Northern way of life) and "Bonnie Blue Flag" (chronicling the cessation of the Southern states at the beginning of the war) are thought by Northern occupation forces to foster anti-Reconstructionist sentiment, which could give rise to Southern rebellion.

1928

Protesters call for a ban on Duke Ellington's song "The Mooche" because they fear the song will inspire rape. The lyrics are considered so provocative that critics blame the song for an increase in the nation's incidents of rape.

1931

Variety refuses to include certain objectionable songs in its chart lists. The magazine's editors worry about the racy titles of several hit songs, and they choose to exclude them from their record charts. Deleted singles include blues classics "Hoochie Coochie Man" and "I'm Gonna Shave You Close," as well as songs by country legends Gene Autry and Jimmy Rodgers.

1940

NBC Radio bans a list of 147 songs from all affiliate stations. Although no stated policy or criterion is established to justify the ban, the network calls the records obscene and believes that they should not receive airplay. The banned record list includes songs by Billie Holiday, Cole Porter, and Duke Ellington.

Songwriter Cole Porter. Several of his compositions were banned during his career.

1944

A songbook by composer Eric Posselt is banned by the military. Officials fear that the songs contained in *Give Out: Songs of, for, and by the Men in the Service* will undermine morale and distract servicemen from their duties.

Record-company executives change the title of the song "Rum and Coca-Cola" to "Lime and Coca-Cola" because they want to secure radio play.

1948

In February, police in Memphis seize records from local retailers and smash those that they find obscene. The seizures are part of a "get tough" campaign against pornography.

Police in Memphis seized and destroyed "obscene" music in 1948.

14

1950s

1951
Several radio stations ban hits by Dottie O'Brien ("Four or Five Times") and Dean Martin ("Wham, Bam, Thank You Ma'am"), fearing they are too suggestive.

1952
The Weavers are blacklisted during the anti-Communist McCarthy Era due to the leftist political beliefs and associations of several members. The action results in the virtual disappearance of the folk group from radio, television, and live performances for the next six years. The group also loses its recording contract as a result of the controversy. Sev-

Folksinger Pete Seeger, leader of the Weavers. The Weavers were blacklisted during the McCarthy Era; the stigma eventually caused the group to disband and followed Seeger through his solo career.

eral of the songs reemerge during the early sixties as hits for other groups.

1953

Lyrics in the song "These Foolish Things" are changed by the publisher because of concerns that the original words are too sexually suggestive. The phrase "gardenia perfume lingering on a pillow" is altered to "a seaplane rising from an ocean billow."

Six counties in South Carolina pass legislation outlawing jukebox operation during certain hours. The laws prohibit the playing of popular music in jukeboxes anytime on Sunday or anytime within hearing distance of a church.

1954

Before playing Stephen Foster songs on the air, radio networks insist on changing the lyrics. Lyrics are edited to remove words such as "massa" and "darky" from the American songwriter's repertoire.

Despite its status as the number-one country and western record in the country, numerous radio stations ban play of Webb Pierce's "There Stands the Glass" because the lyrics offer no moral against drinking. Concern over the song's theme prompts several artists to record "answer" songs with a more appropriate ending.

In February, Representative Ruth Thompson introduces into Congress legislation that is meant to ban the mailing of certain records through the U.S. mail. Thompson wants certain rock records to be added to the list of "pornographic" materials that are illegal to send through the postal service. The Senate Juvenile Delinquency Subcommittee issues a report on the supposed

Representative Ruth Thompson, the earliest proponent of federal regulation of rock music

link between pop music and youth crime. In response to the committee's investigation of music, the senators receive more than twenty thousand unsolicited letters blaming the media, comic books, and music for the apparent rise in crime.

A group of deejays form a "club" to combat the airing of R&B records that "hold the Negro up to ridicule." They plan to enlist as many deejays around the country as possible, set up review committees for new songs, and make suggestions about each record's worthiness. Once the group begins reviews, they also decide to ferret out any songs that contain suggestive sexual references or lingo.

The Boston Catholic Youth Organization begins a campaign against "obscene" records, policing dances and lobbying disc jockeys to stop playing these songs at record hops and on the radio. The group is convinced that the sexual themes they see in R&B music are inappropriate for Catholic youth.

A drug reference convinces ABC to change a line in Cole Porter's classic "I Get a Kick Out of You." Although the song's original lyric, "I get no kick from cocaine," could be construed as an anti-drug reference, ABC still decides to air a version that contains the substitute "I get perfume from Spain." ABC also participates in edits of other Cole classics, such as "All of You" and "My Heart Belongs to Daddy."

An editorial rallying against some rhythm and blues records sparks removal of these songs from jukeboxes. The editorial, "Control the Dimwits," which appears in the September 24 issue of *Billboard*, condemns R&B songs that contain double entendre references to sex. In response, police in Long Beach, California, and Memphis, Tennessee, confiscate jukeboxes and fine their owners. Two national organizations (the Songwriter's Protective Association and the Music Publishers' Protective Association) pass resolutions that endorse the censure of these songs, saying they "show bad taste and a disregard for recognized moral standards." Albert Denver, president of a company that operates more than ten thousand jukeboxes in the New York area, says the company will remove all records that appear on any list of objectionable songs that *Billboard* provides. Several other jukebox vendors and radio deejays suggest establishing screening committees to review records.

In October, WDIA and several other large popular-music radio stations ban several songs for their sexually suggestive lyrics. Those banned include "Honey Love" by the Drifters, along with "Work with Me, Annie" and "Annie Had a Baby" by Hank Ballard and the Midnighters. "Work with Me, Annie" is eventually rewritten into a less offensive hit for Georgia Gibbs, "Dance with Me, Henry." The station periodically runs an on-air announcement saying, "WDIA, your goodwill station, in the interest of good citizenship, for the protection of morals and our American way of life, does not consider this record, [name of song], fit for broadcast on WDIA. We are sure all you listeners will agree with us."[1]

The ABC network bans the Rosemary Clooney hit "Mambo Italiano," saying it does not meet the network's "standards for good taste." The ban becomes official policy after ABC deejay Martin Block refuses to play the record during his show, claiming that the record is obscene and offensive.

The New Jersey division of Alcohol Beverage Control and Order orders two taverns to remove some questionable singles from their jukeboxes. The state agency wants the operators to remove the songs "Hawaiian Tale" and "Joe's Joint," indicating that they may lose their liquor licenses if they do not comply. The agency also warns retaliation if the taverns place any similar records in their machines.

In December, record dealer John Day sends a letter to record stores and radio stations calling for them to "unite and voluntarily take steps to clean out the filth." Day claims that R&B records "are being listened to and purchased by impressionable teenagers almost exclusively."[2]

1955
Former radio deejay Pat Boone begins a career by releasing "sanitized" versions of black R&B hits. Boone's versions of these songs often contain toned-down lyrics, such as substituting "drinkin' Coca-Cola" for "drinkin' wine" in T-Bone Walker's "Stormy Monday" and "Pretty little Susie is the girl for me" instead of "Boys, don't you know what she do to me" in Little Richard's

"Tutti Fruitti." Boone records sixty hit cover singles during his career; six of those reach number one.

In the first congressional hearings on rock music, a committee explores the current rise in juvenile delinquency. Some interest groups suggest that teen crime results from listening to rock and roll music.

Broadcast Music, Inc. (BMI), refuses to grant clearance to more than a hundred songs the company considers objectionable, saying, "You don't have to be dirty to be successful." The action makes it impossible for the song's creators to gain royalties from performance.

In one week's time during April, Chicago radio stations receive fifteen thousand complaint letters protesting their broadcast of rock music. The organized letter-writing campaign—most letters penned by young listeners—arises in response to the increasing popularity of "dirty" music on radio playlists. The campaign begins when a black newspaper, *The Courier,* asks readers to write to disc jockeys. The effort quickly spreads to other groups in the area, who join in the letter-writing campaign.

Also in April, a radio station in Mobile, Alabama, vows to eliminate all rhythm and blues music from the station. In an editorial titled "About the Music You Won't Hear on WABB," station managers promise to censor all controversial music played on the station for the good of the community. The list of banned R&B songs consists entirely of recordings by black artists.

Variety runs a three-part series on what it terms "leer-ics," or R&B songs with obscene lyrics, calling for censorship of the recording industry. The articles compare these songs to dirty postcards and chastises the music industry for selling "their leer-ic garbage by declaring that's what kids want." The stories are widely redistributed throughout the country by wire services. They warn that the recording industry should police itself before others take the initiative to set up regulatory measures.

The Juvenile Delinquency and Crime Commission of Houston, Texas, bans more than thirty songs it considers to be obscene and, therefore, unfit for the ears of Houston's children. The commission's list—including such classics as "Honey Love" by the Drifters, "I Got a Woman" by Ray Charles, "Sixty Minute Man" by the Dominoes, and the 5 Royales' "Too Much Lovin' "—is comprised almost entirely of black artists. All nine Houston radio stations are monitored by an associated review committee.

Fearing outbursts of violence, officials cancel rock and roll concerts scheduled in New Haven and Bridgeport, Connecticut; Boston; Atlanta; Jersey City and Asbury Park, New Jersey; Burbank, California; and Portsmouth, New Hampshire. Observers mistake dancing at concerts for riots and fighting, lending credence to rumors that rock music causes youngsters to break out in spontaneous violence. When news of the bans is covered by the media, an unidentified sociologist is quoted as saying that rock dancing is "caused by the same virus which induces panty raids and goldfish swallowing."[3]

CBS television network cancels Alan Freed's *Rock 'n' Roll Dance Party* after a camera shows Frankie Lymon (leader of the doo-wop

group Frankie Lymon & the Teenagers) dancing with a white girl. Public outrage over interracial coupling inspired by R&B music proves to be too much for network censors.

Deejay and TV personality Alan Freed, on the set of his program *Rock 'n' Roll Dance Party*. The show was canceled permanently for showing interracial dancing.

Florida police force Elvis Presley to stand still while performing, warning him that if he moves at all, he will be arrested on obscenity charges. Officials in San Diego issue a similar warning to Presley following a concert in 1956, saying he will not be allowed to perform in the city again unless he removes all dancing and gestures from his performance.

Radio station KMA in Shenandoah, Iowa, creates its own screening committee to ban records considered "obscene." The campaign, called "The Crusade for Better Disks" removes many songs from the station's playlist, including "Dim, Dim the

Lights" and "Rock and Roll, Baby." A similar review board is established in Boston by six local radio stations and several print journalists.

Responding to radio stations that are removing R&B (read: black) music from their airwaves, R&B singer Jimmy Witherspoon says, "The blacks was starting a thing in America for equality. The radio stations and the people in the South was fighting us." Witherspoon also believes that local radio stations are deliberately hiring program directors who are willing to dissect black music from the airwaves.

1956

ABC Radio Network bans Billie Holiday's "Love for Sale" from all of its stations because of its prostitution theme. While the Holiday version is banned, many stations continue to play instrumental versions of this Cole Porter classic.

An April issue of *Variety* declares that rock music should be banned for causing "a staggering wave of juvenile violence and mayhem." The article quotes a spokesperson for the Pennsylvania Chiefs of Police Association, who speculates that rock music provides "an incentive to teenage unrest."[4]

Also in April, members of the White Citizens Council of Birmingham, Alabama, rush the stage at a Nat King Cole concert and beat the legendary performer. Seeing the reaction of Birmingham's young teen girls to Nat's crooning, the community-minded council members confuse Cole's music with newly popular R&B. They decide to show him just how much they dislike his performances in Alabama. A spokesperson for the group says that the "basic, heavy-beat music of the Negroes [represents] a plot to mongrelize America [by bringing out the] base in man . . . animalism and vulgarity."[5] A similar group, the Citizens' Council of Greater New Orleans, distributes a flier describing how popular music erodes the morals of "white youth."

The Parks Department in San Antonio, Texas, removes all rock and roll records from jukeboxes located at city swimming pools, terming it "jumpy, hot stuff" that is unsuitable for teens. According to one department assistant, "The music attracted a lot of undesirable people who loitered around the pools with no intention of going in swimming."[6]

Cautious network officials ban the novelty hit "Transfusion" by Dot and Diamond from ABC, CBS, and NBC radios in June. According to one NBC executive, "There is nothing funny about a blood transfusion."

1957

Producers of *The Ed Sullivan Show* instruct cameramen to show Elvis Presley only from the waist up on his third and final appear-

ance on the program on Janurary 6. Producers fear the wrath of parents across the country who are concerned about the influence Presley's lewd dancing style has on the nation's youngsters. After Presley performs "Don't Be Cruel," Sullivan addresses the audience: "I want to say to Elvis Presley and the country, this is a real decent, fine boy." The *New York Times* begs to differ, calling the performance "filthy." Eighty percent of the nation's television audience tunes in for Elvis's appearance.

Elvis Presley onstage for *The Ed Sullivan Show* in 1957

Asa Carter, executive president of the North Alabama White Citizens Council, calls for the removal and destruction of jukeboxes. Carter reasons that the National Association for the Advancement of Colored People has brainwashed white teenagers with "vulgar music." If left unchecked, Carter believes, black music will mesmerize large numbers of white youth and destroy civilization.

In March, fearing the effects of the "hedonistic, tribal rhythms" of rock and roll music, Chicago's Cardinal Stritch bans popular music from all Catholic-run schools. Stritch later calls a press conference to educate parents about the negative effects of rock music on their children.

As Elvis Presley's popularity surges, several radio stations across the country pull his records, claiming they are obscene. A Nashville deejay known as Great Scott burns six hundred Elvis records in a city park; WSPT in Minneapolis vows never to air any of Presley's records; and Los Angeles station KMPC refuses to play Elvis's *Christmas Album*, saying it is tantamount to "having Tempest Storm give Christmas gifts to my kids."

Chicago's Cardinal Stritch campaigned against the "hedonistic, tribal rhythms" of rock and roll music.

Congress debates the first national legislation aimed at censoring popular music lyrics. Concerned about teen violence and crime (allegedly caused by exposure to rock and R&B music), Congress considers legislation that requires song lyrics to be screened and altered by a review committee before being broadcast or offered for sale.

1958

The Mutual Broadcasting System drops all rock and roll records from its network music programs, calling it "distorted, monotonous, noisy music." To coincide with the ban, the network changes the title of its twenty-one hours of music programming from "Top 50" to "Pop 50." Songs removed from play included "Splish Splash" by Bobby Darin and Elvis Presley's "Hard Headed Woman."

Catholic youth in Minneapolis begin a campaign against records that promote such immoral acts as "going steady." The group offers radio stations rewritten lyrics to songs such as "Secretly" and "Wear My Ring Around Your Neck," and they issue lists of "wholesome" records that are approved for teen purchase.

When Bo Diddley is booked for a national television appearance, his contract stipulates he cannot move his body while performing. During the program, Diddley forgets to stand still and loses his entire performance fee.

Riding a wave of antirock sentiment in the country, radio stations across the United States remove all rock music from their playlists and run announcements that denounce rock and R&B. Deejays at WISN in Milwaukee stop playing rock music and burn two hundred rock records in their parking lot. San Francisco's KSFR runs an on-air campaign called "I Kicked the Junk Music Habit by Listening to KSFR."

The Senate Committee on Interstate and Foreign Commerce holds hearings on a supposed link between popular music and juvenile delinquency. Though the stated intention of the hearings is to discuss the seriousness of juvenile crime, they are really the result of a fight between the two major music-publishing organizations: the American Society of Composers, Authors and Publishers (ASCAP) and Broadcast Music, Inc. (BMI). BMI had helped popularize R&B and country music, which threatened ASCAP's dominance in the radio industry. During the hearings, Vance Packard, author of the book *Hidden Persuaders,* claims that rock and roll "stirred the animal instinct in modern teenagers" with its "raw savage tone."[7]

1959

Link Wray's instrumental classic, "Rumble," is dropped from radio stations across the country in January—even though it has no lyrics. The title of the song is thought to be suggestive of teenage violence. Censors worry that promoting it could incite violence among otherwise passive teens. When Wray appears on the hit television program *American Bandstand* to perform the song, Dick Clark introduces Wray and his band but refuses to mention the song's title.

Wanting to secure an appearance on *American Bandstand*, singer Lloyd Price agrees to recut the lyrics to his song "Stagger Lee," removing all references to violence. ABC, the network that produces *American Bandstand*, also owns Price's record label.

15

1960s

■

1960

Several radio stations refuse to play Ray Peterson's "Tell Laura I Love Her," calling it "The Death Disk." The song's lyrics detail the injury and death of a stock car driver, considered too graphic for young listeners. The song goes on to be Peterson's biggest hit.

1962

New York Bishop Burke forbids Catholic school students to dance to "The Twist." Burke considers R&B music, and its associated dances, to be lewd and un-Christian.

The Radio Trade Practices Committee recommends that the National Association of Broadcasters review song lyrics before they are broadcast. The committee fears that individual broadcasters will not screen songs for references to sex and violence.

1963

The FBI begins collecting data on folksinger Phil Ochs, alleging that he is a subversive Communist sympathizer who may be a danger to the life of the president. Ochs's "un-American" songs detail the plight of workers and the underclass and strongly criticize the war in Vietnam. The Bureau's file on Ochs eventually grows to more than four hundred pages of information obtained from print articles, credit bureaus, police records, other local and federal agencies, and from interviews with friends and neighbors. FBI Director J. Edgar Hoover says that Ochs's past conduct and statements show a "propensity towards violence and antipathy toward good order and government." The Bureau continues to compile information on Ochs, keeping him on its Security Index until his death in 1976.

Bob Dylan refuses to perform on *The Ed Sullivan Show* in February after producers tell him he cannot sing "Talkin' John Birch Paranoid Blues." CBS's Standards and Practices Department informs the folk singer he is welcome to perform on the program, but he must select more suitable material for their national audience. As a result, Dylan never appears on the popular variety show.

1964

Indiana Governor Matthew Welsh proclaims in Feburary that the Kingsmen hit "Louie, Louie" is pornographic and calls for the song's banishment. After review by the FCC, the agency determines that the song's lyrics are indecipherable and of no danger to impressionable listeners.

1965

After splitting his pants while dancing wildly at a European concert, the boisterous P. J. Proby is uninvited to perform on ABC's music variety show *Shindig*.

Cleveland Mayor Ralph Locher bans all rock concerts in the city following a Rolling Stones performance. Locher says "such groups do not add to the community's culture or entertainment."[1]

The Barry McGuire song "Eve of Destruction" is pulled from retail stores and radio stations across the country after some groups complain that it is nihilistic and could promote suicidal feelings among teens. A study on perceptions of the song reveals that only 36 percent of teens who know the record understand the lyrical themes.

The Curtis Knight & the Squires (featuring Jimi Hendrix) single "How Would You Feel" is given little airplay on radio because the song deals with the plight of blacks and the injustices they have experienced in America.

In June, radio stations across the country ban the Rolling Stones hit "(I Can't Get No) Satisfaction" because they believe that the lyrics are too sexually suggestive.

Many radio stations ban the Who's single "Pictures of Lily" because the song contains a reference to masturbation.

MGM Records alters the Frank Zappa song "Money" because it contains a sexual reference. Executives order engineers to delete the word "balling" from the lyric "I'm not going to do any publicity balling for you." During the same year, some retailers refuse to carry Zappa's album *Cruising with Ruben & the Jets* because they fear customer complaints over the album's themes. Zappa also is fired from the Whisky a Go Go in Los Angeles for saying the word "fuck" on stage.

1966

WLS radio commissions a local group, the Shadows of Knight, to rerecord the Them hit "Gloria" because they object to the lyrics. Station management feels that the lyric "she comes in my room" is too suggestive for broadcast. Substituted for the objectionable phrase is "she calls out my name." The Shadows of Knight version becomes a national top-ten hit; the original stalls at number seventy-one on the charts.

A statement by John Lennon in March, comparing the popularity of the Beatles to that of Jesus Christ, results in widespread Beatles record burnings and protests. Lennon's comments regarding what he perceives as a decrease in Christianity's popularity with teens are taken out of context. He says, "We're more popular than Jesus now." The Reverend Thurman H. Babbs, pastor at the New Haven

Georgia radio station WAYX sponsored a burning of Beatles records, books, and wigs in the summer of 1966 to protest John Lennon's comments concerning the popularity of Jesus with contemporary teens.

Baptist Church in Cleveland, Ohio, vows to excommunicate any church member who listens to Beatles records or attends a Beatles concert. That summer, numerous record burnings are held to protest Lennon's comments. The Ku Klux Klan nails Beatles albums to burning crosses in South Carolina. Legislators in Pennsylvania propose a bill to prohibit the Beatles from ever appearing in the state again. Most protests are organized by religious organizations that use Lennon's comments to illustrate the evils of rock music. One radio station, WAYX in Waycross, Georgia, stages a burning of Beatles records, books, and wigs. The station carries the event live on the radio and vows never to air Beatles songs again.

After radio stations refuse to air the original, the Swinging Medallions are convinced by their record company to rerecord their song "Double Shot (of My Baby's Love)" with more benign lyrics. The original recording contained lyrics that referred to alcohol and illicit sex. The new version substitutes the phrase "the worst *hangover* I ever had" with "the worst *morning* I ever had," the phrase "She *loved* me so long and she *loved* me so hard" with "she *kissed* me so long and she *kissed* me so hard" (emphasis added). The song—with its new lyrics—becomes a top-ten hit. Most collections available today carry the original recording.

In June, Capitol Records recalls all copies of the Beatles' *Yesterday and Today* album following complaints over the album's gory cover art. The "butcher" cover depicts the four Beatles wearing white smocks and surrounded by decapitated baby dolls and raw meat. The Beatles planned the cover as a protest of Capitol's practice of dropping one or two songs from the American release of every British Beatles album, allowing Capitol to create an extra

Beatles album (and gain the associated profits) every few years from the "butchered" tracks. In a cost-saving measure following the album's recall, Capitol simply glues a more acceptable group photo over the top of the controversial butcher cover. Today, well-preserved copies of the original are the most valuable album cover in music history.

Police attempt to shut down a James Brown concert, alleging that the singer's dancing is obscene. During the concert, police intervene after Brown encourages young ladies to come onstage and remove his jacket. During the altercations that follow, concertgoers throw rocks at police, one woman is stabbed, and twenty people are arrested.

The *Gavin Report,* a radio-industry trade publication, routinely identifies songs that it believes condone or promote drug use. One such song, the Byrds' "Eight Miles High," is pulled from several stations after being targeted by Gavin. According to bandleader Jim (Roger) McGuinn, the song actually is about an airplane ride.

After enduring calls for censorship over the song "Rhapsody in the Rain," Lou Christie agrees to change the song's suggestive lyrics. Several portions of the song's lyrics are changed, including "On our first date, we were makin' out in the rain" to "On our first date, we fell in love in the rain," and "In this car, our love went way too far" to "In this car, love came like a falling star." The altered song is heard only on the radio while the original is included on most collections that feature the song.

Atlantic records forces the Who to rerecord a lyric for single "Substitute" before it can be released in America. The phrase "I look all white but my Dad was black" is changed to "I try walking forward, but my feet look back."

1967
The Rolling Stones agree to alter the lyrics to "Let's Spend the Night Together" for an appearance on *The Ed Sullivan Show.* Producers request that singer Mick Jagger alter the title phrase to "Let's spend some *time* together." Following the live performance, Jagger insists he sang the original words; however, the phrase was incomprehensibly mumbled. The song also causes concern among

radio programmers. Several radio stations refuse to play the song despite its high position on the charts.

Against his wishes, Frank Zappa's record company removes eight bars of his single "Let's Make the Water Turn Black." This occurs

when a well-intentioned executive from Verve Records hears the lyric "And I still remember Mama with her apron and her pad, feeding all the boys at Ed's Café." The executive thinks the referred-to "pad" is a sanitary napkin.

Radio programmers pass on Van Morrison's "Brown Eyed Girl" because the lyrics refer to premarital sex and teenage pregnancy. Morrison cuts an alternative version overdubbing the lyric "Laughin' and a runnin' " over top of "Making love in the green grass." The censored version appears on Morrison's *Blowin' Your Mind* and becomes his biggest American hit. The original and censored versions are both found on anthologies available today.

Frank Zappa. Record executives edited his 1967 song "Let's Make the Water Turn Black" because they thought it contained a reference to sanitary napkins.

Producers of *The Ed Sullivan Show* request that Jim Morrison change the lyrics to "Light My Fire" for the band's September appearance on the program. Morrison initially agrees to alter the lyric "Girl we couldn't get much higher" to a more innocuous phrase. During the live performance, Morrison sings the original lyric—with added emphasis—directly to the camera.

Janis Ian's song "Society's Child" is banned from radio stations across the country. The song, detailing an interracial relationship, features themes condemning racism and bigotry.

In an effort to discourage the distribution of songs containing controversial subject matter, Georgia state representative Edwin Mullinax introduces legislation aimed at requiring record labels to carry full information about the song's owner and publisher. The Country Music Association endorses Mullinax's efforts, saying youngsters are "subjected to a constant barrage of recorded music

with lyrics dealing in sex, liquor, narcotics, and profane and disre-
spectful language."[2]

Believing that rock music is responsible for the riots in the Watts
area of Los Angeles, and fearing that the music will only entice
"ethnics" to commit more violence, a jukebox vendor refuses to
stock "inflammatory" titles. David Solish feels that all jukebox
owners should join with those already trying to censor this music
in order to put independent record companies (whom he feels are
responsible for most of the trouble) out of business.

Release of the Velvet Underground's debut album *The Velvet
Underground & Nico,* is delayed nine months over concerns about
the album's themes. Verve Records fears that drug and sexual references in the album's lyrics will make big trouble for the label.

Gordon McLendon, owner of thirteen radio stations in the United
States, starts a campaign against "obscene" songs that glorify sex,
blasphemy, and drugs. McLendon believes that British artists are
responsible for a vast majority of the offending songs, and he suggests a "Wax Party" (similar to the Boston Tea Party) at which
concerned community members can dump records by British
artists. The American Mothers' Committee endorses McLendon's
campaign and rallies more than a hundred radio stations, including ABC, and corporations to join. Participating stations remove
rock songs from their playlists and petition the FCC and major
record companies.

Moby Grape's self-titled debut LP features a photograph of the
group's drummer gesturing with his middle finger. Despite the
band's objections, Columbia Records soon rereleases the record
with the offending finger airbrushed out.

1968
An El Paso, Texas, radio station bans all songs performed by Bob
Dylan because they cannot understand the folk singer's lyrics.
Unable to decipher song lyrics or themes, management worries
that the songs may contain subversive messages. They choose to
completely avoid the songs. The station continues to play recordings of Dylan songs performed by other artists with clearer diction.

Bob Dylan

The Doors' singer, Jim Morrison

The Doors' single "Unknown Soldier" is banned from airplay at many radio stations because of its anti-war theme.

The original cover of the Rolling Stones album *Beggars Banquet* is sanitized to remove a photograph of a bathroom wall covered with graffiti. The altered version, which looks like a formal invitation to a banquet, remains until the album is reissued on CD.

Steppenwolf's "The Pusher" is banned by radio stations for a perceived "pro-drug" message. In fact, the song laments the presence of the drug pusher. In North Carolina, local officials order the band not to sing the controversial lyrics in concert. The band circumvents the order by asking the audience to sing the song.

Sponsors go into an uproar and threaten to pull support after a television program shows interracial "touching." During the taping of a duet between Petula Clark and Harry Belafonte, Clark lays her hand on Belafonte's arm (Clark is white and Belafonte is black).

Jim Morrison is arrested onstage in New Haven, Connecticut, for making lewd gestures and profane remarks during a concert. The arrest is one of several that occur during Doors concerts after Morrison is marked by the FBI and several police organizations as a troublemaker. The mayor of Philadelphia uses a city ordinance from 1879 giving him the right to cancel any performance that may be "immoral in nature or unpleasant and harmful to the community."[3] Las Vegas police bring blank arrest warrants to a Doors performance, empowered to fill them out on the spot if the band does anything that the officers don't like.

Fearing that the Rolling Stones song "Street Fightin' Man" will incite violence during the National Democratic Convention in September, Chicago radio stations refuse to play the song. Nevertheless, violence erupts during the convention, although it is more directly linked to the Vietnam War than to any rock song. During the ban, the single sets all-time sales records in the Chicago area. Following the controversy, several radical political groups adopt the song as an anthem for anarchy.

Mayor Richard Daley felt that censoring the Rolling Stones song "Street Fightin' Man" during the 1968 Democratic National Convention would stem violence. He was wrong.

The American release of Jimi Hendrix's *Electric Ladyland* features live concert photos on the record's cover; the original British release features photos of more than a dozen naked women. Even though the album has been rereleased on several occasions since then, the original photo of the buxom babes is not included.

After being invited by the Smothers Brothers to perform his anti-Vietnam anthem "Waist Deep in the Big Muddy" on their TV show, Pete Seeger is edited out of the program by the censors at CBS. Seeger's checkered past following a run-in with the McCarthy anti-Communist movement and the song's theme cause the network to step in and cut the song before broadcast.

1969

In January, New York police seize thirty thousand copies of John Lennon and Yoko Ono's *Two Virgins* album. The album's art features full frontal nudity of the couple on the cover and full back nudity on the verso. Capitol Records refuses to handle the album, which is released (wrapped in brown paper) on a small independent label. In Chicago, the vice squad closes a retail store carrying *Two Virgins*.

Controversy over the cover of Blind Faith's debut album prompts their label to issue the record with two different covers. The original cover features a photograph of a naked eleven-year-old girl holding a metallic, rather phallic-looking model airplane. The airplane points toward her lower abdomen. Atco Records eventually drops the benign second cover.

The local Roman Catholic diocese runs a two-page ad in the *Seattle Post-Intelligencer* calling for the criminal prosecution of rock musicians and for bans against "rock festivals and their drug-sex-rock-squalor culture."[4] The ads feature photos from local concerts in which nudity and obvious drug use are blacked out.

Controversy over song lyrics delays the release of *Volunteers* by Jefferson Airplane. Record-company officials claim that drug references in the album's lyrics cause the holdup, but the album's overtly anti-war and revolutionary themes are the most likely culprits. Despite having artistic control over its albums' contents, the group eventually establishes its own record label.

One-half of the country's Top 40 stations refuse to play "The Ballad of John and Yoko" because they feel that the lyrics are blasphemous. The song's lyrics contain references to Christ and crucifixion.

The FBI secretly advocates the prosecution of Doors singer Jim Morrison on charges of "lewd and lascivious behavior" based on the data it has collected on the singer since 1963. In a letter to a private citizen who writes to the FBI to complain about the messages contained in Doors albums, Bureau chief J. Edgar Hoover says, "It is repulsive to right-thinking people and can have serious effects on our young people."

After Hudson's, a large department store chain, refuses to carry the debut record from MC5 when it is released in April, the group agrees to delete the expletive "motherfucker." The incident incites the band to take out an advertisement containing the line "Fuck Hudson's." The band's label, Elektra Records, immediately drops them following the ad stunt.

The MC5

16

1970s

∎

1970

A group known as the Movement to Restore Democracy calls for the banning of rock music to end the spread of socialism in America. Joseph R. Crow, speaking at a rally in Minneapolis, says that rock musicians are "part of a Communist movement to incite revolution throughout the world."[1]

MGM Records drops eighteen acts from its record label because the company believes that the performers promote hard drugs in their songs. The effort is an attempt to show the depth of concern the corporation has regarding America's rising drug culture. None of the dropped acts are significant moneymakers for the company. One admitted hard-drug user, Eric Burdon, is not dropped from the roster because his albums are profitable.

Under the direction of President Richard Nixon, Vice President Spiro Agnew ignites widespread interest in censoring popular music by making statements concerning drug imagery in rock music. Agnew believes that rock music is a brainwashing tool that inspires young Americans to use drugs, and he openly endorses government censorship as a control mechanism. Agnew points to songs like "With a Little Help from My Friends" by the Beatles, "Eight Miles High" by the Byrds, and "White Rabbit" by Jefferson Airplane as examples of how the "drug culture" uses pop music to recruit new users. Nixon also calls for radio broadcasters to screen lyrics and ban songs containing references to drugs, war, or violence.

Following the Ohio National Guard's killing of four students at Kent State University during an anti–Vietnam War protest in May, many Ohio radio stations ban the song "Ohio." The governor claims that he fears it will incite further violence on college campuses. Stations worry that public sentiment will turn against them (opinion polls show that more than 60 percent of Ohioans support the Guardsmen's actions). The Crosby, Stills, Nash, and Young song was released just days after the tragedy. "I don't think they'll touch it," says band member David Crosby. "This one names names." Despite the ban, sales of the song are strong throughout Ohio, and no additional violence occurs in the state.

Concerns over drugs and rioting cause a wave of protests of large rock festivals. Citizen groups in Chicago, Houston, Tucson, and Atlanta rally to cancel large, outdoor rock festivals in their cities. When a concert for thirty thousand people is scheduled in Wadena, Iowa (population 231), residents fear that concertgoers will burn down the town. One local farmer becomes so frightened that drug-crazed concertgoers will shoot his cattle, he sells all of his livestock.

Ted Randal, a radio programmer working with more than fifty-five stations across the country, introduces the first ratings system for music. Randal releases a weekly list of songs, each containing symbols that rank the song content for drugs (D), sex (S), language (L), and subcategories such as acceptable (A), marginal (M), and unacceptable (X).[2]

Country Joe McDonald of Country Joe and the Fish is fined five hundred dollars for singing anti-Vietnam protest songs. Law enforcement officials do not find humor in using audience "call and response" (which includes the word "fuck") during the song "I Feel Like I'm Fixin' to Die Rag." They fine McDonald for being a "lewd, lascivious, and wanton person in speech and behavior."

Charles Cleall, a writer for the *Methodist Recorder*, calls for controls and bans of rock music, fearing it could create "states of mind frequently stronger than man's will." While Cleall encourages church leaders to sample rock music, he fears the "thrusting movement of the hips" is far too similar to sexual acts and masturbation.

Janis Joplin is charged with violating local profanity and obscenity laws for her performance after a concert in Tampa, Florida. Joplin is slapped with a two-hundred-dollar fine and "encouraged" to not perform in the city again.

In some locations, Jefferson Airplane is forced to pay cash bonds before performing. Local law enforcement officials are concerned about the group's lyrics protesting the Vietnam War and supporting revolution and drug use. The bond money is forfeited if the group displays any "illegal, indecent, obscene, lewd, or immoral exhibition" during performances. On one occasion, in Oklahoma, authorities forfeit the bond when Paul Kantner uses the word "bullshit" onstage. The group's manager responds by proclaiming that the act is a subversive part of President Nixon's crackdown on rock music.

1971

Several radio stations alter the John Lennon song "Working Class Hero" without the consent of Lennon or his record label. While some stations choose to air a "bleep" over an obscenity in the song, others completely cut the offending word.

A photograph of David Bowie wearing a dress, on the cover of *The Man Who Sold the World*, is changed for the U.S. release. The American version features a cartoon drawing of a cowboy.

Following complaints from retailers, Warner Brothers recalls 100,000 copies of the Faces' *A Nod Is As Good As a Wink* because of concerns over a poster included with the album. The thirty-two-by-forty-four-inch poster contains over 350 photos, some featuring nudity. The offending poster is removed from recalled albums, and they are reshipped to retailers for sale.

Radio stations across the United States ban Bob Dylan's single "George Jackson" over concerns about the song's political theme and the word "shit" in its lyrics.

Following massive protests by retailers, Capitol Records recalls all copies of the debut album by Mom's Apple Pie because the cover shows an innocent-looking farm-wife holding an apple pie with a slice removed and instead of cooked apples in the missing pie, there is an image of an exposed vagina. Capitol reissues the cover with the proper pie contents in place.

The Federal Communications Commission sends all radio stations telegrams threatening their licenses for playing rock music. The message reminds stations that "broadcasting songs 'promoting' or 'glorifying' the use of drugs could endanger station licenses." The agency does not specify which songs it finds inappropriate for broadcast. As a result, WNBC in New York City bans the Brewer and Shipley song "One Toke Over the Line" and other questionable songs. Stations across the country follow suit.

The Illinois Crime Commission publishes a list of popular rock songs that contain drug references. The commission also blames these songs for an increase in substance abuse and calls for their removal from radio and retail stores. Included on the list of "drug-related rock records" are Peter, Paul & Mary's "Puff (the Magic Dragon)" and the Beatles' "Yellow Submarine."

Chrysalis Records changes the lyrics to Jethro Tull's "Locomotive Breath" without the band's knowledge or consent. Label executives fear that radio stations will not play the original, which contains the lyric "got him by the balls." They replace the word "balls" with "fun" by lifting the word from another of the band's songs and inserting it into "Locomotive Breath."

The police chief of Washington, D.C., leads an early-morning raid on a group of seventy thousand people who are waiting for a May Day rock concert (also a protest of the Vietnam War) to begin. Local police and National Guardsmen disperse the crowd, even though the concert has been granted a legal festival permit. Eight thousand attendees are arrested, with most of the charges thrown out of court on constitutional grounds. The raid is endorsed by Attorney General John Mitchell and his assistant, William Rehnquist (Rehnquist eventually becomes Chief Justice of the Supreme Court of the United States).

Pete Seeger's leftist political views result in ABC's banning him from the TV show *Hootenanny*. Earlier, Seeger's career had been sidetracked for several years when his band, the Weavers, was blacklisted during the McCarthy Era. Following his revival as a solo artist, the success of his folk songwriting leads to an invitation to appear on the show, rescinded when censors become aware of Seeger's reputation as a Communist sympathizer. Many other artists boycott the program in support of Seeger.

1972

In January, the Senate Internal Security Subcommittee issues a report on John Lennon and Yoko Ono, advocating the termination of Lennon's visa to live in the United States. The report, which calls the couple "strong advocates of the program to 'dump Nixon,' " describes allegations that they hope to affect election results by holding concerts in states about to have their primary elections. As a result, the FBI begins an investigation into Lennon's political activities that lasts more than four years.

After Indiana Attorney General Theodore Sendak calls rock festivals "drug supermarkets," Hoosier legislators adopt legislation meant to "get tough" on large rock concerts. In the process, the regulation accidentally outlaws the Indianapolis 500 and other large outdoor gatherings. Sendak begins his efforts after making statements that Indiana's popular Bull Island Rock Festival is orchestrated by organized crime.

Two members of the Jefferson Airplane are arrested for criticizing the police present at a sold-out concert in Akron, Ohio. During the show, concertgoers moved into the aisle for more room to dance. Police attempts to move the dancers back into rows erupt in violence. After noticing the beatings, singer Grace Slick jumps into the crowd and is given a black eye by a policeman trying to restrain her.

John Lennon's song "Woman Is the Nigger of the World" is banned by radio stations across the country. The song discusses the subordinate role of women in society, yet it blames women for a lack of "guts and confidence." Lennon later appears on *The Dick Cavett Show* and explains that no racism or sexism is intended. The single makes the playlists of only five U.S. stations.

Radio stations across the country ban John Denver's hit song "Rocky Mountain High," assuming that the song's "high" refers to drugs. More than a dozen years later, Denver passionately defends the song while testifying before Congress:

> This was obviously done by people who had never seen or been to the Rocky Mountains and also had never experienced the elation, celebration of life, or the joy in living that one feels when he observes something as wondrous as the Perseids meteor shower on a moonless, cloudless night, when there are so many stars that you have a shadow from the starlight, and you are out camping with your friends, your best friends, and introducing them to one of nature's most spectacular light shows for the very first time.[3]

1973

Curtis Mayfield's "Pusherman" is edited without his knowledge for a live appearance on *American Bandstand*.

After an initial release in its original form, Harvest Records quickly releases a sanitized version of Pink Floyd's "Money" for radio airplay. The original song contains the lyrical phrase "Don't give me that do goody-good bullshit." The rereleased version contains the word "bull"—with the last syllable clipped out. Accompanying the rereleased record is a note asking DJs to throw away the original. With the low salaries paid to most popular radio DJs, it is not surprising that many sell the original as a collector's item.

Atlantic Records decides to change the title and lyrics of the Rolling Stones' "Starfucker" in order to avoid protests and lawsuits. The song, which contains references to a vagina and performing oral sex on Steve McQueen, is changed to "Star Star" for release. Though the McQueen reference remains (he has agreed not to sue the band over the reference) the word "pussy" is removed from the U.S. release of the song.

New York Senator James Buckley writes a report linking rock music to drug use. He further calls for the record industry to cleanse itself of drug-using or drug-endorsing rock musicians before the federal government takes that step for them. Buckley maintains that rock music holds a powerful influence over young people in America, and rock musicians glamorize drug use and trivialize arrest for drug possession. While Buckley acknowledges that he cannot find a scientific link between rock music and drug use, he contends that the industry should still bear some responsibility, saying, "It is hard to believe that the net effect has not been at the very least to lower the threshold of resistance among the more susceptible."[4] The report fails to generate the attention Buckley hopes for, since his investigations are conducted during the Nixon Watergate scandal.

1974

After witnessing marijuana use at an Elton John concert, Richfield, Ohio, zoning commissioner Richard Crofoot attempts to ban all concerts at the Richfield Coliseum, located outside of Cleveland. Crofoot worries that rock concerts will attract the "wrong element" to the city.

1975

Radio stations across the country refuse to play Loretta Lynn's "The Pill" because of its references to birth control. In the song, intended to be a response to Tammy Wynette's "Stand By Your Man," Lynn declares her newfound sexual freedom and control over her ability to reproduce, thanks to the oral contraceptive.

In November, Reverend Charles Boykin of Tallahassee, Florida, blames popular music for teenage pregnancy. Boykin conducts his own survey of 1,000 unwed mothers and determines that 984 became pregnant while listening to rock music. Boykin decides to dispose of the local stock of "devil's music" by burning thousands of dollars' worth of rock albums.

1976

A billboard advertisement for the Rolling Stones' *Black & Blue* LP features a photo of a battered, bound, and beaten woman and causes massive protests against Time-Warner by women's groups. Several magazines reject versions of the advertisement. Groups that include Women Against Violence Against Women lead boycotts of Time-Warner products that last more than a year, calling the ad a "crime against women."

The RKO radio chain refuses to play Rod Stewart's hit "Tonight's the Night" until the lyric "spread your wings and let me come inside" is edited from the song.

1977

Responding to the popularity of disco music, the Reverend Jesse Jackson insists that dance music promotes promiscuity and drug use. Jackson says he believes that something should be done about the "suggestive lyrics" found in what he calls "sex rock." Examples of this morality-damaging music are "Shake Your Booty," "Let's Make a Baby," and "I Want to Do Something Freaky to You."

1978

British punk band the Sex Pistols are initially denied visas to enter the United States for their first American tour. The American embassy, aware of the band's reputation as troublemakers in the U.K., claims that the visas were denied because of minor criminal records. The U.S. State Department eventually overrules the embassy and allows the band to enter the country.

Producers of *American Bandstand* ban the Trampps' "Disco Inferno." The lyric "burn the mother down" was thought to be too profane for the show's young viewers.

1979

Frank Zappa's song "Jewish Princess" sparks vocal protests from the Anti-Defamation League of the B'nai B'rith. In an attempt to keep the song from being played on radio stations, the group eventually files a complaint with the FCC.

17

1980s

■

1980
Fearing association with its theme, Mercury Records refuses to release Frank Zappa's single "I Don't Wanna Get Drafted." The incident prompts Zappa to leave the label and form his own recording company, Barking Pumpkin.

A representative of the New York State Division of Substance Abuse Services suggests enforcing a tax on musicians whose songs promote drug use. The agency is in charge of providing rehabilitation services to drug addicts, and its director, Julio Martinez, suggests a one-dollar tax every time a song condoning drugs is heard on the radio. Martinez even offers a list of primary offenders, including Jackson Browne, Eric Clapton, Bob Dylan, the Grateful Dead, Jefferson Starship, the Rolling Stones, and Paul Simon.

A record burning at the First Assembly Church of God in Des Moines, Iowa, conducted by the minister, Art Diaz, and the church's youth group

In June, parishioners at the First Baptist Church in Salinas, California, destroy hundreds of rock albums. Church members blame the Beatles for drug use and crime.

In October, youth minister Art Diaz organizes a group of local teenagers who conduct a record burning at the First Assembly Church of God in Des Moines, Iowa. Diaz's group selects thirty albums, breaks them into pieces, and throws them on a bonfire. Albums burned include works by the Beatles, Ravi Shankar, and Peter Frampton. During the burning, Diaz tosses in a copy of the soundtrack from the movie *Grease* for good measure.

1981

Following church services one Sunday afternoon, a church group in Keokuk, Iowa, burns albums to protest the evils they see in contemporary music. They target albums that they believe subliminally influence young people. The list of artists whose recordings are destroyed includes such "subversive" acts as the Carpenters, John Denver, and Perry Como.

A municipal judge in Newark, Ohio, bans rock concerts at the Legend Valley Park because they pose a public nuisance. Judge Laughlin cites excessive noise levels at concerts and unruly crowds as causes for his decision. The ruling is not consistently implemented, as officials use it to forbid only "undesirable" artists from performing and regularly allow personal favorites, such as Bruce Springsteen, to use the facility.

Carroll, Iowa, nightclub owner Jeff Jochims repents his transgressions and sets fire to two thousand dollars' worth of rock records. Jochims has come to believe that rock condones drug abuse and promiscuous sex. Jochims also announces that he will close his club, which has previously featured such sinful activities as mud wrestling and disco dancing.

Ozzy Osbourne: The Man Parents Love to Hate

Both as the lead singer of Black Sabbath and as a solo artist, Ozzy Osbourne has done his share to define the role of "bad-ass rock 'n' roller." If you listen to Ozzy tell it, "I am not a musician, I am a ham." He is a living testament to everything that censors despise: loud music, drugs, alcohol, links to the occult, and general bad behavior.

His behavior on- and offstage has made Osbourne the focus of plenty of controversy and attention during his career. The most infamous example occurred in 1981, when an inebriated Ozzy bit the head off a dove at a meeting with record-company executives. Several months later, he bit the head off a bat that was tossed onstage during a concert in Des Moines (Ozzy thought it was a rubber toy and had to receive a painful series of rabies shots). A year later, Ozzy was banned from performing in San Antonio, Texas, following his arrest for urinating on the wall of the Alamo. In 1991, he was fined for encouraging concert attendees to rush the stage, a situation that exploded into a near-riot. Osbourne's antics have caused him to have trouble securing gigs in many cities across the country, including Boston, Baton Rouge, Corpus Christi, Las Vegas, and Philadelphia.

Bad boy and hard rocker Ozzy Osbourne

Osbourne has taken a lot of heat for the Gothic and occult imagery associated with his music, album artwork, and concert staging. He has been a favorite whipping boy of both the PMRC and religious conservatives, who label him a satanist and occultist bent on destroying the minds of America's youth and luring them into worshipping Beelzebub. Ozzy also was unsuccessfully sued by the families of three young men (one from California and two from Georgia), who claimed that his song "Suicide Solution" goaded their sons into committing suicide. The song's theme actually condemns suicide by lamenting the death of a friend from excessive drug and alcohol abuse.

Osbourne himself has had lifelong battles with alcoholism and drug addiction, including drinking and drug binges that have almost cost him his life on several occasions. His excesses are almost legendary; he once admitted that he and Black Sabbath drummer Bill Ward dropped acid every day for two years.

Despite all the controversy (and perhaps as a result of it), Osbourne has had a very successful career. Nine of his ten solo albums have been certified as platinum, and two have reached multiplatinum status (*Bark at the Moon* and *No More Tears*). Ozzy saw a renewed public interest in his later career, with his successful yearly Ozzfest tours, a popular documentary on VH1, and a reunion with Black Sabbath.

The morals of Provo and Salt Lake City, Utah, residents are saved when two radio stations ban Olivia Newton-John's hit single "Physical." The stations fear that the song's lyrics may be a bit too suggestive for their heavily Mormon audiences.

1982

In February, Ozzy Osbourne is prohibited from performing in San Antonio, Texas, after he is arrested for urinating on the Alamo. The ban lasts for ten years. Osbourne's legal troubles also periodically prevent him from playing in several other cities, including Boston, Baton Rouge, Corpus Christi, Las Vegas, and Philadephia and Scranton, Pennsylvania.

California assemblyman Phil Wyman introduces a bill to outlaw the practice of including subliminal messages in rock records. Wyman is alerted to the dangers of "backmasking" when he is contacted by Monika Wilfrey, a constituent who viewed a segment on the subject that was aired by the PTL network. Wyman justifies his legislation by saying that rock music "can manipulate our behavior without our knowledge or consent and turn us into disciples of the AntiChrist."[1] Later that year, Congressman Robert Dornan presents a similar measure on Capitol Hill.

1983

Following customer complaints over a cover version of the Rolling Stones' "Starfucker," Joan Jett's *Album* is removed from store shelves. Even though the song appears only on the cassette release, all vinyl copies are removed as well. The song reappears on the CD release as "Star Star," the same alternate title used by the Rolling Stones during the song's initial release.

A Baptist youth minister in Emporia, Virginia, petitions the city council to remove MTV from the local cable system. Roger Wilcher's campaign protests the "vulgar and distasteful" programming found on the music channel, and he believes it is the community's duty to "make some moral guidelines."[2] Pembroke Cablevision, the cable provider for the town of forty-eight hundred, is ordered by the council to move MTV from the basic cable service to a pay channel. This action results in MTV fans' paying an additional $120 a year to receive the network. Despite Wilcher's claims of overwhelming community support, a survey determines that only 28 percent of the locals have any interest in regulating MTV.

Voice of America programmer Frank Scott issues a directive to staff that they are not permitted to play music that might offend any portion of their audience. The VOA broadcasts around the world in more than forty languages. One of the songs Scott offers as guidance is Marvin Gaye's hit "Sexual Healing," which he feels is inappropriate for radio airplay.

1984

Rick Allen and his wife express concerns over a Prince album to their local PTA meeting in Cincinnati, Ohio. Allen is angered that he was not informed when purchasing the album that it contained themes and lyrics inappropriate for his young children. He organizes a group of twenty Cincinnati PTA organizations who attend the group's national convention to call for a music ratings system similar to the movie ratings system. This action ignites the mid-eighties music censorship movement that eventually results in the RIAA's universal parental warning sticker.

Following a complaint by Wal-Mart, PolyGram Records changes the cover of the Scorpions' *Love at First Bite*. The original features a partially nude couple locked in an embrace; the man is giving the woman a tattoo on her thigh. The company quickly reissues the album with a less offensive photograph of the band members on the cover.

In May, popular Surgeon General C. Everett Koop speaks out against rock music when he insists that rock video fans have been "saturated with what I think is going to make them have trouble having satisfying relationships with the opposite sex . . . when you're raised with rock music that uses both pornography and violence."[3] Koop makes his statements despite the fact that he has no scientific evidence to support his claims.

Dade Christian School in Miami, Florida, forbids students to attend a local concert by the Jackson Brothers, because school officials fear it will lead the youth to use drugs, drink, behave irresponsibly, and participate in lewd dancing. Any student who attends the concert is guaranteed fifteen demerits.

Critics call for boycotts of Bruce Springsteen's *Born in the U.S.A.* after it is widely rumored that the cover depicts "The Boss" urinating on an American flag. Many opinions circulate regarding the meaning of the album's cover, which shows a hip-cocked Springsteen (from the waist to the knees) facing a flag but facing away from the camera. Springsteen is surprised by the controversial interpretation, saying, "It just turned out that the picture of my butt looked better than the picture of my face."

In December, after issuing a report on violence in music videos, the National Coalition on Television Violence calls for the federal government to regulate rock music on television. The report, filled with statistical oversimplifications and vagaries, notes that MTV airs 17.9 acts of violence each hour and that 22 percent of rock videos contain violent imagery. Presented by the group's founder, a psychiatrist named Thomas Radecki, the report contains a list of videos the group finds objectionable, including "Come Dancing" by the Kinks, "Penny Love" by Lionel Richie, "Eat It" by Weird Al Yankovic, and "Anxiety" by Pat Benatar.

1985

The parents of John McCollum sue Ozzy Osbourne, claiming that the lyrics to his song "Suicide Solution" "aided, or advised, or encouraged" their son to commit suicide. McCollum was found dead after shooting himself in the head with his father's .22-caliber handgun while listening to an Osbourne album. Osbourne counters that the song was inspired by the alcohol-related death of a friend, AC/DC singer Bon Scott, and its theme is anti-suicide and anti-drug. The judge in the case decides that overt lyrics are protected speech and that the evidence is insufficient to connect the song to the suicide.

Following attacks from a conservative group led by the Reverend Jimmy Swaggart, Wal-Mart discontinues sales of all major rock magazines, such as *Rolling Stone, Hard Rock, Spin,* and *Tiger Beat.*

The group Women Against Pornography provides a slide show and lecture program in public high schools about "the sexist and violent content of rock videos."[4] It focuses on rock videos that personify what the group feels is a growing disrespect for women in music videos. The group's intention is to curb youth interest in rock music. While originally intended for parents, the program is adopted for use in schools and presented in dozens of colleges and high schools.

Provo, Utah, apartment-complex owner and Mormon bishop Leo Weidner bans MTV from his tenants' apartments. Weidner says music videos are "pornographic" and feels they will distract his tenants, who are mostly students at nearby Brigham Young University. Weidner later admits that he has never seen a music video.

Following a meeting at St. Columba's Church in Washington, D.C., in early May, Tipper Gore, Susan Baker, and twenty wives of influential Washington politicians and businessmen form the Parents Music Resource Center (PMRC). The group is distressed by the graphic violence and sex its members see in the popular music to which their children are exposed. The PMRC's goals are to lobby the music industry to get lyrics printed on album covers, explicit album covers kept under the counter, a records ratings system similar to that used for films, a ratings system for concerts, reassessment of contracts for those performers who engage in violence and explicit sexual behavior onstage, and a media watch by citizens and record companies that will pressure broadcasters to not air "questionable talent."

Prince: PMRC Poster Boy

Prince can be credited as the catalyst for the creation of the Parents Music Resource Center in 1985. It was his album *1999* that offended Rick Allen to the point that he felt his local PTA in Cincinnati, Ohio, had to do something about vulgar music lyrics. It was Prince's soundtrack album for the film *Purple Rain* that led Tipper Gore to believe that the music her children favored was little more than vile smut.

Prince is one of the rare artists who combines mass popularity with a jaw-dropping arsenal of artistic talents. By the age of fourteen, Prince had taught himself to play piano, drums, and guitar; he received his first recording contract at the age of twenty; and he was one of the first black artists to be played on MTV. He performed every instrument on his first five albums and produced every album he released. Prince's popularity exploded in the early 1980s with the popularity of *1999*. By the time his semiautobiographical film *Purple Rain* was released in 1984, he was on top of the music world. The soundtrack album to *Purple Rain* spent twenty-four weeks at the top of the pop album charts and sold more than ten million copies.

It was around this time that controversy surrounding Prince and his music started to swell. From his first album, *For You* in 1978, Prince's

Prince. Susan Baker once described him as everything the PMRC was founded to fight.

music was laced with sexual innuendo and imagery, including such wholesome topics as incest, fetishism, and group sex. Prince also added an element of sexual theater to his live performances, often stripping down to black thong underwear and gyrating on a brass bed placed on the stage. By the time Prince hit the mainstream with *1999* and *Purple Rain*, parents were shocked. Prince took sex, a prevalent theme in rock and roll since its inception, to a much more overt level. Instead of "I want to love you all night long," Prince got very, very specific.

Prince's career continued to prosper for several years following the birth of the PMRC, and despite being a focal point of their protests, he experienced little resistance to distributing and performing his music. Perhaps the reason was that he was so popular that retailers stood to lose thousands of dollars in sales if they did not carry his albums.

The controversy surrounding Prince reached almost mythic proportions. It was widely rumored that he once turned in an album so controversial that Warner Brothers refused to release it: the infamous *Black Album*. The *Black Album* became the most bootlegged recording in popular music history before Prince released it independently in 1994.

However, as time went on, Prince's eccentricities got the best of him and began to erode his popularity. Prince is a very prolific composer, and he insisted on releasing albums as he produced them (sometimes resulting in multiple albums released in a single year—a kiss of death in the commercial music industry). He rarely grants any interviews and appears awkward and wildly shy and uncomfortable when seen in public.

In addition to his own work as a performer, Prince has had a huge impact on the careers of other performers. Sheena Easton, Sheila E., Sinéad O'Connor, Mitch Ryder, and Chaka Khan all have had hits with Prince-penned compositions.

Also in May, one of the few Christian rock bands to be featured on MTV is banned by the channel because its music video is too violent. MTV objects to imagery of the Antichrist bursting into flames in DeGarmo & Key's video for "Six, Six, Six." The video also shows the Antichrist being attacked by another character. The group thinks that it's been singled out for the Christian theme of the song until MTV presents the members with a list of seventy-five popular acts who also have been rejected by the network. The original, unedited video still appears on the PTL network.

MCA Records sends radio stations an urgent letter that encourages them to stop playing Al Hudson's "Let's Talk." The company fears it may be subject to obscenity prosecutions because of the song's sexually suggestive lyrics.

After receiving a letter from the PMRC expressing concerns over rock lyrics, Eddie Fritts, head of the National Association of Broadcasters, writes a letter to the heads of forty-five major record companies. In his letter, Fritts requests that lyric sheets accompany all songs released to radio. Fritts is concerned about the potential liability issues that surround the broadcast of songs targeted by the PMRC as "porn rock" songs. In a similar letter to more than eight hundred member stations, Fritts warns of the potential trouble for playing controversial music.

The PMRC writes to music-industry presidents and CEOs and requests a rating system for music lyrics and imagery. The letter contains a list of the "Filthy Fifteen" (the artists initially targeted by the PMRC). Those artists are AC/DC, Black Sabbath, Cyndi Lauper, Def Leppard, Judas Priest, Madonna, Mary Jane Girls, Mercyful Fate, Mötley Crüe, Prince, Sheena Easton, Twisted Sister, Vanity, Venom, and W.A.S.P.

Televangelist and presidential candidate Pat Robertson calls for content regulation of rock music on radio and television. The founder of the 700 Club addresses the New York Television Academy during a campaign stop, saying, "Rock groups are singing about drugs and every kind of sex. [They] don't care about free speech. They're just trying to see what they can get away with. They need to be told that they can't go any further than a certain point."[5]

While delivering a speech at the New York Television Academy, Pat Robertson endorses regulation of the music industry, saying, "They [musicians] need to be told that they can't go any further than a certain point."

Determining that music videos are "decadent, morally degrading, and evil,"[6] two women in the Boston suburb of Weymouth, Massachusetts, petition city officials to eliminate MTV from their local cable system. The city responds by ordering the local cable operator to offer subscribers a channel blocker that will prevent MTV from entering the homes of concerned citizens. This does not satisfy the protesters, and the channel is completely eliminated from the Weymouth cable system.

Under the leadership of Mayor (and future Clinton cabinet member) Henry Cisneros, city officials in San Antonio, Texas, pass an ordinance prohibiting children under the age of fourteen from attending rock concerts at any city-owned facility. The ordinance is an attempt to control youth access to "obscene" musical, stage, or theatrical productions. Concerts by groups such as AC/DC, KISS, and Mötley Crüe are also required to carry a warning in all advertisements. That warning reads, "This performance may contain material not suitable for children without supervision. Parental discretion is advised. No child under the age of fourteen years of age will be admitted without a parent or legal guardian." Behavior specifically banned in the ordinance includes "bestial sexual relations" and "sexual relations with a corpse." Local promoters are furious, and

Henry Cisneros, former San Antonio mayor and cabinet member during the Clinton administration

they point out that most children who are old enough to attend alone yet not old enough to drive do not have the required proof of age identification. Cisneros justifies the ordinance to the press by saying that rock concerts are the equivalent of "young people going to the altar to testify for Satan."

At the urging of the Parents Music Resource Center (PMRC), on September 19, the Senate Committee on Commerce, Science, and Transportation holds hearings on music lyrics and proposed systems to rate or sticker albums that contain violent or sexually themed lyrics. Chaired by Senator John Danforth of Missouri, the committee hears testimony from both sides of the issue. Representatives from the PMRC and National PTA, Senator Paula Hawkins, and Dr. Joe Stuessy speak in support of regulating music, while three musicians—Frank Zappa, Dee Snider (of Twisted Sister), and John Denver—speak in defense.

Twisted Sister's Dee Snider testifying before the Senate hearings on record labeling. Snider was the only witness to testify who actually was a target of the PMRC.

Despite the alleged lack of bias of the committee, at least four of the participating senators have wives who are deeply involved in the PMRC. While the stated intention of the hearings is to review the controversy surrounding the music industry, the proceedings are filled with veiled threats regarding possible federal legislation if the problem is not immediately addressed.

The hearings spring from a four-month media blitz conducted by the PMRC in support of a rating system for music releases. Industry insiders are quick to point out that the movie industry creates 325 movies a year to the music industry's more than 25,000 songs. Immediately before the hearings begin, the Recording Industry Association of America proposes a universal warning sticker that can be affixed to those albums that have objectionable themes or imagery. The RIAA is concerned that controversy over music labeling might hurt the chances of one of its pet projects: the Home Audio Recording Act, which will tax all blank audiotapes; the revenue from the tax will be given to the recording industry in place of lost royalties.

Interstate Periodical Distributors, a magazine wholesaler in Wisconsin, refuses to carry the September 1985 issue of *Hard Rock* magazine, despite the fact that no customers have ever complained about it. *Hard Rock*, a New York monthly that covers heavy metal music and culture, often features articles and cover photos of acts that are targeted by the PMRC and other conservative groups. This first boycott results in a chain of events that leads to distributor concerns and the magazine's demise in August of 1986.

During the height of the media blitz surrounding the PMRC and Senate hearings on record labeling, Camelot Music and Video announces it will not carry albums that bear a parental warning sticker. Camelot, the nation's second-largest music retail chain, fears that its mall stores will be picketed, provoking action from mall management that might jeopardize Camelot's leases.

In October, President Ronald Reagan insinuates that "reactionary" and "obscene" rock music does not deserve constitutional protection. Reagan states, "I don't believe that our Founding Fathers ever intended to create a nation where the rights of pornographers would take precedence over the rights of parents, and the violent and malevolent would be given free rein to prey upon our children."[7]

American Bandstand producers refuse to let Sheena Easton perform her hit song "Sugar Walls" because it has been targeted by the PMRC. One producer calls the song "suggestive pornography."

In November, the Recording Industry Association of America strikes a deal with the National PTA and the PMRC to create a universal parental warning sticker that will be placed on all albums containing graphic depictions of sex and/or violence. The agreement gives record companies the option to print song lyrics on the backs of albums. Despite the agreement, the universal sticker does not appear until 1990.

William Steding, vice president of radio station KAFM in Dallas, forms the National Music Review Council, whose mission is to inform broadcasters and parents about music that features controversial themes and lyrics. Steding, who plans to expand the council to cover the entire music industry, hopes that his group will develop a reputation similar to *Good Housekeeping*, with its seal of approval.

Under the direction of the late Marvin Gaye's record company, the title of his song "Sanctified Pussy" is changed to "Sanctified Lady" for a posthumous release, *Dream of a Lifetime*. "Sanctified Pussy," a song extolling the virtues of having sex with churchgoing women, was one of several yet-unreleased songs at the time of Gaye's 1984 death.

Hoping to avoid notice by the PMRC and other conservative groups, Columbia Records wraps the Rolling Stones' *Dirty Work* in dull red plastic, hiding certain words and song titles. Even the album's title appears as simply "Work," because Columbia's plastic wrap covers the word "Dirty" (again, avoiding unwanted attention). According to singer Mick Jagger, the band is also asked to remove certain words from the titles and lyrics, including the word "cunt."

1986
In February, CBS Music sets a strict yet vague companywide policy regarding explicit lyrics. The memo, from CBS's legal department to all A&R and product management personnel, requests that CBS employees warn appropriate personnel if any new releases contain "(a) explicit sex; (b) explicit violence, or (c) explicit substance abuse."[8] The memo outlines CBS's procedure for affixing parental warning labels, but it fails to define any of the three criteria in detail. The memo also implies that CBS executives will encourage artists to alter lyrics rather than suffer the indignities of a warning sticker.

The Cure requests that radio stations pull "Killing an Arab" from airplay following protests from Arabic groups. Though the single was originally released in 1979, it didn't gather much attention until college deejays started connecting a nonexistent anti-Arab theme to the song seven years later. After complaints from groups such as the Arab-American Anti-Discrimination Committee, the band's leader, Robert Smith, appeals to radio stations to not air the song, and he agrees to sticker the Cure's collection of singles (*Standing on a Beach*, which includes "Killing an Arab" as its lead track). The sticker reads, "The song 'Killing an Arab' has absolutely no racist overtones whatsoever. It is a song that decries the existence of all prejudice and consequent violence. The Cure condemns its use in furthering anti-Arab feeling."

Evangelist Jim Brown of the First Church of the Nazarene in Ironton, Ohio, leads seventy-five teenagers in a mass burning of records containing the theme to the television show *Mr. Ed,* claiming the tune contains satanic messages. Brown considers the theme of the show itself (a talking horse) to be the work of the Devil and claims its theme "A Horse Is a Horse" contains the message "Someone sung this song for Satan" when played backwards.

Licensed to Ill, the debut album from the Beastie Boys, had the unfortunate luck of being released soon after record companies started to crack down on artists over explicit content.

A single from the Beastie Boys' debut album *Licensed to Ill* is delayed because there are conflicts with their record distributor's policy on explicit lyrics. The Beastie Boys record for Def Jam Records, which is distributed by CBS. Lyrics in the single "Hold It, Now Hit It" are eventually edited, and the song "The Scenario" is dropped from the B-side.

Assuming that Frank Zappa's status as an anticensorship advocate translates into "dirty words" on his albums, Meyer Music Markets places an "explicit lyrics" warning sticker on Zappa's *Jazz from Hell*—even though the album is entirely instrumental. Meyer, a hundred-store chain based in the Pacific Northwest, adds insult to injury by forbidding sale of the album to minors.

First Lady Nancy Reagan withdraws her support for an eleven-hour anti-drug rock concert because promoters refuse to drop certain acts. Reagan, the figurehead of the "Just Say No" anti-drug campaign of the 1980s, is initially excited at the large number of big-name musicians willing to lend their support to the event. Learning that some of these acts are current targets of the PMRC and other conservative groups, she demands they be forbidden to perform.

The families of two young men sue the British heavy metal band Judas Priest, alleging that their 1978 album *Stained Class* encouraged the young men to commit suicide. The boys, eighteen-year-old Ray Belknap and twenty-year-old Jay Vance, consummate their suicide pact after two days of drinking and smoking marijuana.

In 1990, the judge finds that neither the band nor their record label is liable for the deaths. While the judge does feel that subliminal messages exist, he does not see a connection between the messages and the actions of the young men.

Following the case, the band's guitarist dismisses the notion that his band is deliberately placing hidden messages on its albums, saying, "I didn't even know what 'subliminal' meant [before the trial began]. It'll probably be ten years before I know how to spell it."

Maryland delegate Judith Toth introduces legislation aimed at amending the state's obscenity statutes to include records, tapes, and laser discs. Telling reporters she is inspired by the PMRC's recent attacks on rock music, Toth proposes that retailers segregate "obscene" materials from the rest of their wares. Customers will be required to provide identification (proving they are at least eighteen years of age) before browsing and/or purchasing the products in question. The legislation is voted down, but Toth vows to try again.

Jello Biafra of the Dead Kennedys is charged with violating section 313.1 (distribution of harmful materials to minors) of the California state penal code for a poster included in the band's *Frankenchrist*

LP. The offending poster contains a painting by noted Swiss artist H. R. Giger (best known for his Academy Award–winning art design work for the 1980 film *Alien*) entitled *Landscape #20, Where Are We Coming From?* The painting features about a dozen sets of interlocked male and female genitalia. When examining the painting, it is difficult to tell where one set of genitalia ends and another begins.

The case begins on December 6, 1985, when Tammy Scharwath of Sylmar, California, purchases a copy of *Frankenchrist* at the Northridge Fashion Mall as a Christmas present for her younger brother. Both Scharwath and her brother are minors. The shrink-wrapped album is affixed with a label that states, "Warning: The inside fold-out to this record cover is a work of art by H. R. Giger that some people may find shocking, repulsive, and offensive. Life can be that way sometimes." After their mother, Mary Ann Thompson, discovers the purchase, she writes a complaint letter to the state district attorney's office. Eventually the letter is forwarded to the Los Angeles city attorney's office, which investigates the complaint.

At 6:30 A.M. on April 15, 1986, nine police officers (three from Los Angeles and six from San Francisco) raid the apartment of Dead Kennedys singer Jello Biafra. Though Biafra says he was awake and listening to music at that time, police claim they knocked, received no answer, then forced their way into Biafra's apartment. Police spend approximately two hours searching Biafra's apartment; they seize three copies of the *Frankenchrist* album (with the poster), a copy of *Maximum Rock and Roll*, some of Biafra's personal mail, and business records from Biafra's independent record label, Alternative Tentacles.

Jello Biafra: There's Always Room for Jello

Jello Biafra has spent more than twenty years questioning authority, exploring society's problems, and trying to make a social and political statement through the spoken word and music. He is no stranger to controversy either. He was married in a graveyard, often rants and provokes his audiences from the stage (on several occasions allowing audience members to join him onstage to remove his clothing), and even ran for mayor of San Francisco in 1979 (his campaign slogan was "There's always room for Jello." He finished fourth). For almost ten years, he was the front man of one of the best-known punk bands of all time: the Dead Kennedys. Mixing a punchy British-style beat with cutting lyrical commentary on politics and society, the Dead Kennedys took punk in the United States to a new level with their classic albums *Fresh Fruit for Rotting Vegetables, Frankenchrist,* and *Bedtime for Democracy.* The Dead Kennedys pointed out the problems they saw with society and took the risk of suggesting solutions as well. It was their *Frankenchrist* album that caused the most trouble for Biafra.

Frankenchrist is laced with commentary on gun control, jock culture, racism, classism, corporate influences in the rock and roll industry, and American business's treatment of the working class. The album captures the band at a musical and lyrical high point—but that didn't matter to the Los Angeles County district attorney, who took issue with the H. R. Giger painting featured on a poster included with the album, entitled *Landscape #20.* It's no surprise that Biafra chose to risk financial ruin and jail in order to fight the pornography charges pressed against him. The principle involved was most important to him. Had he simply pled guilty to avoid a protracted court battle, he most likely would have received a small fine and a suspended jail sentence. But he didn't choose that path.

Jello Biafra. Biafra's 1986 indictment on pornography charges marked the first time anyone was criminally prosecuted for the contents of a musical work.

Following the Dead Kennedys' breakup in 1987, Biafra spent his time managing his record label, Alternative Tentacles, releasing six spoken-word albums, touring the lecture circuit, and embarking on a variety of artistic projects with other musicians.

But the Dead Kennedys were in the news again in 1993, when a reissue of their first album was mixed up with a package of Christian radio broadcast CDs and accidentally shipped to Christian radio stations around the country.

He continues to be an ardent fighter against apathy and the mainstream, delivering his unique spin on the truth. If you call his home answering machine, instead of a typical greeting, Biafra fills the announcement with his feelings about what is going on in the world today. As is his style, he points out the problems and suggests a course of action to make life better.

About six weeks later, the Los Angeles attorney's office charges five people with "distribution of harmful matter to minors." Those people are Biafra, Steve Boudreau of Greenworld Distribution, Salvadore Alberti of Alberti Record manufacturing, Michael Bonnano (aka Microwave) of Alternative Tentacles Records, and Ruth Schwartz of Mordam Records. The owner of Wherehouse records (where Scharwath bought the offending album) is not prosecuted after he volunteers to stop carrying the album on his shelves. The charges against Biafra and the other defendants carry a penalty of one year in jail and a two-thousand-dollar fine.

Prosecutor Michael Guarino states, "I didn't think there was much choice but to prosecute. We have made the distinction that this is utterly without socially redeeming importance to minors."[9] Biafra counters,

It's not about pornography, but a political issue. The painting portrayed a vortex of exploitation, that vicious circle of greed where one of us will exploit another for gain and wind up looking over our shoulder lest someone do the same for us in return. I felt that we should include this piece of art work as a kind of crowning statement of what the record was trying to say musically, lyrically, and visually.[10]

All five defendants decide to fight the charges and enter "not guilty" pleas in March of 1987. A trial date is set for August 23, 1987.

At the beginning of the proceedings, charges are dropped against all defendants except Biafra and Microwave. The prosecution tries to prove: (a) that the poster appeals to prurient interests, (b) that the average California adult would deem it offensive to minors, and (c) that it is utterly without redeeming value. The prosecution calls seven witnesses to the stand, including the police lieutenant who led the raid on Biafra's apartment; the album's purchaser, Tammy Scharwath (who commented she thought the poster was "gross" but not harmful), and her mother, Mary Ann Thompson. The prosecution calls no expert witnesses. In their defense, Biafra and Microwave's lawyers call three expert witnesses to establish the legitimacy of Giger's painting as art, the significance of the Dead Kennedys' political messages, and the connection between the poster and the album's theme.

After deliberating thirty-six hours, the jury informs the judge that they are hopelessly deadlocked at seven favoring acquittal and five favoring conviction. The judge declares a mistrial and does not allow the prosecutors to file new charges.

Following the case, prosecutor Guarino attempts to shake hands with Biafra, who refuses. Biafra then hands Guarino a "gift": a copy of Big Black's LP *Songs About Fucking*. Guarino throws the album to the ground and storms out of the building. Biafra is quoted as saying, "We have seen the lengths that vindictive people will go to just get the legal equivalent of a quick ejaculation. Forcing the issue is always worth it. I hope this slams the door on the misuse of judicial power against underground artists with an opposing point of view."[11]

Despite contributions from more than eleven hundred individuals to his defense fund, defending the case financially devastates Biafra. Also, the Dead Kennedys soon disband, and Biafra's marriage ends in divorce.

1987

Fearing eviction, many mall retailers refuse to carry new releases containing the word "fuck" in the title. It is quite common for lease agreements between shopping malls and their tenants (such as chain record stores) to forbid merchants to sell obscene materials. Big Black's *Songs About Fucking* and Leaving Trains' *Fuck* raise concerns about protesting parent groups' forcing retailers to find new homes. Also, the Sam Goody chain refuses to carry the Raunch Hands' *Learn to Whap-A-Dang* because they fear that the cover imagery will provoke controversy. The album's cover features a stylized depiction of a man and woman fighting over an ax.

A part-time record clerk is arrested in April in Callaway, Florida, for selling a copy of 2 Live Crew's album *2 Live Is What We Are* to a fourteen-year-old boy. The arresting officer refers to the album as "hard-core pornography." The owner of Starship Records & Tapes eventually closes the business.

Radio stations in Pittsburgh, New Orleans, Cincinnati, Minneapolis, Denver, and New York ban George Michael's single "I Want Your Sex" because of its explicit sexual content. The well-intentioned programmers are concerned that the song will promote casual or promiscuous sexual relationships at a time when the nation is just beginning to understand the seriousness of the AIDS crisis. Michael defends his song by stating, " 'I Want Your Sex' is about attaching lust to love, not just to strangers."

In an attempt to thwart an upcoming concert by the Beastie Boys, the city of Jacksonville, Florida, passes an ordinance in August that requires all "adult" acts to put a "For Mature Audiences Only" notice on all concert tickets and advertisements. Locals are concerned about the Beastie Boys' stage show, which includes women dancing in cages and a twenty-foot hydraulic penis. The Beastie Boys sue the city, eventually winning a judgment that requires the city to pay the band's attorney fees and issue a public apology calling the ordinance unconstitutional.

An unidentified congressperson commissions a study by the Congressional Research Service to determine if Congress has the constitutional authority to regulate albums that contain explicit lyrics by restricting their sale. The congressperson requesting the report refuses to come forward, and the service refuses to reveal his or her identity. The twenty-nine-page report states that "it would be constitutionally permissible for Congress to restrict access by children to certain records or to impose record labeling requirements, based on its authority to regulate interstate and foreign commerce."[12] The report is kept confidential for longer than two years before being exposed by a Washington journalism newsletter.

MTV refuses to air the video for the Replacements' "The Ledge" because executives fear that it may encourage teens to commit suicide. The video, which contains images of a young boy about to take his life, is thought to be too graphic for MTV. Warner

Brothers Records creates an ad campaign to defend the song, proclaiming that the song's intent is to offer support to those feeling desperate.

1988

Some retailers refuse to stock *Nothing's Shocking,* Jane's Addiction's debut album for Warner Brothers, because of its cover. Featuring a sculpture of two naked Siamese twins with their heads in flames, the cover art was created by the band's frontman Perry Farrell. Warner Brothers stands behind the band, and once the album becomes a hit, most retailers eventually give in and stock it.

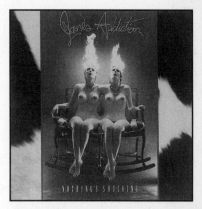

Michael Collazo, a faculty adviser, at a Newark, New Jersey, student radio station, yanks all heavy metal from the station's playlists in April because he fears it will cause young listeners to commit suicide. The station, WSOU, is licensed to the Catholic diocese of Newark,

Jane's Addiction's debut album caused quite a stir when it was released in 1988. Retailers were concerned that the cover's flaming statue of two naked women would spawn protests.

which operates the station as part of Seton Hall University. Several days before the decision is made, a sixteen-year-old suicide victim is found with an Ozzy Osbourne tape in his pocket. Collazo defends his actions by saying it is "only a matter of time before another teen commits suicide and investigators blame the music the child heard on WSOU."[13] Following student and community protests over the metal genre ban, station management reinstates a handful of metal acts, such as Guns N' Roses, Stryper, and Savatage.

Tommy Hammond, co-owner of Taking Home the Hits in Alexandria, Alabama, is arrested in June for selling 2 Live Crew's *Move Somethin'* to an undercover police officer. The local prosecutor considers both *Move Somethin'* and 2 Live Crew's *2 Live Is What*

We Are legally obscene under Alabama's criminal code. The arrest occurs even though Hammond routinely keeps all controversial or stickered albums in a special box behind the counter and will sell those albums only to adults. At a municipal hearing, Hammond is found guilty and is fined five hundred dollars. He requests a jury trial; at the end of a four-day trial, the jury throws out the charges after deliberating just one and a half hours. Hammond's municipal conviction represents the first time in history that someone has been found guilty of an obscenity charge that is based on music.

After initially agreeing to broadcast the world premiere of Neil Young's "This Note's For You" on July 1, MTV refuses to air the video clip. Young's song and accompanying video are a parody of the crass commercialism he sees among popular music's biggest stars. The video parodies MTV artists such as Michael Jackson, Eric Clapton, and Whitney Houston and their endorsements of products like Pepsi, Coke, and Michelob Beer. MTV contends that the ban results from its internal policy not to air videos that endorse or display products. Critics of the video music network contend that MTV is sensitive to the parody because these products are also some of the channel's largest advertisers. In a letter from Young to MTV executives, he calls them "spineless" and wonders, "What does the 'M' in MTV stand for—music or money?"[14] MTV eventually reconsiders the matter and begins airing the video. The clip goes on to win the MTV Award for Video of the Year.

Retailers across the country refuse to carry Prince's *Lovesexy*, despite the fact that the artist's previous two albums reached multiplatinum status. Retailers protest the record's cover, which contains a nude, yet unrevealing, photograph of Prince.

Congress passes the Child Protection and Obscenity Enforcement Act, which is aimed at protecting children from pornographic material. Coming as it does on the heels of the PMRC's efforts to regulate music lyrics and imagery, many supporters and critics of the act think that it can easily be applied to "obscene" popular music as well as to pornographic books, magazines, and films.

Protestors in Santa Cruz, California, picket retailers carrying Guns N' Roses' debut album *Appetite for Destruction,* despite the fact that the offensive cover art has already been replaced. The original cover features a painting by Robert Williams (also titled *Appetite for Destruction*) in which a cartoon character of a woman lies beaten and bloody after a suggested sexual attack. A Santa Cruz–based group known as Media Watch pickets local retailer Cymbaline Records carrying signs that read CYMBALINE SUPPORTS RAPE and CYMBALINE SUPPORTS CHILD MOLESTATION. The only copies of *Appetite for Destruction* available for sale in the store feature the new, benign cover. Protest organizer Jamie Evans says the album is targeted because of its popularity (*Appetite for Destruction* has sold five million copies by this point) and indicates that the group plans to target other stores in the area before moving to other communities in its campaign to promote "healthy images of women and children in the media." Other retailers begin dropping the album from their stores, despite its position as the country's number-two album. "[Pulling the record] is my response to the community uproar," says the manager of Rainbow Records. "Rainbow Records prides itself on fitting into the community."[15]

1989

In January, Yusef Islam, better known as folksinger Cat Stevens, supports the Ayatollah Khomeini's call for the death of *The Satanic Verses* author Salman Rushdie. Following the pronouncement, radio stations across the United States pull his records from play. Radio talk show host Tom Leykis runs a steamroller over a collection of Cat Stevens records in protest.

In an attempt to stop the rampant spread of filth in its community, the city council of New Iberia, Louisiana, enacts an emergency ordinance in February aimed at obscene music. According to the legislation, any materials that might fall under Louisiana's obscenity standard must be kept from the view of unmarried people under age seventeen. Openly displaying potentially obscene music albums can result in a five-hundred-dollar fine and sixty days in jail.

Under pressure from legislators, interest groups, and member companies, the RIAA releases its black-and-white universal parental warning sticker in early March. It reads, "Parental Advisory: Explicit Lyrics." The sticker is to be attached directly to the lower right-hand corner of all controversial records, cassettes, and compact discs. Before the sticker's debut, more than a dozen states had considered regulating and restricting the sale of controversial records through legislation. Following the sticker's debut and immediate implementation, every state, save four, drops its legislation.

In March, a Pepsi commercial set to Madonna's song "Like a Prayer" is pulled after one airing because religious groups are offended. The commercial itself contains no controversial imagery, but the song's video contains scenes of Madonna saving a black man from a lynch mob, making love to him, and then breaking into dance among burning crosses—all inside a church. The Reverend Donald Wildmon, head of the American Family Association of Tupelo, Mississippi, and well known as an ultraconservative and an anti-Semite, calls the video "blasphemous" and threatens a boycott of all Pepsi products. Pepsi actually allows Wildmon to announce that it will no longer air the commercial and will end its business relationship with the singer.

In late March Guns N' Roses is cut from the New York AIDS benefit "Rock and a Hard Place," because of the lyrics to its song "One in a Million." The Gay Men's Health Crisis originally invites the group to "appeal to a new audience," but the group rescinds the invitation after hearing the song's lyrics, which blame immigrants and homosexuals for the spread of AIDS.

Following complaints about the amount of exposed buttocks featured in Cher's video for "If I Could Turn Back Time," several video channels drop or restrict the music clip, featuring the scantily clad Cher singing and dancing for a group of excited sailors on a navy battleship. The city board of directors in Texarkana, Texas, attempts to force the local cable operator to drop MTV after the channel adds the video in heavy rotation. MTV eventually restricts the video to play after 9 P.M. In response to viewer complaints, MTV competitor Hit Video USA drops the clip entirely.

MTV refuses to air a Fuzztones video that contains an oblique reference to condoms. Following pressure from several groups, MTV requests a lyric change in the Fuzztones' song "Nine Months Later" from the group's American debut, *In Heat*. The original lyric contains a double entendre referring to pregnancy: "Well if you don't wanna live this life of shame, be sure to wear your rubbers when it rains." MTV demands that the word "rubbers" (an antiquated term for foul-weather footwear) be changed to "raincoat." The band agrees to change the lyric, and MTV airs the video—but only once.

Five performers, including Gene Simmons of Kiss and R&B singer Bobby Brown, are arrested for "suggestive" performances in Georgia. It is hoped that the prosecutions, initiated under Georgia's obscenity laws, will discourage other performers from engaging in lewd behavior while performing in the state.

The Hastings Record Store chain institutes a policy stating that certain rap and rock titles cannot be sold to minors in its 130 stores nationwide. The store plans to create its own criteria by which titles will be restricted, basing decisions on the opinions of store managers. The chain takes these steps because it fears that it will become the target of parental protests and possible obscenity prosecutions.

Frustrated by the failure to implement a universal parental warning sticker, the Pennsylvania house passes a bill requiring a warning label on all albums with explicit lyrics. The legislation is targeted at songs that "explicitly describe, advocate, or encourage suicide, incest, bestiality, sadomasochism, rape, or involuntary deviant sexual intercourse, [or] advocate or encourage murder, ethnic intimidation, the use of illegal drugs or the excessive or illegal use of alcohol."[16] The Pennsylvania legislators place the burden of enforcement (and criminal liability) on the backs of local retailers.

The Federal Communications Commission launches a campaign to clean up a backlog of radio obscenity complaints, handing out thousands of dollars in fines to stations in order to discourage them from playing risqué music. Novelty songs such as "Makin' Bacon" by the Pork Dudes, "Penis Envy," "Jet Boy, Jet Girl," and "Walk with an Erection" are pulled from stations across the country to avoid possible fines.

Encouraged by the conservative group Focus on the Family, officials at the FBI write to gangsta rap group N.W.A in August, informing the performers that the Bureau does not appreciate their song "Fuck Tha Police." The letter marks the first time a government agency has taken "an official stance" against a work of art. Law enforcement agencies across the country agree with the Bureau, and they stage protests against the group that become so threatening that N.W.A does not perform the hit single on its nationwide tour for fear of arrest. When performing in Detroit, the group attempts to play the song but is chased offstage by waiting police, and the members are held in their hotel rooms for several hours without being arrested.

Also in August, MTV enacts a policy that a lyric sheet must accompany all videos submitted to the network. Songs must pass unwritten lyric guidelines and image criteria set by the video network's Standards Department (which, for the previous five years, consisted of one person). The network attempts to avoid videos it feels endorse or promote violence, illegal drugs, excessive alcohol consumption, or explicit depictions of sexual practices.

After protests from the gay community in September, Los Angeles radio station KDAY pulls from rotation the song "Truly Yours" by Kool G. Rap and D. J. Polo from rotation. Several groups object to the lyric "a sex disease was as common as T.B., but gays today get V.D. and the free-D" because they feel the rap discriminates against gays. The rapper's record label initially offered stations a "radio-safe" version of the song, which substitutes the word "people" for "gays," but KDAY broadcasts the original album version. In a statement about the song, Kool G. Rap insists the song is about a relationship between a man and a woman: "I wasn't trying to discriminate against the gay community by any means."

In Texarkana, Texas, city officials force the Dimension Cable Service to offer channel blockers to prevent MTV from entering the homes of concerned families. The city's board of directors originally attempts to force the cable operator to drop MTV after residents bitterly complain about the imagery contained in many popular videos. After the channel blockers are offered free of charge to Dimension's twenty-two thousand subscribers, only forty units are requested by customers.

18

1990s

1990

Frustrated by the lack of progress on the RIAA/PMRC universal warning sticker, Missouri legislators introduce a bill in January that forbids the sale of records containing lyrics that are violent, sexually explicit, or perverse. An exception is made to those albums that carry a warning label and the lyrics printed on the cover. Similar measures are introduced in twenty other states.

Despite claims by the PMRC and other conservative and anti-rock crusaders, statistics demonstrate that music labeling is not a priority for a large majority of Americans. Surveys conducted by the Recording Industry Association of America (the industry group that created the warning sticker) show that 22 percent of parents believe that records should bear mandatory parental warning labels. Twenty-four percent of parents feel the concept is wrong and that music should not be labeled.

Citizens in Westerly, Rhode Island, hold a town council meeting to discuss concerns regarding an upcoming 2 Live Crew concert in the city. Citizens worry about "possible rowdy behavior" and obscene lyrics at the event. In light of "public safety" concerns, the council passes an ordinance that forces the promoter to appear in court to justify why his entertainment license should not be revoked for sponsoring the band's appearance. A judge grants an injunction against the town's ordinance, saying that the town failed to demonstrate sufficient proof of imminent danger as a result of the concert.

Within a year after the music industry adopts the uniform parental warning sticker, many major recording companies (such as MCA, Arista, Atlantic, Columbia, Electra, Epic, EMI, and RCA) establish committees to review upcoming releases for objectionable material. Most committees also are charged with counseling artists about potential ramifications (for the artist and label) that could result from releasing controversial materials.

Three county prosecutors in eastern Pennsylvania warn retailers that they may be prosecuted if they sell 2 Live Crew's *As Nasty as They Wanna Be* to minors. Prosecutors in Chester and Delaware counties join Montgomery County prosecutor Michael Marino in declaring the album obscene.

Disc Jockey, a retail chain with nearly two hundred stores, announces it will not carry any album with the warning sticker. Another large retailer, Trans World (with more than four hundred stores) announces they will require proof of age before selling stickered products.

After receiving a tip from local attorney Jack Thompson, the Broward County, Florida, sheriff's department embarks on a campaign to eliminate 2 Live Crew records from the country—this act leads to the country's first federal court judgment that popular music can be obscene. Before the incident, 2 Live Crew was a rap group popular primarily with black urban fans. The racy themes found on their album *As Nasty as They Wanna Be* began to attract fans from among white suburban teens, who were becoming large consumers of rap music. The album's sexual content came to the attention of Thompson (best known for his run against then-

District Attorney Janet Reno—during which he insisted Reno sign a statement declaring her sexual preference), who began a campaign to alert police departments about the album's content and the possibility that it could be considered obscene under Florida law. On February 26, with the blessing of Broward County sheriff Nick Navarro, Deputy Mark Wichner purchases a cassette copy of *As Nasty as They Wanne Be* and presents it to County Circuit Court Judge Mel Grossman for review. On March 9, Grossman declares that there is probable cause that the album is obscene under Florida's "sale of harmful material" statute.

Sheriff Nick Navarro hounded 2 Live Crew both in and out of the courtroom. After the high-profile confrontation, Navarro lost a bid for reelection.

The sheriff's office immediately mails copies of the judge's ruling to record retailers in the county. They follow up with visits to more than a dozen record stores to inform retailers that they face potential arrest and prosecution as felons if they continue selling the record. Almost immediately, most copies of *Nasty* disappear from stores shelves in Broward County.

Skyywalker Records, 2 Live Crew's record label, has two potential courses of action: To fight the sheriff's department's threats, retailers or the band itself could allow themselves to be arrested and prosecuted and then fight the issue in the criminal courts. Although this course of action will most likely result in a definitive ruling in their favor, neither the band members nor the retailers are willing to risk possible conviction. The second, riskier option (and the one chosen by 2 Live Crew) is to file suit in federal court and ask for declaratory judgment as to whether the sheriff's actions violated the band's First Amendment rights.

Nine days after the band files suit, Sheriff Nick Navarro files a separate lawsuit asking the court to declare *Nasty* legally obscene. The trial date is set for May 14.

After hearing two days of testimony, Federal Judge Jose Gonzalez, Jr., declares that *As Nasty as They Wanna Be* is obscene under both preponderance and clear-and-convincing evidentiary standards. In a small victory for the band, the judge finds that the sheriff's actions constituted prior restraint (punishing someone for something before a crime is committed), violating the band members' First and Fourteenth Amendment rights. In his opinion, Gonzalez declares that rap music has significantly less artistic merit than "melodic" music. He also theorizes that the focus of rap music is its lyrics. Therefore, based solely on the themes embodied in an album's lyrics, it could be deemed legally obscene. Thompson obviously, is elated with the decision, saying, "Will it mean more prosecution of 2 Live Crew? Probably. Will there be prosecutions of [comedian] Andrew Dice Clay and others? Maybe. People can't be so self-expressive and self-absorbed that they ignore the community standards."[1] Despite the prior-restraint ruling, the damage is done; the sheriff's office has the declaration it needs to go ahead with prosecutions.

And that's exactly what it did. Despite an anticipated appeal of Gonzalez's decision, the sheriff arrests Charles Freeman two days after the ruling is handed down by the judge. Freeman is the only Broward County record retailer still selling *Nasty* on his shelves. When he is found guilty by a six-member jury in October and is fined a thousand dollars, Freeman is the first person ever convicted of selling obscene music in the United States (while Dead Kennedys frontman Jello Biafra was the first to be prosecuted, his case was eventually thrown out of court).

Two days later, three members of 2 Live Crew are arrested while performing at an adults-only show in Hollywood, Florida. The performers are charged with violating Florida's obscenity law for performing material from the *Nasty* album. A jury acquits them of the charges in October.

Despite the fact that Gonzalez's ruling applies only to a three-county area in Florida, retailers across the country begin pulling 2 Live Crew material (along with anything else that they think might upset conservatives) because they fear prosecution on obscenity and racketeering charges. Jack

Luke Skyywalker (Campbell) of 2 Live Crew after a jury found him not guilty of obscenity charges for performing the group's songs in a nightclub

Thompson, fueled by his apparent success and with the support of the group Focus on the Family, plans protests and picketing at retailers across the country who carry the album—including those who carried the edited version of the album, *As Clean as They Wanna Be*.

About eighteen months later, the U.S. Court of Appeals for the Eleventh Circuit reverses Gonzalez's ruling, siding with the band. Despite the national uproar caused by the album, its supporters, and its detractors, the reversal receives little media coverage. The issue is finally settled several months later when the U.S. Supreme Court announces, without comment, that it will let the appeals court's reversal stand—thus allowing the issue to be decided permanently in favor of the band.

Thereafter, 2 Live Crew quickly fades from public view, selling few records. Sheriff Nick Navarro later loses his attempt to be reelected as Broward County sheriff.

In March, Record Bar, a retail chain with more than 170 stores, announces that it will pull all 2 Live Crew recordings from its stores due to the controversy surrounding the band. The chain also refuses to carry any edited or "sanitized" versions of the group's releases.

Waxworks, a chain music retailer, refuses to stock any product that carries a parental warning sticker for fear of potential protests and obscenity prosecutions. According to company president Terry Woodward, the decision stems from "an unfortunate local incident," adding, "at the time, we just thought it was the labels' problem. The retailer is too much at risk."[2] Following customer complaints and the adaptation of the music industry's standard sticker, the chain reverses its decision.

A Tennessee judge rules that 2 Live Crew's *As Nasty as They Wanna Be* and N.W.A's *Straight Outta Compton* are obscene under state law. Joe Baugh, district attorney general for Williamson County, reviews copies of the albums that were purchased at a local record store by the county commissioner. Although no prosecutions are planned, anyone arrested for selling the records could face fines of from ten thousand dollars to one hundred thousand dollars, depending upon the involvement of minors in the offense.

In April, an Indianapolis record store falls victim to a private sting when John Price, a local attorney, state senate candidate, and head of the group Decency in Broadcasting, wires a twelve-year-old boy and a fourteen-year-old girl and sends them into a local Karma Records and Entertainment store to purchase 2 Live Crew's *As Nasty as They Wanna Be*. Price holds a press conference outside the store to announce that if he is elected, he will push for felony convictions of anyone caught selling that album, or any other obscene recording.

Following the controversy surrounding 2 Live Crew's obscenity battle in Florida, six states pass legislation declaring the band's album *As Nasty as They Wanna Be* legally obscene. The states are Florida, Indiana, Ohio, Pennsylvania, Tennessee, and Wisconsin.

Convinced that the RIAA/PMRC universal sticker will not adequately protect children from pornographic music, Utah Republican Howard Nielson introduces a resolution in Congress that calls for a stricter labeling system for controversial recordings. Nielson warns that if the industry does not take its role in regulating music more seriously within the next eighteen months, more drastic action (by the federal government) may be necessary.

In May, a Hamilton, Ohio, record-store owner is pressured by local law enforcement officials to stop carrying 2 Live Crew's *As Nasty as They Wanna Be*. Upon receiving a letter from Florida crusader Jack Thompson alerting local officials that the album is being sold in their community, officers from the local sheriff's office visit the only record store in the county that carries the album. After reviewing a copy of the lyrics and hearing the opinions of local law enforcement, the retailer voluntarily pulls the record and avoids possible criminal proceedings.

Also in May, Fred Meyer Music, a hundred-store retailer with outlets in six states, creates its own stickering system to warn parents of objectionable lyrics. Dissatisfied with the parental warning sticker system agreed upon between major record labels and groups like the National PTA and PMRC, Meyer Music creates its own sticker and internal criteria for what constitutes objectionable material. The chain vows to follow its own sticker policy and restrict sales of stickered products to minors until the recording industry creates a more standardized system for dealing with warning stickers.

In San Antonio, Texas, a record-store owner is jailed for selling a copy of 2 Live Crew's *As Nasty as They Wanna Be* to the twenty-year-old son of an antipornography activist. Before the June arrest, the San Antonio police department had telephoned eighty-four local record stores to inform them that under state law the record might be considered obscene. The veiled threats and arrest occurred even though police had no judicial ruling regarding the album's obscenity under Texas law.

Also in June, James Anders, county solicitor in Columbia, South Carolina, gives local record stores ten days to remove 2 Live Crew's *As Nasty as They Wanna Be* from their shelves. According to Anders, "We reviewed it, and we definitely feel it's obscene."[3]

Fearing the effects of exposure to controversial songs and performers, the city of Memphis bans minors from attending concerts that feature "potentially harmful" material. The ordinance mimics several others passed in cities such as San Antonio, Texas, and Jacksonville, Florida.

In June, a Nebraska radio station leads a boycott of k d lang for her anti-meat beliefs. Management at KRVN in Lexington feels that lang, a card-carrying member of People for the Ethical Treatment of Animals (PETA), could destroy a huge percentage of their listeners' livelihoods as cattle ranchers. The station concedes that it rarely plays lang's records, so their action is largely symbolic. The boycott occurs despite the fact that none of lang's music addresses the topic of meat consumption.

Louisiana considers a bill to criminalize the sale or distribution of stickered products to any unmarried persons under the age of seventeen. Although vetoed by Louisiana's governor, Buddy Roemer, the bill is reintroduced into the legislature on two other occasions over the next several years.

After receiving multiple complaints from retailers who threaten to refuse to carry the album, Jane's Addiction releases a second cover for its album *Ritual de lo Habitual*. The original cover is a photograph of a sculpture created by the group's singer, Perry Farrell. It features a nude, anatomically correct threesome (one of whom is Farrell, the other two unidentified women) lying in each other's arms. Though partially covered with a red cloth, the Farrell character shows an exposed penis. Says Farrell, "Every time we were at a meeting, they'd bring up the fact that they find the penis objectionable. Like the cock's too much."[4] The alternative cover shows the band's and album's names and the text of the First Amendment to the U.S. Constitution. Once both album covers are put out for sale, Warner VP Charlie Springer says, "The original cover is not meeting with as much resistance as we thought it would."[5]

Members of the New York rock band Too Much Joy are arrested in August in a Florida nightclub for performing 2 Live Crew songs. About two months earlier, members of 2 Live Crew were arrested in the same club for performing the same material (from their controversial album *As Nasty as They Wanna Be*). Too Much Joy, staging the concert in support of 2 Live Crew, is arrested by Sheriff Nick Navarro (the same person 2 Live Crew sued to fight the album's obscenity ruling) and faces a fine and a one-year prison term for performing the songs. The band is found innocent by a jury that deliberates for thirteen minutes and later chastises police for wasting its time.

Record World refuses to carry the debut album by Professor Griff in any of its stores, calling it "totally obscene." Professor Griff (aka Richard Griff) never sings about sex, drugs, or alcohol and rarely uses foul language on the album. The content objected to by Record World executives is the album's controversial political message. Previously, Griff has been accused of making anti-Semitic and black-separatist statements. The chain continues to sell other albums containing controversial racist statements, such as those of Guns N' Roses.

In October, the lead singer of the heavy metal parody band GWAR, is arrested in Charlotte, North Carolina, on charges of "disseminating obscenity" at one of the band's performances. David Murray Brockie, who goes by the stage name Oderus Urungus, is arrested for "depiction of anal intercourse, masturbation, and excretory functions." The club's owner also is arrested for "knowingly allowing a crime on the premise of a business with an alcohol license." While arresting Brockie, police confiscate one of the band's stage props—a "two and a half foot rubber penis," which the band describes as a rubber fish. Commenting on the charges, Brockie says the incident is "a mirror image of the true obscenities of the culture we live in. That's what they're really afraid of."[6]

After promoting its premier in a daylong "Madonnathon," MTV refuses to air Madonna's video for "Justify My Love" because it contains scenes of sado-masochism, homosexuality, cross-dressing, and group sex. In a statement to the press, Madonna asks, "Why is it that people are willing to go to a movie and watch someone get blown to bits for no reason and nobody wants to see two girls kissing or two men snuggling?"[7] Stating that "nobody" wanted to see it is far from the truth. Warner Home Video sells more than eight hundred thousand retail copies of the video.

Madonna caused considerable consternation regarding her open embrace of sexuality in her music and videos.

1991

Wal-Mart, the nation's largest retailer, announces it will not carry any stickered albums in its stores. The chain will carry "clean" or "edited" versions of albums that it considers to be in conflict with customers' "family values." Record companies begin altering album artwork, lyrics, and songs (by such artists as White Zombie, Nirvana, Beck, Outkast, and Rob Zombie) in order to maintain access to Wal-Mart's considerable customer base.

In June, Tele-Community Antenna, a cable service provider with fifty-three systems in six states, pulls MTV from all its systems. One TCA executive calls MTV "borderline pornographic" and uses a handful of complaints about the channel to justify yanking it from 420,000 households. TCA initially wants to move MTV from the basic service to a pay channel, but it cancels MTV entirely when negotiations with the network fail. Following the cancellation, several grassroots efforts campaign for MTV's reinstatement. Although denying that negative publicity influences the decision, TCA restores MTV to most of its systems within two weeks.

In November, one of the nation's largest cable providers, with fifty-five systems in nineteen states, announces it plans to replace MTV with the less controversial Video Jukebox Network. Sammons Communications says some families do not want MTV in their homes, and MTV's refusal to become a pay service forces Sammons to drop the channel. Disgruntled subscribers form a group called Viewers Voice for MTV, which begins a petition and publicity campaign to lobby for MTV's reinstatement. MTV airs several ads that feature artists such as Paula Abdul and Phil Collins, who suggest that viewers contact Sammons and ask for the channel to be restored. Sammons relents and returns MTV to its basic cable service four months later.

Country Music Television and its parent company, The Nashville Network, both ban Garth Brooks's video for "The Thunder Rolls" because it graphically depicts domestic violence. They take this action despite the fact that both networks aired the video up to six times a day for several weeks without receiving a single complaint. The video shows a husband, played by Brooks, having an adulterous affair and then returning home and abusing his wife. The video then shows the wife shooting the husband. The networks pull the video after Brooks refuses to add a spoken message at its conclusion. Brooks eventually edits the song and accompanying video to remove the domestic violence footage.

Also in November, the Simon Wiesenthal Center, a Jewish human-rights group, lobbies four major record chains to remove Ice Cube's *Death Certificate* from their shelves. The center objects to anti-Semitic references throughout the record and, in particular, to a lyric in the song "No Vaseline" that advocates violence against Jews and claims, "You can't be the nigga for life crew with a white Jew telling you what to do." A spokesperson for the center calls the record a "cultural Molotov cocktail"[8] and identifies additional racist hate messages in *Death Certificate* directed at Koreans and homosexuals. The center has previously protested albums by Public Enemy, Madonna, and Guns N' Roses—but it never before called for an album's withdrawal. *Billboard* magazine joins in the condemnation of the album, which is promptly dropped by hundreds of retail stores. Despite the controversy, the album debuts at number two on the album charts.

1992

MTV refuses to air Public Enemy's video for "Hazy Shade of Criminal" because it violates the network's standards for violence. The video contains graphic footage of violence during a political demonstration and riot in Africa.

Washington State legislators pass a law in February banning the sale of "erotic music" to minors; the bill amends the state's "harmful to minors" statute to include musical recordings. In the process, lawmakers inadvertently outlaw the sale of classical musical compositions by Mozart, Beethoven, Verdi, and Richard Strauss. The law holds retailers liable for selling music that "appeals to the prurient interests of minors in sex; which is patently offensive because it affronts contemporary community standards relating to . . . sexual matters or sadomasochistic abuse; and is utterly without redeeming social value."[9] Opponents feel that the bill will lead to adult-only sections in music stores. Eventually the law is overturned, but it is reintroduced in 1994.

Following the controversy surrounding Ice Cube's album *Death Certificate,* the state of Oregon makes it illegal to display Ice Cube's image in any retail store. The ban even extends to ads for St. Ides Malt Liquor, which uses Ice Cube as a spokesperson.

The police chief of Guilderland, New York, threatens local retailers who sell albums bearing the universal parental warning sticker. The officer warns local record stores that if they sell those albums, they will be prosecuted for the "illegal sale" of stickered products under New York obscenity laws.

Super Club Music Corporation releases a memo in April restricting sales of stickered and nonstickered rap titles to minors. The Marietta, Georgia–based company owns three hundred Record Bar,

Tracks, Rhythm Views, and Turtles retail stores. The memo begins by saying, "We believe in First Amendment rights of freedom of speech and creative, artistic expressions." It goes on to warn managers to "pay particular attention to pronouncements from local judges and district attorneys" and pull albums immediately when "a judge with jurisdiction over your market declares his intention to prosecute the sale of a particular title."[10]

Furthermore, the chain encourages managers to "restrict the sale of certain titles to customers eighteen and older, whether they carry a warning label by the manufacturer." With the exception of three albums by Andrew Dice Clay, the list of restricted artists is comprised entirely of rap artists. To help enforce the policies, Super Club announces it will use computerized monitoring to ensure that customers produce proof of age before purchasing questionable products.

In a sting coordinated by a group calling itself Omaha for Decency, four music stores in Omaha, Nebraska, are charged with "distributing material harmful to minors" for selling 2 Live Crew's *Sports Weekend* to teenagers. Charges are dropped when the stores cut a deal with prosecutors and make a public statement that they will not sell *Sports Weekend* and will refrain from selling any questionable material to minors.

John Moran's *The Manson Family* becomes the first classical recording to carry a parental warning sticker. As the title indicates, the opera deals with murders committed by the followers of Charles Manson. The recording label, Phillips Classics, sees the promotional value in the labeling and orders promotional materials that include prominently displayed parental warning stickers.

In July, following intense public pressure and protest, Ice-T drops the song "Cop Killer" from his *Body Count* album. One month after the album is released, police organizations across the country protest Ice-T, begin boycotting all Time-Warner products, and threaten to divest the Time-Warner stock owned by police pension funds. Alabama Governor Guy Junt calls for all record stores to stop carrying the album. Two months after protests begin, Ice-T announces that he is asking Warner Brothers to reissue the album without the song. The company immediately recalls all copies of *Body Count* and halts production. Law enforcement groups say that protests and boycotts will continue until Ice-T issues an apology. The thirty-five thousand member National Black Police Association refuses to join in the boycotts because, according to the group's executive director, "Where were these police groups when the police beat up Rodney King?"[11] The controversy leads to a number of record companies pulling anti-cop songs from rap releases, such as "Shoot 'Em Down" by Boo-Yaa Tribe, Tragedy's "Bullet" and the albums *Bush Killa* by Paris and *Live and Let Die* by Kool G Rap and DJ Polo.

After Irish singer Sinéad O'Connor tears up a photograph of Pope John Paul II during a December performance on *Saturday Night Live*, critics quickly call for boycotts of her albums. Sinéad issues a statement saying, "The story of my people [the Irish] is the story of the African people, the Jewish people, the Amer-Indian people, the South African people. My story is the story of countless millions of children whose families and nations were torn apart for money in the name of Jesus Christ."[12] In addition to suffering boycotts and widespread public outrage, O'Connor is booed offstage at a New York concert honoring Bob Dylan.

1993

Protests erupt after Guns N' Roses releases its album *The Spaghetti Incident,* which contains a cover version of a song written by Charles Manson. Previous legal judgments against Manson force Guns N' Roses to pay royalties from the song to the child of one of the Manson Family's seven murder victims. Guns N' Roses' record label, Geffen Records, offers to make a donation to the Doris Tate Crime Victims Bureau (named for the mother of Sharon Tate, another Manson Family victim), but the victims' group still vows to boycott all Geffen-related music, movies, and other creative endeavors. Members of the Guardian Angels picket Geffen's New York and Los Angeles offices, calling for the label to remove the song from the album.

In October, two urban-contemporary radio stations announce they will begin to screen rap songs according to their own standards of decency. Taking the stance of "Enjoyability with Responsibility," WBLS-FM in New York and KACE-FM in Los Angeles hold that some popular rap music contains indecent or negative views of black urban life. Management announces that the stations will not air songs that mention violence, gangs, sex, or drugs, nor will they air songs that contain references to women as "bitches" and "hoes." Other stations use the controversial songs to facilitate on-air dialogues with listeners about the themes.

In November, Wal-Mart and Kmart refuse to stock Nirvana's second album, *In Utero*, because they object to the cover art and one of the song titles. Shortly before singer Kurt Cobain's death and shortly after the record becomes the number-one-selling album in the country, the mass merchandisers strike a deal to carry the album. The album's back-cover art is subdued (images of pink fetuses are removed), and the title of the offending song is changed from "Rape Me" to "Waif Me."

1994

Pennsylvania legislators consider a bill aimed at preventing retailers from selling stickered records, tapes, and compact discs to minors. According to sponsor T. J. Rooney, the bill will help to "protect our children from negative, violent, sexual, and potentially harmful influences."[13] Following its failure, the bill is reintroduced the following year.

The House Energy and Commerce Subcommittee holds hearings in April to determine the necessity of rating gangsta rap records. Fearing that exposure to gangsta rap provokes violence among teens, the congressional subcommittee considers a ratings system similar to that proposed for rock music by the PMRC nine years earlier. The hearings are organized at the urging of singer Dionne Warwick.

Also in April, House Speaker Newt Gingrich tells *Broadcasting and Cable* magazine that he strongly encourages advertisers to pull all advertisements on radio stations that broadcast rap music. Gingrich refuses to identify those specific artists and songs he finds offensive.

Singer Marilyn Manson is arrested by police in Jacksonville, Florida, for violating the Adult Entertainment Code. During his performance earlier that evening, Manson doused himself with water, shaking violently to spray it onto his audience. At the time, Manson was dressed in rubber underpants with an extension in the front to hold his penis. Police observed the act and thought Manson was inserting a dildo into his anus while urinating on the audience. The charges were quickly dropped.

1995

Time-Warner CEO Gerald Levin asks Warner Music executives to draft a more specific ratings system to replace the current RIAA universal sticker. Warner is at the center of fierce controversy over the company's roster of gangsta rap artists.

Following protests that Michael Jackson's song "They Don't Care About Us" is anti-Semitic, Jackson changes the song's lyrics. The offending phrases "Jew me" and "kike me" are changed to "do me" and "strike me."

2 Live Crew

Lawyer and evangelical Christian Jack Thompson wanted to keep 2 Live Crew records out of the hands of children at any cost. Little did he know that the attention he created for the band propelled them to a level of fame they would never have received otherwise. If it weren't for Thompson's efforts to censor 2 Live Crew, you might have never heard of the group.

2 Live Crew had enjoyed an unexceptional career as a rap troupe for five years before *As Nasty as They Wanna Be* was released in 1989. Although their singles "We Want Some Pussy," "The Fuck Shop," and "Head Booty and Cock" didn't exactly burn up the charts, the group (featuring Luther "Luke Skyywalker" Campbell, Christopher "Fresh Kid Ice" Wong-Won, Mark "Brother Marquis" Ross, and David "Mr. Mixx" Hobbs) was starting to build a reputation in the rap underground as a salacious but forgettable comedy rap group. They followed in the footsteps of "blue-humored" records by Redd Foxx and Richard Pyror and the work of pioneering rapper Blowfly.

No one questions whether the lyrics of *As Nasty as They Wanna Be* were sexually suggestive (the album contains eighty-seven references to oral sex alone). The real question was whether or not it was obscene. The answer volleyed back and forth for several years, finally being settled in 1993 when the Supreme Court refused to hear an appeal of the case, letting the decision stand that *As Nasty as They Wanna Be* was constitutionally protected speech. The Supreme Court, however, did hear another case involving 2 Live Crew.

In 1989, the band had created a rap version of the Roy Orbison classic "Pretty Woman." 2 Live Crew's version described "big, hairy," "bald-headed," "two-timing women." The band had applied for and been denied license to include song samples from the original from Nashville publishing giant Acuff-Rose. Upon the song's release, Acuff-Rose sued the band. 2 Live Crew claimed that its version did not require license since it was a

parody of the original (thus falling under the "fair use" provisions of the First Amendment). The case was repeatedly appealed, until it finally reached the Supreme Court. In 1994, the Supreme Court ruled that 2 Live Crew's version was indeed a parody.

By the time these legal troubles ended, 2 Live Crew had slipped out of the public eye. Later albums failed to remain on the record charts and produced little interest in the group's musical talent. Bandleader Luther Campbell eventually filed for bankruptcy in 1995 after

Luke Skyywalker (Campbell), leader of 2 Live Crew, during his arrest on obscenity charges for performing material from *As Nasty as They Wanna Be* in a Florida club. When Campbell was found not guilty by a jury, one of the jurors asked the judge if she could deliver their verdict in the form of a rap.

several failed business ventures involving the band's record label, which he owned and managed.

In May, conservative William Bennett and National Political Congress of Black Women chairwoman C. Delores Tucker speak at a Time-Warner shareholders' meetings and urge the company to drop all Warner Music's rap artists who use violent and/or sexually degrading lyrics. Following the speech, the pair begins a public campaign against rap music. This includes a letter-writing campaign under the banner of Mr. Bennett's conservative think tank, Empower America.

Ten years after the PMRC's creation, the organization's executive director, Barbara Wyatt, renews the call for a records ratings system that is similar to the system in place for films and television. By 1995, none of the four original members are still active in the PMRC, and the group's reduced prominence has brought its annual budget to less than fifty thousand dollars and its paid staff to just one employee.

In December, during their lunch hours, fifteen state employees drive to Boston's WBCN-FM to picket the station for playing music from *Hempilation,* a CD released as a fund-raiser for the National Organization for the Reform of Marijuana Laws. Driving state vehicles and accompanied by a DEA agent and the executive director of the Governor's Alliance Against Drugs, the protestors demand that the station pull all the album cuts currently in rotation, including songs from Black Crowes, Cypress Hill, and Ziggy Marley.

1996

Religious and civic leaders push for the cancellation of a January White Zombie concert in Johnson City, Tennessee. After several area residents object to the performance, the city's municipal attorney announces that city officials will cancel the performance at the ironically named Freedom Hall Civic Center. While officials and protesters are mum after the cancellation, bandleader Rob Zombie quips, "It always amazes me how these God-fearing freedom fighters are so ready to spit on the First Amendment."[14]

Wal-Mart refuses to carry Sheryl Crow's self-titled second album because one of the songs contains an unflattering comment about the discount retailer. The ban occurs after Crow refuses to delete the lyric "Watch our children while they kill each other with a gun bought at the Wal-Mart store" from her song "Love Is a Good Thing." Wal-Mart does not sell guns to minors, although it does sell rifles and other weapons in its stores. Wal-Mart had sold one out of every ten copies of Crow's debut album.

1997

In New Braunfels, Texas, eighteen-year-old John Schroder is arrested in a local grocery store and charged with making an obscene display for wearing a Marilyn Manson T-shirt. Other customers had called police after seeing the shirt, which depicted singer Marilyn Manson and was inscribed with the words I AM THE GOD OF FUCK on the back. A Kentucky woman also is prosecuted and fined for wearing the shirt in public.

A group calling themselves Oklahomans for Children and Families urges the Oklahoma City city council to cancel a lease with a concert promoter who is planning a Marilyn Manson concert at the State Fairgrounds. After reviewing a lyric sheet provided by the group, council member and attorney Jerry Foshee deems the songs obscene under state law and says the group will be prosecuted if they perform in Oklahoma. After public hearings, the council passes a resolution urging the State Fair board to ensure that Marilyn Manson complies with all state obscenity laws. Oklahoma Governor Frank Keating is disappointed that the concert will take place, but he hopes people will not attend the event. "If no one comes to listen to their trash, this group will go elsewhere and not come back," says Governor Keating. He continues by calling the band "bent on degrading women, religion, and decency, while promoting satanic worship, child abuse, and drug use." Upon questioning, Keating admits he has never heard the band but bases his comments on information provided to him by others.

Tale of a Marilyn Manson Concert Tour

During the band's 1997 concert tour, Marilyn Manson attracted protests and censors like honey attracts flies. Here is a month-by-month list of the high jinks:

February: Shows are protested by religious groups in Salt Lake City; Oklahoma City; Lubbock, Texas; and Fitchburg, Massachusetts (where protesters offer the city council a check for five thousand dollars to cancel the Manson concert at the city-owned venue). School officials in Milwaukee ban the Goth-rock look from schools to discourage students from emulating band members.

March: The city council in Anchorage, Alaska, warns concert promoters that the performance could violate state obscenity laws. According to Councilwoman Cheryl Clementson, "There will be no eating of little animals on the stage, or oral sex, or anything else that they have claimed to do."

Marilyn Manson on tour in 1997

April: Religious groups protest shows in LaCrosse, Wisconsin; Evansville, Indiana; Normal, Illinois; and Columbia, South Carolina. Legislators in Mississippi write to concert promoters and ask that they refrain from bringing the band's "counter-cultural and/or radical messages" to the state. In Jacksonville, Florida, five thousand people contact the mayor's office to urge him to cancel the show. In Saginaw, Michigan, a local minister collects twenty thousand signatures that support canceling a Marilyn Manson concert at a city-owned venue. In Fort Wayne, Indiana, religious protesters claim to have acquired the ability to "bind" evil spirits. They post a prayer on the Internet that they claim will restrict the powers of the demons accompanying the Marilyn Manson concert tour and force the group to cancel its local concert.

OUTRAGEOUS!!!

*"Kill your parents"
(on t-shirts)

*"Each age has to have at least one brave individual that tried to bring an end to Christianity. No one has managed to succeed yet, but maybe through music we can do it."

*"I am the All-American Anti Christ."

*Indecent exposure ON STAGE, obscenities beyond description, "Kill God" props.

*Lyrics and ideas too far out even for MTV without editing..."Totally Offensive" (as described by their own writer/singer).

These are the quotes/actions/merchandise of Marilyn Manson and his rock-metal group of the same name, appearing at the Fitchburg Civic Center on February 21st.!!!!!!!

DISGUSTED TOO? Join us.

At a protest, Civic Center, Feb. 15, 5:50 p.m.
At Fitchburg City Council Meeting, Tues., Feb. 18,7:30 p.m.

OUR KIDS NEED YOUR PARTICIPATION
Paid for by Mass State Council, Knights of Columbus

A flyer advertising a meeting for parents to force the cancellation of a Marilyn Manson concert in Massachusetts

May: Local politicians in Richmond, Virginia; Utica, New York; and Washington, D.C., argue for the cancellation of local Marilyn Manson concert dates. According to D.C. councilwoman Nadine Winter, "It's time to stop creating a platform for people who say, 'Kill your mother, kill your father.' " In Richmond, City Manager Robert Bobb calls the band's "satanic" performances "animalistic."

June: Officials overseeing New Jersey Meadowlands threaten to cancel Ozzfest '97 unless Marilyn Manson is removed from the bill. A federal judge rules against the venue, calling their case "groundless."

Three owners of Lyric Hall in Oxford, Mississippi, are arrested and handed six-month jail terms for booking a performance by 2 Live Crew. Judge Glen Anderson refuses to hear testimony from witnesses for the defense during the sentencing. In addition, despite the prosecutor's endorsement, he rejects a request for a plea bargain.

Officials at New Mexico State University cancel an upcoming Marilyn Manson concert. They claim it has nothing to do with protests by conservative groups; rather, they cannot find thirty security officers to work during the performance. Local police wonder why the university doesn't simply hire a security firm.

The Philadelphia Fraternal Order of Police sues the Crucifucks and their label, Alternative Tentacles, for featuring a photo of a dead policeman on the cover of the band's album *Our Will Be Done*. The photo, taken of a very-much-alive Philadelphia police officer who posed for an FOP advertisement used during 1986 union contract negotiations, was used on the album cover without securing the proper licensing agreement. According to FOP spokesman Richard Costello, the intent of the suit is to punish the defendants for their apparent endorsement of violence against police. He says, "I'm hoping for every last dime these people have, up to the penny in their loafers, if we can get it."

City officials in Richmond, Virginia, attempt to cancel a Marilyn Manson concert because they feel the group's songs promote rape, murder, and self-mutilation. After receiving word that the state's chapter of the American Civil Liberties Union is planning a lawsuit, the city council votes to allow the concert. Robert C. Bobb, Richmond's city manager, tells reporters that the band is still not welcome and that police will heavily monitor the concert.

In June, Insane Clown Posse's *The Great Milenko* is pulled from stores and the band is dropped from its record label within hours of the album's release. The band's label, Hollywood Records, receives its marching orders from the parent company, Disney, even though company officials have known of the album's content for nearly a year. The about-face happens shortly after Southern Baptists vote to boycott all Disney-affiliated products, calling the company "immoral" and "reprehensible" and saying Disney has established an "antifamily agenda" by promoting homosexuality, drugs, and violence.

Rap duo Insane Clown Posse. The group was dropped by its record label on the same day its debut album was released, due to controversial lyrics.

Also in June, Texas Governor George W. Bush signs into law a rider to a state appropriations bill. The rider requires state pension funds to divest any assets that are invested in record companies that produce "obscene" albums. During debate on the measure, Republican State Senator Bill Ratiff distributes CDs of Snoop Doggy Dog, Marilyn Manson, and Nine Inch Nails, citing them as examples of works partly funded by Texas retirement plans. Country music legend (and Texan) Willie Nelson writes a letter to legislators urging them to vote against the bill, saying, "Like a great many artists, I speak quite frankly with my audience. Often times it is the only way to talk about certain subjects and situations that some may find unpleasant but are a very real part of America."[15] In an attempt to bypass First Amendment concerns, the legislation is carefully written to avoid mentioning the words "obscenity" and "offensive." Specifically, the measure prohibits investment in any company which "records or produces any song, lyrics, or other musical work that explicitly describes, glamorizes, or advocates: 1) acts of criminal violence, including murder, assault, assault on police officers, sexual assault, and robbery; 2) necrophilia, bestiality, or pedophilia; 3) illegal use of controlled substances; 4) criminal street gang activity; 5) degradation or denigration of females; or 6) violence against a particular sex, ethnic group, sexual orientation, or religion."[16]

Local authorities ban a group of Cuban musicians from performing in Miami in September. The musicians hope to play at an international trade show to showcase the talent of Latin American and

Caribbean artists. Officials blame the ban on local regulations. Latin pop star Gloria Estefan accuses Dade County of pandering to right-wing Cuban-Americans, saying, "I can't imagine how we could explain to the people of Cuba, who have suffered so much oppression, that the very freedom that they so desperately desire and deserve are [*sic*] being annihilated in their name."[17]

Senator Sam Brownback, surrounded by lyrics to Marilyn Manson and Master P songs, during his 1997 hearings concerning rock lyrics. Brownback jumped on the antirock bandwagon again following the school shootings in Littleton, Colorado.

Kansas Senator Sam Brownback leads the Senate Commerce Committee in a November hearing on popular music lyrics and the effectiveness of the Recording Industry Association of America's universal parental warning sticker. Despite dozens of offers from rap and rock musicians, the two-hour hearing features only one "supporter" of the music industry, RIAA president Hillary Rosen. There are more than half a dozen speakers rallying against the violent, lewd, and sexual messages contained in popular rock and rap music.

Senator Brownback opens the hearing by describing the jump in teen suicide rates, pregnancy, crime, and drug use. Brownback feels that society has grown "coarser, meaner, and more alienated." Despite a complete lack of evidence linking music to the problems he mentions, Brownback says, "it stands to reason that prolonged exposure to such hate-filled lyrics . . . could have an effect on one's attitudes, assumptions, decisions, and behavior. Understanding the nature and extent of the influence of music violence may well be the first step . . . for ensuring a more civil society."[18] When committee member Senator Joseph Lieberman speaks at the hearing, he focuses on America's "broken culture," a culture in which children are better armed than police.

Another speaker is Raymond Kuntz, who tells the heart-wrenching story of his wife's finding their son shortly after he committed suicide. The son was wearing headphones, with Marilyn Manson's

Antichrist Superstar still in the CD player. Kuntz calls Manson a "drug fiend" who once took LSD before visiting Disney World. He accuses Manson of engaging in disgusting antics during his live shows, such as exposing his genitalia, sodomizing himself with a stick that he later throws into the audience, and inviting the crowd to spit on him (Senator Lieberman remarks that in the era of AIDS, it's shameful to ask people to spit on you).

The final speaker is C. Delores Tucker, who repeats much of the same rhetoric she's been expounding to the press for several years. Despite the fact that dozens of people have volunteered to address the session (and been turned down), Mrs. Tucker urges Senator Brownback to allow the young man who has accompanied her to the hearing to speak. The request is granted, and the youth states that it is extremely easy to purchase stickered products in record stores (in fact, it is completely legal for minors to purchase stickered products). He also describes how "satanic" fans invaded his neighborhood and committed random acts of violence before a Marilyn Manson concert.

No legislation is proposed as a result of the hearings.

Students at Southview High School in Fayetteville, North Carolina, are suspended in December after protesting a ban on rock and rap T-shirts in their school. Principal Tony Parker initially bans only T-shirts featuring the group Marilyn Manson, but he later expands the ban to include shirts that feature Wu-Tang Clan and Tupac Shakur. Eighteen students who protest the order by leaving class are told to return to class or face suspension. Half of the students choose suspension. Sherrie Ellis, mother of one of the nine suspended students, says she is proud of her daughter's act of protest, "I'm ecstatic. I'm the happiest momma in North Carolina."[19]

Following protests by groups such as the National Organization for Women, Kmart and Wal-Mart pull Prodigy's *The Fat of the Land* from shelves—even though they have sold the CD for nine months. Pressure groups interpret the song "Smack My Bitch Up" as condoning violence against women. The song's lyrics consist of only two sentences: "Change my pitch up. Smack my bitch up." According to the band's lead singer, Liam Howlett, the phrases refer to doing anything with intensity and have nothing to do with women. Before the ban, Wal-Mart and Kmart had sold 150,000 copies of the album without a single customer complaint.

1998

Legislators in South Carolina introduce legislation that requires concerts to carry ratings similar to those featured on television programs and movies. Concert promoters and First Amendment advocates consider the legislation to be completely unenforceable and potentially nightmarish. The measure fails.

Eighteen-year-old Eric Van Hoven is suspended from Zeeland High School in Holland, Michigan, for wearing a T-shirt promoting the band Korn, even though the shirt contains no images or words save the band's name. Zeeland's conduct code forbids clothing bearing any references to obscenity, drugs, violence, or sex. Assistant Principal Gretchen Plewes calls the shirt "vulgar, obscene, and insulting" but fails to describe precisely why the band's name is so upsetting or violates school policy.

Police arrest Shawn Thomas in March after reading the lyrics to his new album 'Til My Casket Drops. Thomas—better known as gangsta rapper C-Bo—had been paroled in early 1997 after serving nine months on a weapons-related conviction. Thomas's parole agreement states that he is not permitted "to engage in any behavior which promotes the gang lifestyle, criminal behavior and/or violence against law enforcement." But "Deadly Game," a song on the new CD, contains lyrics criticizing California's "three strikes and you're out" law: "You better swing, batter, swing 'cause once you get your third felony, yeah, 50 years you gotta bring . . . Fuck my P.O., I'm going A.W.O.L . . . bound for another state, me and my crew . . . California and Pete Wilson can suck my dick." Within days of the album's release, Thomas is arrested and charged with parole violation.

Florida legislators withhold $104,000 in state funding for public radio station WMNF because they object to the station's programming. Republican state senator John Grant initiates a move to slash one-eighth of the station's budget when he hears on-air praises for Kurt Cobain, broadcasts of Iris DeMent's "Wasteland of the Free" (containing the lyric "We got CEO's makin' 200 times the worker's pay. But they'll fight like hell against raisin' the minimum wage"), and the song "Undone" by Robert Earl Keen (which includes the lyrical phrases "back seat sex" and "son of a bitch"). Using state money to intimidate others is familiar territory for Grant, who has previously attempted to revoke funding from the University of Southern Florida for inviting gay Olympian Greg Louganis to speak on campus.

At a Fort Worth, Texas, conference entitled "Marilyn Manson Awareness Training," sponsored by Crime Prevention Resource Center (CPRC), representatives of several local police departments advocate the forced hospitalization of Marilyn Manson fans. Other proposals include the development of databases that will track the musical tastes and Internet usage of "suspicious youth." According to CPRC director Ramon Jacquez, "There's no difference between a Manson fan and a Crips gang member."[20] Jacquez also wants to classify groups of "Goth rock" fans as street gangs.

A free concert by the Indigo Girls scheduled in April for a South Carolina high school is canceled when the school's principal learns the performers are gay. Irmo High School principal Gerald Witt receives some complaints from parents and cancels the performance, even though Witt had earlier reviewed the content of several of the Grammy Award–winning group's CDs. Witt says, "I don't see us as a platform for community kinds of issues."[21] The resultant controversy and adverse publicity lead to cancellations of Indigo

The Indigo Girls. The duo had several concerts canceled after school officials learned that the two women were lesbians.

Girls concerts in two Tennessee schools. Thirteen students are suspended for protesting the cancellations. The director of the South Carolina ACLU chapter says, "Homophobia in the South is becoming what race was thirty years ago."[22]

William Bennett and C. Delores Tucker renew their calls against rap music, this time joined by U.S. Senators Joseph Lieberman and Sam Nunn. At a Washington, D.C., press conference in June, the group says that they want record companies to stop selling music with "blatantly pro-drug" lyrics and music they consider to be "obscene." Examples of the group's targets include Wu-Tang Clan, Notorious B.I.G., Geto Boys, the Dogg Pound, Tupac Shakur, Gravediggaz, Cypress Hill, Lords of Acid, Black Crowes, and Blues Traveler.

Michigan legislators consider a bill that will require minors to be accompanied by their parents to certain rock concerts. The proposed legislation also requires all artists whose albums carry a parental warning label to provide a similar warning to parents of minors who wish to attend a live concert. Under the bill, advertisements for such concerts must include a warning label like that on CDs and cassettes.

Westerly, Rhode Island, high school student Robert Parker is suspended for wearing a shirt inscribed with a "devilish" message. The shirt features the numbers "666" and a rendering of singer Rob Zombie. School officials feel that the satanic implications of the number "666" may be disruptive in the classroom. The Rhode Island ACLU steps in to remind school officials that satanic messages are indeed religious, and banning religious messages—even sacrilegious ones—violates the student's civil rights.

The high school band at Fort Zumbald North High School in St. Louis is forbidden to play the Jefferson Airplane hit "White Rabbit" because of drug references in the song's lyrics, even though the band's version of the song is entirely instrumental. The school's principal doesn't want to "give the wrong idea about drugs" and believes that the song's lyrics are explicit enough to warrant banning the instrumental version.

Many retailers refuse to carry the soundtrack for the movie *Kama Sutra* because of concerns over the album's cover art. The cover features an image of a man and woman locked in a passionate embrace (although no private body parts are revealed). The image duplicates the promotional posters and advertisements for the film, which have been displayed at movie theaters and published in many newspapers. The record company eventually alters the cover to appease retailers.

1999

Police organizations across the country call for the cancellation of a sold-out concert scheduled for New Jersey's Continental Arena. The concert, featuring headliners Rage Against the Machine, the Beastie Boys, and Bad Religion, is a fund-raiser for death-row inmate Mumia Abu-Jamal. Abu-Jamal was convicted of murdering a police officer in 1981, and plans are to use proceeds to fund his defense appeals. New Jersey officials claim to have been deceived about the fund-raising aspect of the concert. Promoters offer to refund money to any of the sixteen thousand fans who bought concerts tickets. However, few people actually return their tickets.

In February, the city council of Richmond, Virginia, unanimously passes an ordinance outlawing any "pornographic" performance if minors might view such performances. The council defines a pornographic performance as "one that contains a display of male or female genitalia; sadistic, masochistic or violent sexual relationships; sexual relations with a child, corpse, or animal; rape or incest; any sex act, including sexual intercourse."[23] Richmond's council has previously attempted to ban Marilyn Manson from performing at the city-owned Richmond Coliseum. Although the city's ordinance acknowledges the Constitution's ban on prior restraint, it stresses its obligation to balance the "right of free expression against the interest of society in protecting its children and providing for their normal maturation and emotional development."

State representatives in Georgia and North Dakota introduce legislation forbidding the sale of stickered CDs and cassettes to minors. Both states have seen similar bills introduced (and killed) in the legislature before. North Dakota's bill is voted down; however, Georgia's is tabled to allow the recording industry to show how it is discouraging sales of stickered product to children. Says Jim Flatow, government affairs director for the RIAA, "We are happy to work with them or any other legislator to get out the good word on our parental advisory program and parents getting involved in what their children listen to. Ultimately, that's what this is about. We share the same goal."[24]

Starting in February, high school students at Kettle Moraine High School in Wales, Wisconsin, are required to show ID to view *Rolling Stone* magazine in their school library. School board member Gary Vose calls the music and culture magazine "pornographic" and attempts to ban it from school shelves. The school board decides that students must be eighteen years of age to view the magazine's contents, even though a child of *any* age could purchase it at local stores.

Michigan passes legislation aimed at creating a concert ratings system that is similar to the system used to rate movies. In the bill, parental warnings must be attached to all tickets, print advertisements, or radio spots that promote a concert by artists who have released (within the last five years) recordings that bear the RIAA universal parental warning label. "I don't anticipate that there's going to be much criticism," says Mark Lemoine, a spokesperson for the state senator who has introduced the bill. "We're just echoing the voluntary system the recording industry has already put into place."

Local residents pressure the school board in Streetsboro, Ohio, after the board agrees that school facilities can be used for "Spring Mosh '99." The city's mayor has originally denied a permit for the event, citing safety concerns during the concert. The school board then circumvents the mayor's decision when it decides that the event does not require a permit for use of the school's facilities. The concert, a benefit for the high school's student-run radio station, features a variety of local and regional rock acts whose songs do contain some profanity and sexual innuendo. According to local resident Dave Hamner, "This is a war against the classroom. The views of the bands undermine the educator's work in the classroom."[25]

Following a customer complaint about obscene lyrics, both Wal-Mart and Kmart pull Godsmack's self-titled debut album, even though the band's label (Universal) does not feel the album lyrics warrant a parental warning sticker. Kevin Clarke of Cleveland bitterly complained to a local Wal-Mart store that the album, which contains the word "motherfucker" nine times, is unfit for teenagers. Before Clarke's protest, Kmart and Wal-Mart had stocked the album for more than a year, selling seventy thousand copies of the record without receiving one customer objection.

State Assemblyman Robert D'Andrea introduces a bill in the New York legislature aimed at banning the sale of targeted recordings to minors. D'Andrea's legislation would forbid sales to minors of any recording that features suicide, sodomy, rape, incest, bestiality, violent racism, religious violence, sadomasochism, adultery, sexual assault, sexual activity, murder, morbid violence, and illegal use of drugs or alcohol. In a similar bill D'Andrea submitted in 1995, he even specified the size, color, and type style of the sticker affixed to such titles.

In the wake of the school shootings in Littleton, Colorado, presidential candidate Dan Quayle suggests that conservatives publish the names and addresses of record-company executives and board members. Quayle feels that the information may prove useful so "neighbors can go to their fancy cocktail parties and make them ashamed."

Kansas Senator Sam Brownback holds a congressional hearing before the Senate Commerce Committee into the link between teen violence and the entertainment industry. The witness list includes several other senators, conservative commentator William Bennett, and representatives of several industry and advocacy groups; however, no representatives participate to defend music, movies, or video games. Says Brownback, "Over the past several years, our society seems to have become increasingly flooded with music with lyrics that glorify suicide, torture and murder."

A school superintendent in Portsmouth, New Hampshire, forbids students to wear Marilyn Manson T-shirts or other Goth attire. Superintendent Suzanne Schrader does not want a reprise of the violence in Littleton, Colorado, at one of her schools. Says Schrader, "When kids come back from vacation, they better not even think about wearing Marilyn Manson [shirts]. Parents are welcome to challenge me in court."

State park officials in Kentucky uninvite blues singer Bobby Rush, because they fear his act is too sexually suggestive. Originally officials offer Rush a contract to perform at the annual Hot August

Blues and BBQ Festival at Kenlake State Park Resort in Hardin, Kentucky. They later revoke the invitation (even though none of the officials in charge of the festival has ever seen Rush perform). Everett Huffman of the Kentucky Civil Liberties Union says, "I think it's shortsighted for park officials to basically strike him for his music because they think his music is outside the mainstream. After all, they are sponsoring a blues festival."

The city council of Fresno, California, unanimously passes a resolution that condemns musicians whose music is filled with "anger and hate." Says Councilman Henry Perea, "If people were on the street and engaged in some of the same behaviors that [Manson] demonstrates onstage, they'd probably be arrested."[26]

President Clinton requests, and Congress approves, government inquiries into any possible link between teen violence and the entertainment industry. The measure charges the Federal Trade Commission and the Justice Department to investigate if the entertainment industry targets advertising for violent products at children (similar to an investigation of the tobacco industry two years earlier). It also directs the National Institutes of Health to examine the effects of violent movies, video games, Internet sites, and music on young children and grants a limited antitrust exemption for the entertainment industry to establish a "code of conduct" for various entertainment products.

A Jewish advocacy group calls for boycotts of the rap group Public Enemy over the single "Swindler's Lust," claiming that the single is anti-Semitic. Abraham Foxman, national director of the Anti-Defamation League, says the song is rife with anti-Semitic references, including allusions to Jews controlling the banking industry, plus the words "six" and "millions"—referring to the number of people who died in the Holocaust. Public Enemy's Chuck D says no harm was intended toward anyone, clarifying that "six" refers to the six major record companies, and the only mention of "millions" refers to the Million Man March on Washington, D.C., in 1995.

Kmart refuses to stock Ministry's *Dark Side of the Spoon* because the company objects to the album's cover, which features an overweight nude woman wearing a dunce cap and facing a chalkboard. Written repeatedly on the chalkboard is the phrase "I will be

God." Despite its history of making similar decisions, Wal-Mart stores decide to carry the album.

Senator Sam Brownback writes a letter to Seagram's/MCA (parent company to Interscope Records), asking them "to cease and desist profiteering from peddling violence to young people" and suggesting that the company cease production of all Marilyn Manson records. The bill is cosigned by several other senators, including John Ashcroft of Missouri, Ben Nighthorse Campbell and Wayne Allard of Colorado, Susan Collins of Maine, Tim Hutchinson of Arkansas, Rick Santorum of Pennsylvania, and Kent Conrad and Byron Dorgan of North Dakota. The letter continues, "Out of respect for the 13 innocent victims in Colorado, sympathy for their grieving families, and concern for young people everywhere, we ask you to strongly reconsider which lyrics the Seagram's corporation chooses to legitimize and popularize."[27]

The parish-city council of Lafayette, Louisiana, passes an ordinance that requires truth in concert advertising, following an appearance of the Family Values Tour (featuring hard-core and rap acts such as Korn, Orgy, Ice Cube, and Limp Bizkit) at the area's Cajundome. The council's measure requires the "content of ads to be consistent with the content of the concert." Apparently some parents felt deceived by the concert's name, not realizing it was a parody. According to council president Walter Comeaux, "When government is able to provide the tools to protect children, I believe it is their obligation."[28]

Church groups and community members in Georgia campaign for the cancellation of the Hard Rock Rockfest, fearing the music of some of the artists will incite attendees to commit violent acts that are similar to those recently experienced at schools in Colorado and Georgia. The protesters do not approve of two of the artists scheduled to perform: the Offspring (for their songs "Beheaded" and "Cool to Hate") and Silverchair (for their song "Suicidal Dream"). The concert features more than half a dozen other artists, such as Everlast, Collective Soul, the Mighty Mighty Bosstones, and Better Than Ezra. Despite protests by more than 100 demonstrators, the concert goes on as scheduled, with over 127,000 people attending; however, both Silverchair and the Offspring drop the controversial songs from their set lists for the performance. According to Mighty Mighty Bosstones signer Dicky Barrett, "To protest the song lyrics, that's really getting picky, like you're just looking for someone to blame. It's just music, dude. Take it for what it's worth."[29]

Senators Joseph Lieberman of Connecticut and Sam Brownback of Kansas initiate a campaign entitled "An Appeal to Hollywood," asking the entertainment industry to "take modest steps of self-restraint" about the "increasingly toxic popular culture." The appeal contains cosignatures from former Presidents Ford and Carter; former Generals Colin Powell and Norman Schwarzkopf; political figures William Bennett and Mario Cuomo; entertainers Naomi Judd and Steve Allen; and ten thousand other concerned citizens. After introducing the campaign, Lieberman warns the entertainment industry, "If you don't use your rights with some sense of responsibility . . . there is a danger that those very rights will be endangered."

Congressman Henry Hyde of Illinois, best known as the lead prosecutor in the Clinton impeachment trial, introduces legislation that would require music retailers to provide lyric sheets to parents "on demand." Backlash to Hyde's proposal is so severe that he retracts his legislation two days later, yet he vows to introduce new legislation that will ban the sale to minors of movies, video games, and music that contains graphic sex or violence.

Senators John McCain of Arizona and Joseph Lieberman of Connecticut introduce to the Senate the 21st Century Media Responsibility Act of 1999. The measure proposes changing the Cigarette Labeling and Advertising Act (which strictly regulates how tobacco products can be advertised) to include entertainment products. The bill would also require the entertainment industry to devise its own ratings system. Lieberman hints that entertainment executives and artists could be criminally prosecuted under the measure.

The county commission in Birmingham, Alabama, passes a resolution to "eliminate violent, vulgar concerts" from the Birmingham-Jefferson Convention Complex. The commissioners are upset by a concert that featured Rob Zombie, Korn, and Videodrome. The commissioner who proposed the resolution, Bettye Fine Collins, says that such concerts only encourage young people to get "off track."

Officials at the P.S. 1 Contemporary Art Center in Long Island City, New York, cancel a musical performance presented by Bedroom Productions featuring a group of deejays and electronic musicians. Officials received complaints from local residents about the performance, which contained obscenities directed toward police.

The national Fraternal Order of Police announces a mass boycott against musical artists who support a new trial for death-row inmate Mumia Abu-Jamal. The group specifically targets Rage Against the Machine and the Beastie Boys, but plans to keep an updated list on its Web site once it has compiled a list of all the musicians who support Abu-Jamal. According to FOP national president Gilbert Gallagos, "We want to provide our members and the general public with the information they need to inflict economic punishment on the supporters of this cop-killer." The group is also investigating a group of musicians, including REM singer Michael Stipe, ex–Talking Head David Byrne, and Sting, who signed their names in a 1995 *New York Times* advertisement supporting a new trial for Abu-Jamal.

The group Rock for Life urges mass boycotts and cancellations of Rage Against the Machine over the content of its album *The Battle for Los Angeles*. According to Rock for Life director Erik Whittington, "These guys support baby killing and hate Christians. Because music fans continue to buy Rage Against the Machine CDs and concert tickets, the band is given a huge platform to spew their hateful propaganda while thousands numbfully accept it as gospel."

Four hundred police officers picket a Rage Against the Machine concert at the Worcester Centrum in Massachusetts after calling for the concert's cancellation. The protesters are angered by the band's support of convicted murderer Mumia Abu-Jamal.

Third Eye Blind gives in to record company pressure to remove the song "Slow Motion" from its second album, *Blue*. The song, originally intended as an antiviolence song, contains multiple references to drugs, violence, and youth murders similar to the Columbine shootings earlier in the year. The move to remove the song started with Elektra Records chairwoman and CEO Sylvia Rhone, who justified her action by saying the song "didn't work in the context of the current social climate."

The National Football League drops a series of four commercials based on rapper Eminem's song "My Name Is" because they feel the song is too controversial, even though the commercials contain none of the original lyrics. The NFL campaign features new lyrics and is called "My Name Is Joe," highlighting the careers of football stars Joe Namath, Joe Gibbs, Joe Montana, and "Mean" Joe Greene. A spokesperson for the league says that they were unaware of the Eminem song's controversial nature.

In December, after the high school senior class in Belen, New Mexico, votes Ozzy Osbourne's "Goodbye to Romance" as their class song, the school board steps in to review their choice, deciding that the song is inappropriate. According to school board member Robert White, who admits he has never heard the song or read the lyrics, "Ozzy could be singing 'Mary Had a Little Lamb' and I would have a problem with it because of his history as someone who presents a negative message and a negative world view."[30]

19

2000

2000

During his annual State of the Union speech in January, President Bill Clinton calls for a voluntary, uniform ratings system for the entertainment industry. Clinton's proposal would replace the current movie, television, video game, and music rating and warning systems with a universal system.

Police officers in Northwood, Ohio, order fourteen-year-old Daniel Shellhammer to remove his shirt, which features slogans for the rap group Insane Clown Posse. The officers inform Shellhammer that Insane Clown Posse clothing is "banned" in Ohio and that they will tear the shirt off his back and arrest him if he does not comply. The T-shirt features the name of the band on the front and a picture of Santa Claus with a bullet in his head on the verso. Shellhammer and his family sue the police officers for civil rights violations.

Police in New Iberia, Louisiana, close down a roller-skating rink in February and seize more than sixty CDs after a fight breaks out in the rink's parking lot. Police accuse the rink's management of instigating the incident by playing music over the rink's PA system. The rink's owner and manager are charged with contributing to the delinquency of juveniles for playing "vulgar" music. Among the confiscated CDs are ones by Britney Spears and Christina Aguilera and the popular tunes "The Chicken Dance," "Rudolph the Red Nosed Reindeer," "The Hokey Pokey," and "Jingle Bells."

A private school in San Antonio, Texas, suspends four students for attending a Backstreet Boys concert in March. The students are suspended for one day for violating a school policy forbidding "involvement in inappropriate music [or] dancing." The school justifies its action, saying, "our conduct must be moral and upright twenty-four hours a day." Three of the four students served their sentence; one student's parents withdrew him from the school.

Tennessee's state Senate and General Assembly consider the Tennessee 21st Century Media Market Responsibility Act of 2000, which requires state's Department of Children's Services to screen movies, video games, and music. The legislation also calls for a ratings system for all violent entertainment media, which will decide on the appropriateness of material for young people.

After airing it for over a month, MTV requests edits in the video for the Bloodhound Gang's "The Bad Touch." The request comes after complaints from the Gay and Lesbian Alliance Against Defamation. In the clip, the group, dressed as monkeys, assaults a pair of sailors walking through Paris arm in arm, feeding each other french fries. According to GLAAD spokeperson Scott Seomin, "I know it's a satire, but a gay-bashing scene in any context in today's climate is not acceptable."

The rap group the Murderers see their album *Irv Gotti Presents the Murderers* delayed three times over their label's concerns about lyrics that use derogatory terms for homosexuals and slurs aimed at police. Executives from the BET music channel say the group is too negative for play on the channel.

Students at the University of Maryland and the University of Wisconsin ask for the cancellation of performances by the Bloodhound Gang over lyrical content of an unreleased song. The song, entitled, "Yellow Fever," details the protagonist's desire to have sex with Asian women. The four-year-old song has never been commercially released and has rarely been performed in concert. Shveta Kulkarni of the Associated Students of Madison Diversity Committee says the issue has surfaced now because of the group's increasing popularity. The concerts go on as planned, but groups of Asian-American students turn their backs to the band during the shows.

The New York Fraternal Order of Police places Bruce Springsteen on its boycott list and calls for the cancellation of his New York performances after Springsteen debuts a song about the shooting of Amadou Diallo, entitled "American Skin." The song condemns the police shootings that resulted in Diallo's death. Diallo was shot forty-one times when police mistook his wallet for a gun. Speaking of Springsteen, NYFOP president Bob Lucente says, "He's turned into some type of fucking dirtbag. He has all these good songs and everything, American flag songs and all that stuff, and now he's a floating fag. You can quote me on that."

In August, two Michigan concerts of the Up in Smoke tour (starring Dr. Dre, Snoop Dogg, Ice Cube, and Eminem) cause police intervention over violent and sexual imagery. During the concert, a video is shown that features a robbery and partially naked women. During Eminem's set, he planned to bring a blow-up sex doll onstage. Police threaten arrests and legal action against the venue, concert promoters, and artists if the show goes off as planned. Following last-minute negotiations in Detroit with police, the tour management agrees not to play the videos. The following evening, police in Auburn Hills make similar requests, but the concert management refuses to comply. As a result, Dr. Dre is ticketed for violating the city's nudity ordinances. Dr. Dre files suit against the police for civil rights violations.

The Federal Trade Commission holds hearings before the U.S. Senate contending that the entertainment industry (including record companies) should be regulated and sanctioned for deliberately marketing violent and sexual content to children. Among the many witnesses to testify in these election-season proceedings is Lynn Cheney, the wife of then–vice presidential candidate Dick Cheney, who feels that record companies should be shamed for releasing excessively violent or sexual titles and who advocates censorship of controversial artists. Speaking of music by rapper Eminem, Cheney says, "It is despicable. It is horrible. This is dreadful. This is shameful. This is awful." FTC Chairman Robert Pitofsky informs legislators that he has asked his staff to look at whether action could be brought against the industry for unfair and deceptive advertising.

Notes

"Freedom of Speech"—An Overview of Music Censorship
1. White, *Anatomy of Censorship,* p. 31.
2. Christenson and Roberts, *It's Not Only Rock & Roll,* p. 238.
3. Christenson and Roberts, p. 239.
4. *Music Trades,* 1981, p. 30.
5. Christenson and Roberts, pp. 158–59.
6. Christenson and Roberts, p. 24.
7. White, p. 41.

"Banned in the USA"—The PMRC and Music Labeling
1. Gore, *Raising PG Kids in an X-Rated Society,* p. 17.
2. Gore, p. 18.
3. Denisoff, *Inside MTV,* p. 282.
4. Denisoff, p. 284.
5. Marsh, *The New Book of Rock Lists,* p. 503.
6. Holland, "Congress Can Regulate Lyrics" p. 70.
7. Wolmuth, "Parents vs. Rock," p. 48.
8. Kennedy, "Frankenchrist versus the State," p. 138
9. Goldstein, 1985, contained in the record of Senate hearing 99–529.
10. Wolmuth, p. 50.
11. Clark, " 'As Nasty As They Wanna Be,' " p. 1486.
12. Wolmuth, p. 48.
13. Jaeger, 1985, contained in the record of Senate hearing 99–529.
14. Goldstein, 1985, contained in the record of Senate hearing 99–529.
15. Goldstein, 1985, contained in the record of Senate hearing 99–529.
16. Gore, p. 25.
17. Senate hearing 99–529, p. 2.
18. Senate hearing 99–529, p. 2.
19. Senate hearing 99–529, p. 11.
20. Senate hearing 99–529, p. 12.
21. Senate hearing 99–529, p. 13.
22. Senate hearing 99–529, p. 17.
23. Senate hearing 99–529, p. 49 [emphasis added].

24. Senate hearing 99–529, p. 53.
25. Senate hearing 99–529, p. 54.
26. Senate hearing 99–529, p. 56.
27. Senate hearing 99–529, p. 58.
28. Senate hearing 99–529, p. 65.
29. Senate hearing 99–529, p. 65.
30. Senate hearing 99–529, p. 74.
31. Senate hearing 99–529, p. 75.
32. Holland, "Dole Blasts Industry for Drug Imagery," p. 68.
33. Kennedy, "Frankenchrist versus the State," p. 139.
34. Zappa, *The Real Frank Zappa Book*, p. 284.
35. Clark, p. 1493.
36. Kennedy, p. 137.
37. Billboard, "Free Speech Outweighs Minority Concerns," p. 11.
38. "Record Industry Misunderstands PMRC," p. 9.
39. Gundersen, "Tipper Gore faces the music," p. 1D.

"Happiness Is a Warm Gun"—Violence

1. Bruni, "Senate Looks for Clues on Youth Violence," p. 1.
2. O'Connor, "Colorado Tragedy Continues to Spook Manson Bashing," p. 1.
3. Waliszewski, "Don't Underestimate the Power of Media on Teen Rage," p. 1.
4. Waliszewski, p. 1.
5. Katz, "Other Side of Littleton Story," p. 1.
6. O'Connor, p. 1.
7. O'Connor, p. 3.
8. Associated Press, "Full Senate Commerce Committee hearing scheduled," p. 1.
9. Manson, "Columbine, Whose Fault Is It?" pp. 1–3.
10. Heins, *Sin, Sex, and Blasphemy*, p. 81.
11. Bronson, "A Selected Chronology of Musical Controversy," p. N40.
12. Martin and Segrave, *Anti-Rock*, p. 31.
13. Banks, *Monopoly Television*, p. 189.
14. Zukerman, "Coalition Blasts Violence in Clips," p. 35.
15. Senate hearing 99–529, p. 13.
16. Broyde, "Metal Ban at Catholic WSOU Still an Exception," p. 10.
17. Senate hearing 99–529, p. 12.
18. Adelson, "Osbourne is distressed," p. 9.
19. Solotaroff, "Subliminal Criminals," p. 34.
20. Peters, *Why Knock Rock?*, p. 157.
21. Peters, p. 159.
22. Peters, p. 154.
23. Christenson and Roberts, *It's Not Only Rock & Roll*, p. 204.
24. Christenson and Roberts, p. 205.
25. Raschke, *Painted Black*, p. 169 [emphasis added].
26. Walser, *Running with the Devil*, p. 146.
27. Christenson and Roberts, p. 135.
28. Christenson and Roberts, p. 157.

"Cover Me"—Album Cover Art
1. Morris, "Jane's Addiction," p. 31.
2. Biafra, "The Far Right and the Censorship of Music," p. 11.

"I Want My MTV"—MTV and Music Videos
1. Shales, "The Pop Network That's Dim & Ditzy to Décor," p. B9.
2. Goldberg, "MTV's Sharper Picture," p. 62.
3. Levy, "Ad Nauseam: How MTV Sells Out Rock & Roll," p. 33.
4. Banks, *Monopoly Television: MTV's Quest to Control the Music*, p. 3.
5. Seidman, "An Investigation of Sex-Role Stereotyping in Music Videos," pp. 209–15.
6. Banks, p. 186.
7. Denisoff, *Inside MTV*, p. 291.
8. Wire service UPI release, May 15, 1984.
9. Goldberg, p. 63.
10. Banks, p. 183.
11. Dawes, " 'This Note's for You': Neil Young Criticizes MTV's Ban of Parody," p. 58.
12. Darling, "R&B Denied?" p. 4.
13. Connelly, "Rick James Blasts Vanity 6," p. 47.

"Ebony and Ivory"—Race
1. White, "Trouble in Music, Trouble in Mind 99," p. 5.
2. Mahon, *The Black Rock Coalition and the Cultural Politics of Race in the United States*, p. 154.
3. Szatmary, *A Time to Rock: A Social History of Rock 'N' Roll*, p. 24.
4. Mahon, p. 197.
5. Szatmary, p. 28.
6. Szatmary, p. 24.
7. Szatmary, p. 25.
8. Szatmary, p. 151.
9. Senate Judiciary Committee, 1992, p. ii.
10. D, *Fight the Power*, pp. 1, 2, and 48.
11. Szatmary, p. 338.
12. Szatmary, p. 330.
13. Lusane, "Rap, Race, and Power Politics," p. 39.
14. *The Progressive*, "Free speech for rappers," p. 9.
15. Landler, "Coalition Challenges Time-Warner Over Gangsta Rap," p. B10.
16. Landis, "Record Protest," 1D.
17. Pareles, "Pop View: Should Ice Cube's Voice Be Chilled?" Sec. 2 p. 30.

"Dear God"—Religion
1. Pardun and McKee, "Strange Bedfellows," p. 442.
2. Pardun and McKee, p. 445.
3. Lewisohn, *The Complete Beatles Chronicle*, p. 212.
4. Lewisohn, p. 212.
5. Lewisohn, p. 213.
6. Hamerlick, "MTV and Morality," p. 43.

7. Bronson, "A Selected Chronology of Musical Controversy," p. N42.
8. Larson, *Rock,* p. 15.
9. Godwin, *"Dancing with Demons,"* p. 25.
10. Godwin, p. 37.
11. Godwin, p. 88.
12. Menconi, *Today's Music: A Window to Your Child's Soul,* p. 40.
13. Manson, *The Long Hard Road Out of Hell,* p. 32.
14. Supplement included in Senate hearing 99–529, p. 6.
15. Walser, *Running with the Devil,* p. 139.
16. Raschke, *Painted Black,* p. 166.
17. Bill, *Rock and Roll,* p. 17.
18. Godwin, p. 129.
19. Menconi, p. 42.
20. Nathan, "The Devil Makes Them Do It," p. 12.

"Comfortably Numb"—Drugs

1. Federal Communications Commission, "In the Matter of Licensee Responsibility to Review Records Before Their Broadcast" FCC 71-205, p. 409.
2. Federal Communications Commission, FCC 71-205, p. 412.
3. Federal Communications Commission, FCC 71-428, p. 77.
4. Federal Communications Commission, FCC 71-428, p. 78.
5. Federal Communications Commission, FCC 71-803, p. 386.
6. Federal Communications Commission, FCC 71-803, p. 386.
7. Buckley, Congressional Report.
8. Buckley.
9. Buckley.
10. Buckley.
11. *Rock and Rap Confidential,* 1996, p. 2.

"I Want Your Sex"—Sex

1. Greenberg, *Media, Sex, and the Adolescent,* p. 1.
2. Szatmary, *A Time to Rock: A Social History of Rock 'N' Roll,* p. 24.
3. Leo, "Polluting Our Popular Culture," p. 15.
4. Martin and Segrave, *Anti-Rock,* p. 123.
5. Martin and Segrave, p. 168.
6. Thompson, Walsh-Childers, and Brown, *Media, Sex, and the Adolescent,* edited by Greenberg, et al., p. 248.

"What's So Funny 'Bout Peace, Love, and Understanding?"—Politics and Protest

1. Szatmary, *A Time to Rock: A Social History of Rock 'N' Roll,* p. 93.
2. Orman, *The Politics of Rock Music,* p. 124.
3. Szatmary, p. 197.

"I Fought the Law and the Law Won"—Law

1. *Regina* v. *Hicklin,* 1868.
2. *Roth* v. *United States,* 354 U.S. 476 (1957).

3. *Miller* v. *California,* 413 U.S. 15 (1973).
4. White, *Anatomy of Censorship,* p. 7.
5. White, p. 8.
6. *Chaplinsky* v. *New Hampshire,* 315 U.S. 568 (1942).
7. California State Penal Code, Sec. 313.1
8. Kennedy, "Frankenchrist versus the State," p. 139.

1950s

1. Martin and Segrave, *Anti-Rock,* p. 18.
2. *Billboard,* 1954, "Letter Asks Clean-up of Filth Wax," p. 12.
3. Martin and Segrave, p. 30.
4. Heins, *Sex, Sin, and Blasphemy,* p. 81.
5. Szatmary, *A Time to Rock,* p. 24.
6. Martin and Segrave, p. 31.
7. Szatmary, p. 24.

1960s

1. Martin and Segrave, *Anti-Rock,* p. 133.
2. Martin and Segrave, p. 194.
3. Martin and Segrave, p. 124.
4. Bronson, "A Selected Chronology of Musical Controversy," p. N42.

1970s

1. Dougherty, "From 'Race Music' to Heavy Metal," p. 53.
2. *Variety,* "Disk Programmer Sets Own 'Morality' Ratings, " p. 1.
3. Senate hearings 99-529, p. 65.
4. Orman, *The Politics of Rock Music,* p. 13.

1980s

1. Denisoff, *Inside MTV,* p. 290.
2. Denisoff, p. 292.
3. UPI, "Koop speaks out against violence and sex in music videos," p. 1.
4. Love, " 'Washington Wives' set their sights on video," p. 18.
5. Denisoff, p. 311.
6. Banks, *Monopoly Television,* p. 185.
7. Powell, "What Entertainers Are Doing to Your Kids," p. 46.
8. Johnson, David (CBS company memorandum, 1986, February 20).
9. Kennedy, "Frankenchrist versus the State," p. 132.
10. Kennedy, pp. 134–35.
11. Baldwin, "Punk rock and the First Amendment," p. 62.
12. Holland, "Congress Can Regulate Lyrics, '87 Study Says," p. 1.
13. Broyde, "Metal Ban at Catholic WSOU Still an Exception," p. 10.
14. Dawes, " 'This Note's for You': Neil Young Criticizes MTV's Ban of Parody," p. 58.
15. Morris, "Guns 'N Roses," p. 80.
16. Clark, " 'As Nasty As They Wanna Be': Popular Music on Trial," p. 1493.

1990s

1. Haring, "Crew's 'Nasty' Ruled Obscene in Florida," p. 98.
2. Terry, "Trade Unites on Self-Labeling," p. 83.
3. Mayfield, "Not just fans greet raunchy rappers in Georgia," p. 3A.
4. Morris, "Jane's Addiction Has a Habit of Sparking Album-Art Furors," p. 31.
5. Morris, p. 32.
6. Mills, "Singer Arrested in N.C. for 'Obscene' Performance," p. 83.
7. Banks, *Monopoly Television*, p. 183.
8. Pareles, "Pop View: Should Ice Cube's Voice Be Chilled?" Sec. 2 p. 30.
9. Serrano, "Bill Would Ban Sales of 'Dirty Music' to Minors," p. A1.
10. Neely, "Record-Chain Blacklist," p. 18.
11. Landis, "Record Protest," p. 1D.
12. *Rock and Rap Confidential*, 1992, p. 1.
13. *Legal Intelligencer*, 1995, p. 6.
14. Deggans, "Ban doesn't stop White Zombie," p. 2B.
15. Goldberg, "Protesting Rock and Rap Censorship," p. 1.
16. Goldberg, p. 1.
17. ACLU, "Cuban Musicians Stir Free Speech Debate," p. 1.
18. Crowley, "The Microphone Archive" (online), p. 1.
19. ACLU press release, December 17, 1997. "ACLU Complains About T-Shirt Discipline in North Carolina."
20. *Rock and Rap Confidential*, 1998, p. 2.
21. Crowley, p. 2.
22. ACLU press release, December 17, 1997. "ACLU Complains About T-Shirt Discipline in North Carolina."
23. Hickey, "Pornographic performances outlawed," p. 23.
24. Taylor, "Senate passes plan ordering study of violence in entertainment," p. 1.
25. Dyer, "Concert complaints resurge," p. C1.
26. O'Connor, "Rockers, Industry Folks Slam Clinton for Attacks on Entertainment," 1999, p. 1.
27. Associated Press, "Full Senate Commerce Committee hearing scheduled," p. 1.
28. Associated Press, "Truth in concert advertising measure becomes law in Lafayette, LA," p. 1.
29. Whitaker, "Offspring, Silverchair Leave Controversial Songs Off Setlists," p. 4.
30. Sanchez, "Senior Song Irks Official," p. 1.

Glossary

A&R Short for "Artists and Repertoire." The department at record companies that recruits and oversees those artists who have been signed to record for the label.

A-side The featured single on a two-sided record; usually the "hit" song.

Backmasking The practice of adding subliminal or indistinguishable messages into musical recordings. Often, it is suggested that these messages are taped in reverse, making them even more difficult to locate or decipher.

B-side A song or songs added to the verso of an "A-side" hit single.

Cover song Performance or recording by an artist of a song written, performed, or generally associated with another performer.

Drop When an artist is "dropped" from a record label, he or she is not offered a contract extension or renewal for additional recordings. In essence, the record company ceases to do additional new business with that artist.

Gold record A status level achieved with retail sales of half a million units.

Label A recording company or division of a recording company. A "brand" under which artists release their recordings.

Lyrics The words to songs.

Minor An individual under the age of eighteen.

Platinum record A status level achieved with retail sales of one million units.

PMRC The Parents Music Resource Center, founded in 1985 by Tipper Gore, Susan Baker, Pam Howar, and Sally Nevius.

Bibliography

"ACLU Complains About T-Shirt Discipline in North Carolina" (1997, December 19). ACLU press release.

Adair, Benjamin (1998, March 20). "Jailhouse Rap: Sacramento Rapper Becomes First Imprisoned for His Lyrics." *OC Weekly*, 22.

Adelson, David (1986, February 1). "Osbourne is distressed." *Cashbox*, 9.

Aranza, Jacob (1983). *Backward Masking Unmasked*. Shreveport, La.: Huntington House.

Aranza, Jacob (1985). *More Rock, Country and Backward Masking Unmasked*. Shreveport, La.: Huntington House.

Associated Press (1991, May 5). "Two cable channels ban a country music video."

Associated Press (1999, June 14). " 'Truth in concert advertising' measure becomes Lafayette, Louisiana."

Associated Press (2000, August 3). "Owner asks judge to reopen skating rink closed for playing 'vulgar' music." *The Freedom Forum*, Internet: http://www.freedomforum.org

Baker, Soren (2000, March 11). "No Album Out Yet but Rappers Still Under Fire." *LA Times*, Internet: http://www.clanedarlive.com/music

Baldwin, Doug (1987, Summer). "Punk rock and the First Amendment." *Critique of America*, 62.

Banks, Jack (1996). *Monopoly Television: MTV's Quest to Control the Music*. Boulder: Westview Press.

"Ban that tune" (1991, January 11). *USA Today*, 1D.

Bargreen, Melinda (1992, April 12). "New Law Bans Chunks Of Classical Music." *Seattle Times*, K1.

Bauder, David (1996, November 19). "Music: Business or art?" *Tampa Tribune*, 4.

Baxter, R. L., DeReimer, C., Landini, A., Leslie, L., and Singletary, M. W. (1985). "A content analysis of music videos. *Journal of Broadcasting and Electronic Media*, 333–40.

Benesch, Connie (1994, November 26). "Rap: The Good, The Bad, and The Censored." *Billboard*, 42, 44.

Berry, Cecelie, and Wolin, David (1986, Summer). "Regulating Rock Lyrics: A New Wave of Censorship." *Harvard Journal on Legislation,* 595–619.

Berry, Jahna (2000, July 12). "Dr. Dre's Up in Smoke Tour Comes Under Fire." *Sonicnet,* Internet: http://www.sonicnet.com

Biafra, Jello (1987, April 17). "The Far Right and the Censorship of Music." *Harvard Law Review.*

Bill, J. Brent (1987). *Rock and Roll.* Old Tappan: Power Books.

"Bloodhound Gang draws protesters to U. Maryland concert" (2000, May 8). *U-Wire,* 1.

"Bloodhound Gang lyrics spark protest plans at U. Wiconsin, U. Maryland" (2000, May 8). *U-Wire,* 1.

Bliss, Karen and Vineyard, Jennifer (2000, May 5). "Bloodhound Gang Respond to Maryland Protest." *Rolling Stone Online,* Internet: http://www.rollingstone.com

Bloom, Howard (1989, January 21). "It's Time to Campaign Against Censorship." *Billboard,* 13.

"BMI Tightens Controls on Song Lyrics" (1955, March 5). *Billboard,* 9.

Boehlert, Eric (1997, August 21). "Culture Skirmishes." *Rolling Stone,* 29, 32.

Boehlert, Eric (1999, June 7). "Godsmack Album to Be Emblazoned With Advisory Sticker." *Rolling Stone Online,* Internet: http://www.rolling-stone.com

Boehm, Mike (1990, October 4). "Popbeat." *Los Angeles Times,* F3.

Borzillo, Carrie (1993, October 30). "KACE Clears Air Of 'Negative' Songs." *Billboard,* 78.

Bronson, Fred (1994, March 26). "A Selected Chronology of Musical Controversy." *Billboard,* N38–43.

Brown, J. D. and Shulze, L. (1990). "The effects of race, gender, and fandom on audience interpretations of Madonna's videos." *Journal of Communication,* 88–102.

Brown, Mark (1993, October 24). "Radio Station Takes Stand." *Orange County Register,* F11.

Brownback, Sam (1998, May 15). "Free Speech: Lyrics, Liberty and License." *Vital Speeches of the Day,* 454–56.

Broyde, Sharon (1988, June 18). "Metal Ban at Catholic WSOU Still an Exception." *Billboard,* 10.

Bruni, Frank (1999, May 5). "Senate Looks for Clues on Youth Violence." *New York Times Online,* Internet: http://www.nytimes.com

Buckley, James (1973, November 21). *Congressional Report,* vol. 119, no. 180.

Bundy, June (1954, November 27). "Miss Clooney's 'Mambo' Nixed by ABC." *Billboard,* 11.

Bundy, June (1954, December 25). "Mr. J. Q. Grows Up; He's Less Prudish About Music on Air." *Billboard,* 1.

"C-Bo's Criminal Content" (1998, March 20). *OC Weekly,* 22.

Charen, Mona (1992, August 5). "The good guys won one on Ice-T and 'Cop Killer.'" *Atlanta Journal and Constitution,* A7.

Christenson, Peter G. and Roberts, Donald F. (1998). *It's Not Only Rock & Roll*. Cresskill, N.J.: Hampton Press.

Clark, Anne (1990, December), " 'As Nasty As They Wanna Be': Popular Music on Trial." *New York University Law Review*, 1481–1531.

Cocks, Jay (1985, September 30). "Rock Is a Four-Letter Word." *Time*, 70–71.

Connelly, Christopher (1983, April 14). "Rick James blasts Vanity 6, charges MTV with racism." *Rolling Stone*, 47.

"Control the Dim-Wits!" (1954, September 25). *Billboard*, 33.

"County Judge Rules Juke Box Ban Illegal" (1954, January 9). *Billboard*, 58.

"Cuban Musicians Stir Free Speech Debate" (1997, October 3). ACLU press release.

D, Chuck (1997). *Fight the Power*. New York: Delacorte.

Darling, Cary (1981, November 28). "R&B Denied?" *Billboard*, 4, 62.

Dawes, Amy (1988, July 6). " 'This Note's for You': Neil Young Criticizes MTV's Ban of Parody." *Variety*, 58.

DeCurtis, Anthony (1986, April 24). "Eleven-hour antidrug concert planned." *Rolling Stone*, 13.

Deggans, Eric (1996, February 1). "Ban doesn't stop White Zombie." *St. Petersburg Times*, 2B.

Denisoff, R. Serge (1988). *Inside MTV*. New Brunswick, N.J.: Transaction Publishers.

"Disco music makes pigs deaf and mice gay" (1981, March). *Music trades*, 30.

"Disk programmer sets own 'morality' ratings" (1970, May 13). *Variety*, 1.

"DJ's Would Ban Smut and Racial Barbs on Disks" (1954, February 27). *Billboard*, 9.

Dolan, Michael (1985 September 18). " 'Porn Rock' Hearing Hot Ticket in D.C.; Zappa Lashes PMRC." *Variety*, 73–74.

Dougherty, Steven (1985, September 16). "From 'Race Music' to Heavy Metal: A Fiery History of Protests." *People Weekly*, 52–53.

Dunn, Jancee (1993, November 11). "Wal-Mart: No Utero' " *Rolling Stone*, 13.

Dyer, Stephen (1999, March 12). "Concert complaints resurge." *Beacon Journal*, C1, C4.

Erlewine, Michael (Ed). (1996). *All Music Guide to Rock*. San Francisco: Miller Freeman Books.

"Experts Easier on TV, Radio than Public Is" (1954, February 20). *Billboard*, 8.

Federal Communications Commission (1971). *In the Matter of Licensee Responsibility to Review Records Before Their Broadcast* (FCC 71-205), 409. Washington, D.C.

Federal Communications Commission (1971). *In the Matter of Licensee Responsibility to Review Records Before Their Broadcast* (FCC 71-428), 77. Washington, D.C.

Federal Communications Commission. (1971). *In the Matter of Licensee Responsibility to Review Records Before Their Broadcast* (FCC 71–803), 386. Washington, D.C.

Feldman, Paul (1986, July 6). "ACLU Will Aid Rock Singer in Poster Dispute." *Los Angeles Times*, Part 2, 3.

Fischer, Blair (1999, June 11). "Kmart bans Ministry's 'Dark Side of the Spoon.' " *Rolling Stone Online*, Internet: http://www.rollingstone.com

Flanagan, Bill (1990, July 28). "Radio Moo-ves to Ban Anti-Beef lang Are Un-American." *Billboard*, 9.

"Free speech for rappers" (1994, April). *The Progressive*, 9.

"Free Speech Outweighs Minority Concerns" (1989, November 25). *Billboard*, 11.

"Full Senate Commerce Committee hearing scheduled," (1999, May 4). Associated Press, 1.

Gamerman, Ellen (1998, June 17). "Critics decry violent music." *Baltimore Sun*, 1F.

Garofalo, Reebee (1993). *Rock and Popular Music: Politics, Policies, Institutions*. New York: Routledge.

Ginell, Richard S. (1986, November 27). "Opera's Hot Lyrics Could Curl Censor's Hair." *Chicago Tribune*, C15.

Glassenberg, Bob (1970, June 27). "Nation's PDs Giving Disk Lyrics Once-Over in No-Preaching Drive." *Billboard*, 32.

Godwin, Jeff (1988). *Dancing with Demons*. Chino, Calif.: Chick Publications.

Goldberg, Michael (1986, April 24). "CBS Sets Policy on Explicit Lyrics." *Rolling Stone*, 13.

Goldberg, Michael (1986, January 30). "Crackdown on 'obscene' shows." *Rolling Stone*, 9.

Goldberg, Michael (1990, February 8). "MTV's Sharper Picture." *Rolling Stone*, 62–64, 118.

Goldberg, Michael (1998, July 7). "Protesting Rock and Rap Censorship." *Sonicnet*, Internet: http://www.sonicnet.com

Goodwin, Andrew (1992). *Dancing in the Distraction Factory*. Minneapolis: University of Minnesota Press.

Gore, Mary Elizabeth (Tipper) (1987). *Raising PG Kids in an X-Rated Society*. Nashville: Abingdon Press.

Gore, Tipper, and Baker, Susan (1989, February 11). "Record Industry Misunderstands PMRC." *Billboard*, 9, 68.

Gowen, Alice (1993, April 15). "Tipper Gore quits PMRC." *Rolling Stone*, 20.

Greenberg, Bradley S., Brown, Jane D., and Buerkel-Rothfuss, Nancy L. (Editors) (1993). *Media, Sex, and the Adolescent*. Creskill, N.Y.: Hampton Press.

Gundersen, Edna (1992, July 22). "Tipper Gore faces the music." *USA Today*, 1D.

Hiatt, Brian (2000, June 9). "Cop Group President Calls Springsteen 'Dirtbag' Over Song." *Addicted to Noise*. Internet: http://www.addict.com/MNOTW/lofi

Hall, Claude (1971, April 10). "U.S. Aide Puts Down View That Music Turns Up Youth to Drugs." *Billboard*, 1.

Hall, Mildred (1971, June 5). "FCC 'Clarification' Notice on Drug Lyrics Draws Challenge." *Billboard*, 1, 58.

Hall, Mildred (1973, April 7). "Judge Terms FCC's Drug Lyric Edict 'Obfuscating.' " *Billboard,* 3.

Hamerlick, John (1995, January). "MTV and Morality." *Popular Condition,* 43.

Haring, Bruce (1990, June 16). "Crew's 'Nasty' Ruled Obscene in Florida." *Billboard,* 5, 98.

Harrington, Richard (1995, June 14). "Verse 2 for the Lyric Labelers." *Washington Post,* p. C7.

"Harrisburg." (1995, January 27). *Legal Intelligencer,* 6.

Heins, Marjorie (1993). *Sex, Sin, and Blasphemy.* New York: The New Press.

Henderickson, Matt (1998, April 16). "Grapevine." *Rolling Stone,* 26.

Henry III, William A. (1990, July 30). "Did the Music Say 'Do It'?" *Time,* 65.

Hertzberg, Hendrick (1987, December 7). "Tipper de doo dah, Tipper Gore." *The New Republic,* 22.

Hetter, Katia (1994, May 9). "Can she censor the mayhem?" *U.S. News & World Report,* 44.

Hiatt, Brian (1999, June 3). "Columbine Teens to Rally Against Offspring, Silverchair Show." *Sonicnet,* Internet: http://www.sonicnet.com

Hiatt, Brian (1999, May 25). "Silverchair, Offspring Lyrics Spark Call to Ax Atlanta Rockfest." *Sonicnet,* Internet: http://www.sonicnet.com

Hiatt, Brian (1999, August 20). "Cop Group Boycotts Rage Against the Machine, Beastie Boys Over Mumia Abu-Jamal." *Sonicnet,* Internet: http://www.sonicnet.com

Hickey, Gordon (1999, February 23). "Pornographic performances outlawed." *Richmond Times Dispatch,* 23.

Holden, Stephen (1987, June 2). "AIDS Fears Lead to Ban on Record." *New York Times,* C13.

Holland, Bill (1989, June 10). "Congress Can Regulate Lyrics, '87 Study Says." *Billboard,* 1, 84.

Holland, Bill (1995, June 24). "Stickering Review an RIAA Priority; Latest Lyrics Bill Blocked in Louisiana." *Billboard,* 5.

Holland, Bill (1996, September 28). "Dole Blasts Industry for Drug Imagery." *Billboard,* 6, 99.

Holland, Bill (1998, May 9). "Righting past wrongs." *Billboard,* 84.

Hudson, David (2000, January 28). "Ohio teen who was ordered to take off offensive T-shirt takes city to court." *The Freedom Forum,* Internet: http://www.freedomforum.org

Hull, Anne (1990, December 5). "Who's that with that girl?" *St. Petersburg Times,* 1D.

Husney, Owen (1992, June 27). "Hardcore Rappers Are Voice of the Underclass." *Billboard,* 6.

"Increased Government Censorship Looms on the Horizon" (1997, November 6). ACLU press release.

Katz, Jon (1999, April 26). "Other side of Littleton story: Anti-oddball hysteria." *The Freedom Forum,* Internet: http://www.freedomforum.org

Katz, Jon (1999, May 28). "Crime stats belie effects of on-screen violence." *The Freedom Forum,* Internet: http://www.freedomforum.org

Katz, Jon (1999, July 1). "Why do kids kill?" *The Freedom Forum*, Internet: http://www.freedomforum.org

Kaufman, Gil (1999, January 22). "Cops Protest Rage Against the Machine's Abu-Jamal Benefit." *Sonicnet*, Internet: http://www.sonicnet.com

Kaufman, Gil (1999, November 16). "Third Eye Blind Drop Song at Label's Request." *Sonicnet*, Internet: http://www.sonicnet.com

Keen, July (1990, July 19). "Band: No subliminal message in songs." *USA Today*, 3A.

Keller, Julie (1999, November 15). "Eminem: Too Hot for NFL." *Excite News*, Internet: http://www.excite.com

Kennedy, David (1988). "Frankenchrist versus the State: The New Right, Rock Music, and the Case of Jello Biafra." *Journal of Popular Culture*, 24n1, 131–48.

Kirby, David (1999, July 11). "Neighborhood Report: New York Up Close." *New York Times*, Sec. 14, p. 6.

"Koop speaks out against violence also in music videos" (1984, May 16). UPI wire report, 1.

Landis, David (1992, June 18). "Record Protest." *USA Today*, 1D.

Landis, David, and DeQuine, Jeanne (1990, October 22). "The fight's not over for Brew." *USA Today*, 2D.

Landler, Mark (1995, June 1). "Coalition Challenges Time-Warner Over Gangsta Rap." *New York Times*, B10.

Larkin, Colin (Editor) (1997). *The Virgin Encyclopedia of Popular Music*. London: Virgin.

Larson, Bob (1984). *Rock*. Wheaton, Ill.: Living Books.

LeMoyne, James (1990, June 12). "Three Men Who Took Aim at Rap Group." *New York Times*, A14.

Leo, John (1990, July 2). "Polluting our popular culture." *U.S. News & World Report*, 15.

Leo, John (1990, March 19). "Rock 'n' roll's hatemongering." *U.S. News & World Report*, 17.

"Letter Asks Clean-Up of Filth Wax" (1954, December 18). *Billboard*, 12.

Levin, Eric (1985, November 4). "Lay Off of Them Blue Suede Shoes." *People Weekly*, 42–45.

Levy, Steven (1983, December 8). "Ad Nauseam: How MTV Sells Out Rock & Roll." *Rolling Stone*, 33–37, 74–78.

Lewis, Gregory (1992, January 12). "Taking the Rap: Where to Draw the Line?" *San Francisco Examiner and Chronicle*, D5.

Lewisohn, Mark (1992). *The Complete Beatles Chronicle*. New York: Harmony Books.

Lowenthal, David (1999, August 23). "The Case for Censorship." *Weekly Standard*, p. 21.

Love, Robert (1985, October 10). " 'Washington Wives' set their sights on video." *Rolling Stone*, 18.

Lusane, Clarence (1992, December). "Rap, Race, and Power Politics." *The Black Scholar*, 37–51.

Mahon, Maureen (1997, May). *The Black Rock Coalition and the Cultural*

Politics of Race in the United States. Doctoral dissertation, New York University, New York.

Males, Mike (1999, May 9). "Why Demonize a Healthy Teen Culture?" *Los Angeles Times*, B13.

Manson, Marilyn (1998). *The Long Hard Road Out of Hell*. New York: HarperCollins.

Manson, Marilyn (1999, May 28). "Columbine: Whose Fault Is It?" *Rolling Stone*, 13.

"Marilyn Manson to Perform" (1997, April 23). ACLU press release.

Marcus, Amy Dockser, and Hayes, Arthur S. (1990, August 27). "CBS Is Found Blameless in Music Suicides." *Billboard*, B4.

Marsh, Dave (1990, May 29). "Perception: Protection, Reality: Censorship." *Village Voice*, 85–86.

Marsh, Dave, and Bernard, James (1994). *The New Book of Rock Lists*. New York: Fireside.

Martin, Linda, and Segrave, Kerry (1988). *Anti-Rock*. New York: Da Capo Press.

Mayfield, Mark (1990, June 15). "Not just fans greet raunchy rappers in Georgia." *USA Today*, 3A.

McLeod, Douglas M. (1997, April). "Support for censorship of violent and misogynist lyrics: An Analysis of the third-person effect." *Communication Research*, 153–74.

Menconi, Al (1990). *Today's Music: A Window to Your Child's Soul*. Elgin, Ill.: Cook Publishing.

Mifflin, Lawrie (1999, May 9). "Many Researchers Say Link Is Already Clear on Media and Youth Violence." *New York Times*, Section 2, p. 1.

Mills, Fred (1990, October 6). "Singer Arrested in N.C. for 'Obscene' Performance." *Billboard*, 6, 83.

Moran, Terence (1985, August 12). "Sounds of Sex." *The New Republic*, 14–16.

Morris, Chris (1988, November 5). "Guns N' Roses." *Billboard*, 80.

Morris, Chris (1990, August 25). "Jane's Addiction Has a Habit of Sparking Album-Art Furors." *Billboard*, 31–32.

Morris, Chris (1993, December 18). "Manson Royalties from GN'R Song Go to Victim." *Billboard*, 8, 129.

Morris, Chris (1994, March 26). " . . . While Its Home State Passes 'Adult Music' Bill." *Billboard*, 12, 121.

Morris, Chris, and Jeffrey, Don (1995, June 18). "Chains Wary of Stickered Albums." *Billboard*, 6.

Morris, Edward, and Haring, Bruce (1990, April 7). "2 Live Crew, N.W.A Called Obscene by Tenn. Judge." *Billboard*, 4, 93.

Moss, Corey (2000, March 2). "Gay-Bashing Complaint Spurs Edit of Bloodhound Gang Video." *Sonicnet*, Internet: http://www.sonicnet.com

"Music Is Crime . . . " (1998, December). *Rock and Rap Confidential*, 2.

Nathan, David (1989, September 16). "L.A. Radio Station Pulls Rap Tune After Protests from Gay Listeners." *Billboard*, 82.

Nathan, Debbie (1991, July 24). "The Devil Makes Them Do It." *In These Times,* 12, 13.

Neely, Kim (1992, August 20). "Record-Chain Blacklist." *Rolling Stone,* 18.

Nelson, Chris (1998, August 31). "Hard Rockers Weigh In on Music Censorship Bills." *Sonicnet,* Internet: http://www.sonicnet.com

Nelson, Chris (1999, June 23). "Jewish Group Decries Public Enemy's 'Swindler's Lust.' " *Sonicnet,* Internet: http://www.sonicnet.com

Nelson, Chris (2000, March 9). "Students Suspended for Immoral Behavior: Seeing the Backstreet Boys." *Sonicnet,* Internet: http://www.sonicnet.com

Newman, Melinda (1989, March 25). "Guns N' Roses Cut from AIDS Benefit." *Billboard,* 80.

"Northwest Dealer Launches Six-State Sticker Policy" (1990, May 5). *Billboard,* 5, 81.

Nunziata, Susan (1990, March 7). "Record Bar Pulling 2 Live Crew Recordings from All Its Stores." *Billboard,* 5, 106.

" 'Obscenity' Rap Snags WB LP" (1971, September 25). *Billboard,* 8.

O'Connor, Christopher (1999, April 23). "Manson Show Called Off; Cops Seize Colorado Suspects' CDs." *Sonicnet,* Internet: http://www.sonicnet.com

O'Connor, Christopher (1999, April 27). "Colorado Tragedy Continues to Spark Manson Bashing." *Sonicnet,* Internet: http://www.sonicnet.com

O'Connor, Christopher (1999, May 3). "Politicians Go on Offensive Against Manson." *Sonicnet,* Internet: http://www.sonicnet.com

O'Connor, Christopher (1999, May 12). "Rockers, Industry Folks Slam Clinton for Attack on Entertainment." *Sonicnet,* Internet: http://www.sonicnet.com

O'Connor, Christopher (1999, May 27). "Michigan Senate Passes Concert Regulations." *Sonicnet,* Internet: http://www.sonicnet.com

O'Connor, Christopher (1999, June 3). "Godsmack Debut Yanked from Wal-Mart, Kmart Stores." *Sonicnet,* Internet: http://www.sonicnet.com

O'Connor, Christopher (1999, June 8). "Senators Seek Uniform Labeling of Music, Movies, Video Games." *Sonicnet,* Internet: http://www.sonicnet.com

O'Connor, Christopher (1999, June 10). "Proposed Law Requires Retailers to Provide Lyrics On Demand." *Sonicnet,* Internet: http://www.sonicnet.com

O'Connor, Christopher (1999, June 10). "Congressman Won't Demand Record Stores Provide Lyrics." *Sonicnet,* Internet: http://www.sonicnet.com

"Op Warned on Dirty Records" (1954, November 20). *Billboard,* 54.

Orman, John (1984). *The Politics of Rock Music.* Chicago: Nelson-Hall, Inc.

Ostling, Richard (1990, March 19). "No Sympathy for the Devil." *Time,* 55, 56.

Pardun, Carol, and McKee, Kathy (1995, June). "Strange Bedfellows." *Youth and Society,* 438–49.

Pareles, John (1991, December 8). "Pop View: Should Ice Cube's Voice Be Chilled?" *New York Times,* Sec. 2, p. 30.

Pareles, John (1987, May 3). "Pop View: A Case Against Censoring Rock Lyrics." *New York Times,* Sec. 2, p. 22.

Parham, Betty, and Ferris, Gerrie (1992, September 14). "Q & A on the News." *Atlanta Journal and Constitution,* A2.

Perry, Robert J. (1992, June 26). "Important Ruling in the War Over Pop Music Censorship." *New York Law Journal*, 5.

Peters, Dan and Steve (1984). *Why Knock Rock?* Minneapolis: Bethany House.

Porter, Everett (1998, July 14). "Dionne and friends." *Village Voice*, 66.

Postman, David (1995, August 12). "Rockers' PAC Seeks Funds Nation-wide—Organizers Commend Lowry for Veto on 'Harmful to Minors' Bill." *Seattle Times*, A11.

Powell, Stewart (1985, October 28). "What Entertainers Are Doing to Your Kids." *U.S. News & World Report*, 46–49.

"The President's Drug Strategy: Has It Worked?" (1992, September). Majority Staff of the Senate Judiciary Committee and the International Narcotics Control Caucus.

"Protesting Rock and Rap Censorship." (1998, July 7). *Sonicnet*, Internet: http://www.sonicnet.com

"Rage Against the Machine tear it up" (1999, November 30). *Boston Globe*, D6.

"Random Notes" (1970, July 19). *Rolling Stone*, 4.

Raschke, Carl (1990). *Painted Black*. San Francisco: Harper & Row.

"Record Labeling: Hearing before the Committee on Commerce, Science, and Transportation, United States Senate. First Session on Content of Music and the Lyrics of Records." (1985). Senate Hearing 99–529. Washington, D.C.: U.S. Government Printing Office.

Reeves, Jay (1999, June 1). "Concert ban proposal raises free-speech questions." *Associated Press*, 1.

Riley, Gail Blasser (1998). *Censorship (Library in a Book)*. New York: Facts On File.

Robichaux, Mark (1995, February 8). "It's a Book! a Shirt! a Toy! No, Just MTV Trying to Be Disney." *Wall Street Journal*, A1, A9.

Roblin, Andrew (1985, May 4). "Antichrist Cooled Down for MTV Debut." *Billboard*, 37.

"Rock Mag Folds As Distribs Fear Pressure Groups" (1986, August 20). *Variety*, 1, 93.

Rohde, Stephen (1989, July). "The Sounds of Lawsuits: Rock Lyrics on Trial." *USA Today*, 86, 87.

Romanowski, Patricia, and George-Warren, Holly (Editors) (1995). *The Rolling Stone Encyclopedia of Rock & Roll*. New York: Fireside.

Rosen, Bradley C. (1990, March 10). "Labeling Laws Violate U.S. Constitution." *Billboard*, 13.

Samuels, Anita (1998, March 14). "Rapper's Lyrics Bring Parole Arrest." *Billboard*, 6.

Sanchez, Arley (1999, December 27). "Senior Song Irks Official." *Albuquerque Journal*, Internet: http://www.abjournal.com

Seidman, Steven (1992, Spring). "An Investigation of Sex-Role Stereotyping in Music Videos." *Journal of Broadcasting and Electronic Media*, 209–15.

Serrano, Barbara (1992, February 18). "Bill Would Ban Sales of 'Dirty Music' to Minors." *Seattle Times*, A1.

Shales, Tom (1985, August 1). "The Pop Network That's Dim & Ditzy to Decor." *Washington Post*, B1, B9.

Silverman, Edward R. (1992, July 30). "Groups Still Target 'Cop Killer.' " *Newsday*, 8.

Snider, Eric (1992, December 9). "Controversy = bucks is a pathetic new cliché." *St. Petersburg Times*, 7B.

Sobel, Robert (1971, April 10). "RIAA Acts vs. FCC; ACLU: Delay Edict." *Billboard*, 1.

Solotaroff, Ivan (1990, September 4). "Subliminal Criminals: Judas Priest in the Promised Land." *Village Voice*, 24–34.

"South Carolina School Cancels Indigo Girls Concert" (1998, May 4). ACLU press release.

"Stations Turn Against No. 1 Drinker Song" (1954, January 30). *Billboard*, 22.

Stolder, Steve (1992, November 2). "Aren't stickers enough?" *Rolling Stone*, 30.

Stolberg, Sheryl Gay (1999, May 9). "By the Numbers: Science Looks at Littleton, and Shrugs." *New York Times*, Sec. 2, p. 1.

Strauss, Neil (1996, November 12). "Wal-Mart's CD Standards Are Changing Pop Music." *New York Times,* 1, C12.

Street, John (1986). *Rebel Rock: The Politics of Popular Music.* New York: Basil Blackwell.

Szatmary, David (1996). *A Time to Rock: A Social History of Rock 'N' Roll.* Upper Saddle River, N.J.: Prentice-Hall.

Talbot, David (1999, April 28). "Media probe urged after Colorado shootings." *Boston Herald*, 1.

Taylor, Phillip (1999, May 14). "Senate passes plan ordering study of violence in entertainment." *The Freedom Forum,* Internet: http://www.freedomforum.org

"Telling It Straight" (1971, October 16). *Billboard*, 1.

Terry, Ken (1990, March 24). "Trade Unites on Self-Labeling." *Billboard*, 1, 81, 83.

"Texas Governor Signs Off on 'Censorship' Bill" (1998, June 20). *Sonicnet,* Internet: http://www.sonicnet.com

"Trade Fears 'Nasty' Consequences of Crew Ruling" (1990, June 23). *Billboard*, 5.

" 'Truth in concert advertising' measure becomes law in Lafayette, LA." (1999, June 14). Associated Press, 1.

"Up Against Wal-Mart" (1996, September 14). *The Economist*, 30.

Viles, Peter (1993, December 13). "Three stations, two responses to rap: KACE, WBLS ban violent or offensive lyrics; KPWR opens dialogue with listeners; radio." *Broadcasting & Cable*, 90.

Volz, Edward J. (1991, July). "You Can't Play That: A Selective Chronology of Banned Music: 1850–1991."

Waliszewski, Bob (1999, April 27). "Don't Underestimate the Power of Media on Teen Rage." Focus on the Family press release.

Walser, Robert (1993). *Running with the Devil*. Hanover, Conn.: Wesleyan University Press.

Wener, Ben (1997, December 12). "So who needs smacking up in this case?" *Orange County Register,* F49.

Whitaker, Lang (1999, June 7). "Offspring, Silverchair Leave Controversial Songs Off Setlists." *Sonicnet,* Internet: http://www.sonicnet.com

White, Harry (1997). *Anatomy of Censorship.* Lanham, Calif.: University Press of America.

White, Timothy (1999, February 6). "Trouble in Music, Trouble in Mind 99." *Billboard,* 5.

Winfield, Betty Huchin, and Davidson, Sandra (Editors) (1999). *Bleep: Censoring Rock and Rap Music.* Westport, Conn.: Greenwood Press.

Woods, John (2000, March 6). "Tennessee Considered Censorship of Music, Movies, and Video Games." Rock Out Censorship Online, Internet: http://www.theroc.org

Wolmuth, Roger (1985, September 16). "Parents Vs. Rock." *People Weekly,* 46–51.

Zappa, Frank (1989). *The Real Frank Zappa Book.* New York: Poseidon Press.

Zukerman, Faye (1984, December 22). "Coalition Blasts Violence in Clips." *Billboard,* 35–36.

Online

"Rock and Rap Confidential." Internet: http://www.rockrap.com/rockrap

"Rock Out Censorship." Internet: http://www.theroc.org

"Rolling Stone Online." Internet: http://www.rollingstone.com

"Sonicnet Music News of the World." Internet: http://www.sonicnet.com

"The Freedom Forum Online." Internet: http://www.freedomforum.com

Crowley, Nina. "The Microphone Archive." (1998). Internet: http://www.ultranet.com/~crowleyn/microarchive.html

High Priestess LaDonna, aka LaDonna Smith. "The Cult of Fuzz—Official Rudi Protrudi & the Fuzztones Home Page." (1998). Internet: http://www.geocities.com/SunsetStrip/Alley/1216

Interviews

Ellis, Len (via telephone). 1999, February 4.

Gilmore, Peter (via telephone). 1999, April 27.

Larson, Bob (via telephone). 1999, August 8.

Music Buyer, Wal-Mart, Inc. (via telephone). 1999, January 27.

Protrudi, Rudi (via telephone). 1998, December 29.

Seeger, Pete (via telephone). 1999, February 4.

Wyatt, Barbara (via telephone). 1999, June 15.

Thanks

**I would maintain that thanks are
the highest form of thought, and that
gratitude is happiness doubled by wonder.**
—G. K. Chesterton

First, my thanks to God. For providing me with a passion and voice to speak the truth. And for blessing me with such a beautiful life.

Right after God, my sincerest thanks to Pamela R. Anderson, a great friend who spent countless hours poring over a year's worth of edits to the early drafts of this text ("Eric, I just don't understand what you are trying to say here").

To Gary Harwood, for offering his boundless enthusiasm and support, not to mention his talent, by shooting over a third of the photographs that appear in this book.

Special thanks to all those who donated their personal time and effort to helping out and gathering information used in this book: the High Priestess LaDonna (aka LaDonna Smith), Noah Adams, Dr. Kevin Pearce, Ken Paulson and Laurie Woods of the Freedom Forum, Nina Crowley, and Kelly DeBaer, plus all the social scientists, rock critics, writers, and theorists whose work informed and enlightened me in the process of creating this book.

To those who have affected my thinking about music: Laura Patterson, David Olson, John and Adam Mercer, Chuck Rutzen, Dave Evans, Rob Brantz, Steve Bennett, Dave McFarland, and Doug Dickson.

To those who have affected my thinking on justice: the Reverend Ora Calhoun, my group leader friends, and the ten other people in Canton, Ohio, who opposed the Gulf War.

To Peter Buck for answering his mail.

To the current and past staff of WKSU-FM, for teaching me daily about excellence.

To Shauna Yule, Bob and Kevin Burford, Peter and Kim Bell, Wendi Koontz, Paula Phillips, and Brian Siewiorek for forcing me to take sanity breaks.

To my many colleagues who work so hard to make public radio a national treasure.

To all my friends for their understanding and interest.

To my parents and family for unqualified support and encouragement ("All that I am or hope to be, I owe to my Angel Mother."—Abraham Lincoln).

To my agent, Marian Young, for helping to inform, guide, and protect me. And to David Sedaris, for introducing me to Marian.

To my faithful cat, Buster, for giving up his favorite spot in front of the computer keyboard and biting me when I'd spend too much time writing and not enough time playing.

To Yung Kim and Tom Dupree for shepherding this project through its final stages.

To my editor (for most of this project) and friend, Ben Schafer, for believing in me from day one, for fighting for me and for this project. I could never thank you enough.

And finally, and most important, to Katherine Kendall. Without her, this book, and so many other wonderful things in my life, would still be distant dreams.

Thank you.

Index

Page numbers in **bold** indicate sidebars and illustrations.

PHOTOGRAPHIC CREDITS

All albums photographed for this book are from the personal collections of Eric Nuzum, Gary Harwood, and Al Bartholet.

p. 4—AP/Wide World Photos
p. 17—Photo by Gary Harwood
p. 21[left]—©Chester Simpson/
Pix Int'l.
p. 21[right]—Corbis
p. 26—CORBIS/Wally McNamee,
used with permission
p. 29—AP/Wide World Photos
p. 36—Linda Matlow/Pix Int'l., used
with permission
p. 41—Photo by Gary Harwood
p. 57—Corbis/Bettmann-UPI
p. 58—©Terry Sesvold/Pix Int'l.
p. 69—Photo by Gary Harwood
p. 70—Photo by Gary Harwood
p. 71—Photo by Gary Harwood
p. 71—Photo by Gary Harwood
p. 72—Photo by Gary Harwood
p. 72—Photo by Gary Harwood
p. 73—Photo by Gary Harwood
p. 73—Photo by Gary Harwood
p. 74—Photo by Gary Harwood
p. 74—Photo by Gary Harwood
p. 75—Photo by Gary Harwood
p. 75—Photo by Gary Harwood
p. 76—Photo by Gary Harwood
p. 76—Photo by Gary Harwood
p. 79—Photo by Gary Harwood
p. 79—Photo by Gary Harwood
p. 80—Photo by Gary Harwood

p. 80—Photo by Gary Harwood
p. 81—Photo by Gary Harwood
p. 81—Photo by Gary Harwood
p. 81—Photo by Gary Harwood
p. 81—Photo by Gary Harwood
p. 82—Photo by Gary Harwood
p. 82—Photo by Gary Harwood
p. 93—The Fuzztones, used with
permission
p. 95—©Terry Sesvold/Pix Int'l.
p. 104—AP/Wide World Photos
p. 108—©1996 Linda Matlow/Pix
Int'l.
p. 111[top]—Bob V. Noble
p. 111[bottom]—Starline/Paniccioli
p. 113—Corbis
p. 114[top]—Photo by Gary Harwood
p. 114[bottom]—©Linda
Matlow/Pix Int'l.
p. 117—AP/Wide World Photos
p. 121—AP/Wide World Photos
p. 122—CORBIS/Bettman, used
with permission
p. 129—CORBIS/S.I.N, used with
permission
p. 132—Photo by Gary Harwood
p. 140—AP/Wide World Photos
p. 156—Corbis/Bettmann-UPI
p. 157—Archive Photos/Express
Newspapers, used with permission

About the Author

Eric Nuzum is a pop-culture critic and regularly contributes to the *Cleveland Free Times, Public Arts,* and Music.com. He has contributed essays to National Public Radio and the public radio business program *Marketplace.* Nuzum also is the program director of WKSU-FM, Kent State University's National Public Radio affiliate. His favorite food is peanut butter, and his current life quest is to read or reread each of the 100 greatest novels of the twentieth century (he has finished fourteen). He lives in Kent, Ohio.